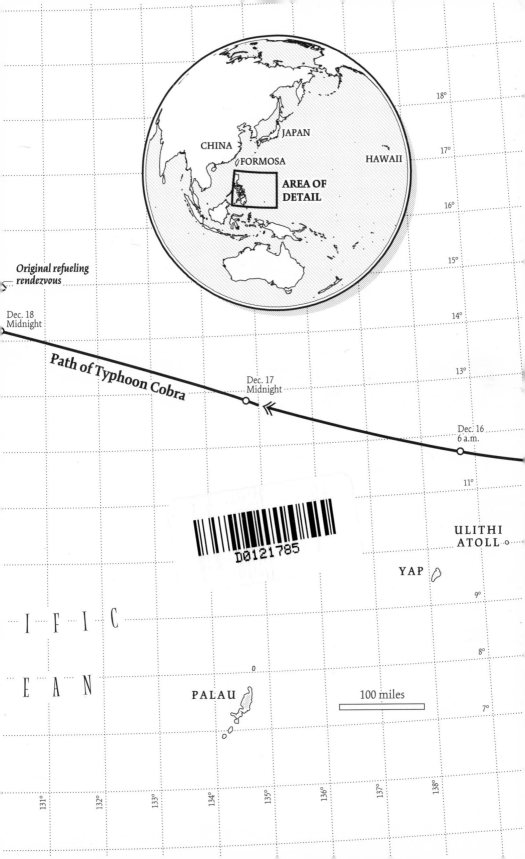

18°

CHINA   JAPAN

FORMOSA   17°

HAWAII

AREA OF
DETAIL   16°

15°

*Original refueling
rendezvous*   14°

Dec. 18
Midnight

13°
Dec. 17
Midnight

Path of Typhoon Cobra

Dec. 16
6 a.m.

11°

ULITHI
ATOLL

YAP

9°

I F I C

8°

E A N

PALAU   100 miles   7°

131° 132° 133° 134° 135° 136° 137° 138°

HALSEY'S TYPHOON

HALSEY'S TYPHOON

The True Story of a Fighting
Admiral, an Epic Storm, and
an Untold Rescue

BOB DRURY
AND
TOM CLAVIN

Atlantic Monthly Press
New York

Published simultaneously in Canada
Printed in the United States of America

FIRST EDITION

Library of Congress Cataloging-in-Publication Data

Drury, Bob.
    Halsey's typhoon : the true story of a fighting admiral, an epic storm,
and an untold rescue / Bob Drury & Tom Clavin.
       p. cm.
    Includes bibliographical references and index.
    ISBN-13: 978-0-87113-948-1
    ISBN-10: 0-87113-948-0
    1. United States. Navy. Fleet, 3rd—History. 2. World War, 1939–1945—
Naval operations, American. 3. Typhoons—History—20th century.
4. Shipwrecks—Philippine Sea—History. 5. Survival after airplane accidents,
shipwrecks, etc. 6. Halsey, William Frederick, 1882–1959. I. Clavin,
Thomas. II. Title.
    D773.D78 2007
    940.54'5973—dc22   2006049948

Atlantic Monthly Press
an imprint of Grove/Atlantic, Inc.
841 Broadway
New York, NY 10003

Distributed by Publishers Group West

www.groveatlantic.com

07 08 09 10 11 12   10 9 8 7 6 5 4 3 2

To the 793 who
perished with honor, with
dignity, and with courage.

Size of Ships Versus Height of Waves
in *Halsey's Typhoon*

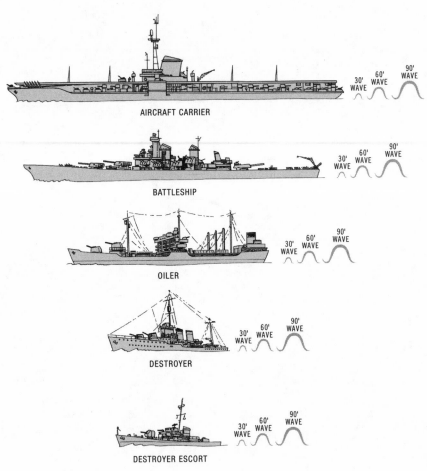

AIRCRAFT CARRIER

30' WAVE · 60' WAVE · 90' WAVE

BATTLESHIP

30' WAVE · 60' WAVE · 90' WAVE

OILER

30' WAVE · 60' WAVE · 90' WAVE

DESTROYER

30' WAVE · 60' WAVE · 90' WAVE

DESTROYER ESCORT

30' WAVE · 60' WAVE · 90' WAVE

CONTENTS

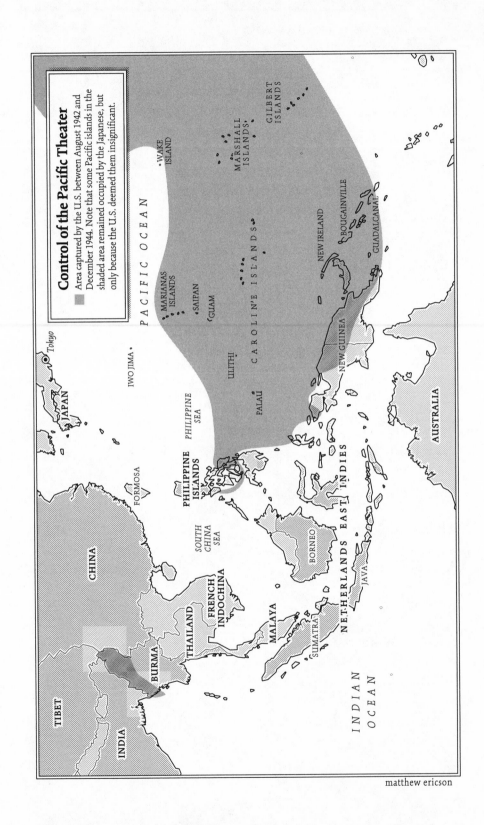

Control of the Pacific Theater

Area captured by the U.S. between August 1942 and December 1944. Note that some Pacific islands in the shaded area remained occupied by the Japanese, but only because the U.S. deemed them insignificant.

matthew ericson

DRAMATIS PERSONAE

Third Fleet

Adm. William Halsey, Commander of Third Fleet
Adm. John McCain, Commander of Task Force 38
Comdr. George Kosco, Chief Aerologist of Third Fleet
Adm. "Mick" Carney, Halsey's Chief of Staff
Capt. Jasper Acuff, Commander of Task Group 30.8
Capt. Preston Mercer, Commander of Destroyer Squadron 1
Lt. (j.g.) Jerry Ford, USS *Monterey*
Capt. Charles Calhoun, USS *Dewey*
Capt. William Rogers, USS *Aylwin*
Capt. Stuart Ingersoll, USS *Monterey*
Capt. R. W. Bockius, USS *Cape Esperance*
Capt. Michael Kernodle, USS *San Jacinto*
Capt. Raymond Toner, USS *Robert F. Keller*
Capt. H. P. Butterfield, USS *Nehenta Bay*

USS *Tabberer*

Capt. Henry Lee Plage
Lt. Bob Surdam, Executive Officer
Lt. (j.g.) Howard Korth, Gunnery Officer
Louis Purvis, Bosun's Mate 1st Class
Paul "Cookie" Phillips, Ship's Cook 1st Class
William McClain, Mailman 3rd Class
Leonard Glaser, Shipfitter 3rd Class

John Cross, Signalman 3rd Class
Ralph Tucker, Chief Radioman
Tom Bellino, Gunner's Mate
Lt. Frank Cleary, Medical Officer

USS *Hull*

Capt. James Marks
Lt. Griel Gherstly, Executive Officer
Lt. (j.g.) Lloyd Rust, CIC Officer
Archie DeRyckere, Chief Quartermaster
Pat Douhan, Petty Officer 2nd Class
Ray Schultz, Chief Bosun's Mate
Tom Stealey, Fireman
"Spiz" Hoffman, Ship's Cook 1st Class
Nick Nagurney, Fireman 1st Class

USS *Monaghan*

Capt. Bruce Garrett
Keith Abbott, Radar Technician
Joe McCrane, Watertender 2nd Class
Evan Fenn, Fireman
Joe Guio, Gunner's Mate

USS *Spence*

Capt. James Andrea
Lt. (j.g.) Alphonso Krauchunas
Bob Ayers, Gunner's Mate Striker
George Johnson, Chief Watertender
Floyd Balliett, Radar Technician

Other Officers

Adm. Ernest King, Chief of U.S. Naval Operations

Gen. Douglas MacArthur, Field Marshal, Combined
American-Filipino Army

Adm. Chester Nimitz, Commander of Pacific Naval Operations
(CINCPAC)

Arleigh Burke, Commander, DesRon 23, "Little Beavers"

Adm. Raymond Spruance, Commander of Fifth Fleet

Rear Adm. Thomas Kinkaid, Commander of (MacArthur's)
Seventh Fleet

GLOSSARY

Abaft—toward the stern of a boat; behind

Abeam—on a line at right angles to a ship's keel

Aft (also stern)—the rear part of a ship

Amidships—in or toward the center

Beam—the width of a ship at its widest part

Bow (also prow)—the forward part of a ship

Bridge—the raised platform on a ship from which it is navigated

Bulkhead—a vertical partition separating compartments

CINCPAC—commander in chief, U.S. Pacific Fleet (Nimitz)

Coaming—a vertical piece around the edge of a cockpit, hatch, etc., to prevent water on deck from running below

Comdr.—commander

CPO—chief petty officer

CWO—chief warrant officer

Following sea—an overtaking sea that comes from astern

Helm—the wheel or lever controlling the rudder of a ship

Hull—the frame or body of a ship (excluding masts, yards, and rigging)

Keel—the longitudinal plate extending along and projecting from the center of the bottom of a ship

Leeward—away from the direction of the wind; opposite of windward

Line—nautical term for a rope

Locked in Irons—unable to escape the liquid gorge formed by parallel waves on either side of a ship

Pilothouse (also wheelhouse)—the deckhouse for a ship's helmsman containing the steering wheel and navigating equipment

Port—the left side of a ship

Starboard—the right side of a ship

Stern—the rear of a ship
TBS—talk-between-ships
Watch—four-hour period when a sailor is on duty
Windward—toward the direction from which the wind is coming

PREFACE

December 18, 1944
The Philippine Sea, 500 Miles East of Luzon

Chief Quartermaster Archie DeRyckere was more astonished than frightened. He craned his neck to stare at the massive waves, churning gouts of water, some reaching ninety feet in height. The seas were not only mammoth, but confused by a backing wind that slammed into the sheer, flint gray walls of ocean and seemed to suspend them in midair, like looming, petrified hills. The USS *Hull* rolled at unprecedented angles, slip-sliding nearly stern-first into the trough.

DeRyckere had sailed through weather before, none like this. The rain blew hard, horizontal, pelting the bridge like grapeshot and pocking the skin of any seaman who had the hard luck to face it. As another huge comber marbled the *Hull*'s deck with whitewater, the chief was reminded of a set of tumblers clicking into place, locking the 2,100-ton destroyer in irons.

For the better part of the morning DeRyckere had listened with mounting disbelief from his station on the bridge as the *Hull*'s TBS (talk-between-ships) ship-to-ship wireless flashed scratchy distress calls from across the whole upheaval of the Philippine Sea. Vessels unaccounted for. Men swept overboard. Fighter planes blown into the sea off the decks of carriers. Cruisers dead in the water. The 170-odd ships comprising Adm. William F. Halsey Jr.'s Third Pacific Fleet, the United States Navy's Big Blue Fleet, had been ambushed by a tropical cyclone, and the most powerful armada in the world was scattered and running for its life. This was far worse, DeRyckere thought, than anything the Japanese had thrown at them over the past three days.

As the long swells rocked the *Hull*, DeRyckere kept a wary eye on the ship's inclinometer, the device used to measure the angle of a vessel's horizontal sway. The wind and waves were beginning to push the instrument's needle to its stop limit of 73 degrees. After each roll the destroyer would rebound painfully, as if wounded, and begin the slow, vertical climb to right herself. Belowdecks, pumpers and bucket brigades were encountering nightmares. With each seismic heel, sailors grabbed onto fittings and projections in the overhead, their feet hanging free of the deck. On some rolls they lost both their footing and their grips, and pitched shoulder-deep into water that sloshed up against the bulkheads.

DeRyckere remembered the *Hull's* variance; she had been certified to recover from a maximum roll of 72 degrees. Soon enough, he feared, there would come a heel from which the ship would not recoup. She was too top-heavy. The destroyer, one of the old *Farragut*-class "gold platers," had been designed in the mid-1930s as a 1,500-tonner. Compared to the cumbersome four-stackers of the Great War, her lines and living quarters were considered luxurious. But over the course of this conflict the addition of radar mounts on the tip of her mast and extra armament on her deck had pushed her well past her projected sailing weight.

In the pilothouse, beneath the starboard portal, DeRyckere watched as Joe Jambor was knocked to his knees as the *Hull* was rocked by another mountainous surge. Jambor was the ship's chief electrician, a pale, willowy sailor who looked as if daylight would kill him. The chief read the expression on Jambor's face as he scrambled to his feet; it was as if he were mentally composing a suicide note. He told DeRyckere that water was pouring in through blown hatches from stem to stern, yet the ship's pumps were not operating to full capacity because her new skipper, Lt. Comdr. James Alexander Marks, refused to divert electricity from the engine room.

The bilges were already overflowing, Jambor said, and he couldn't pump them out. "He's going full power because he's getting reports from all over the fleet that ships are in trouble," he said, his face turned away from the captain. "He thinks he can save them."

Jambor wiped his brow with a dirty neckerchief. "Maybe he'd better think about saving us first."

Then Jambor was gone, scrambling down the outside skipper's ladder, bent double against the wind lashing the sea-washed deck. In seconds his silhouette disappeared behind a veil of gray rain and scud, and DeRyckere turned back toward Marks.

At six-foot-three, with wide, strong shoulders tapering down to a wasp waist, DeRyckere towered over the *Hull's* commander. Four days shy of his twenty-fifth birthday, the chief cut a figure with his jutting chin, long aquiline nose, and broad forehead shading hooded blue eyes that seemed to flicker with some hidden delight. Among the crew he was known for his self-deprecating humor and sea chest full of stories—including the time he'd inadvertently helped load the *Hull's* antiaircraft guns with star-shell flares instead of frags during the Japanese attack on Pearl Harbor. "We're trying to kill the bastards, not illuminate them!" an angry gunner's mate had finally shouted.

His scant formal education belied DeRyckere's intelligence, and he had "booked up" from seaman second class to chief quartermaster in his four years on the *Hull*. Chiefs were the backbone of the U.S. Navy, and DeRyckere fit the template. He was an adroit helmsman, skilled at navigation and celestial sailing, and one of his collateral duties was to synchronize each of the ship's clocks. As such he was also considered a "walking newspaper" on his daily rounds belowdecks, spreading scuttlebutt, making small talk—a fair posture from which to take the temperature of the destroyer's complement of 263 sailors.

He told friends that he'd inherited his affinity for the sea from his paternal forebears, one of whom, a Spanish sailor, had gone down with the Armada in 1588 and washed up on the lowland shores of the Netherlands. There he'd anglicized his name and begun a line of DeRyckeres that extended to Archie's father, who'd emigrated to the United States, settled in Laurel, Montana, outside of Billings, and married a Norwegian girl whose parents still lived in the tiny arctic circle village of Sunndal.

DeRyckere liked to joke that it was from his mother's side of the family that he'd acquired his "Viking blood." But in truth, though a strong swimmer in lakes and rivers as a boy, he had never glimpsed the ocean until he enlisted in October 1940 with the notion of becoming a fighter pilot. He had spent part of his youth as a section hand, a gandy dancer, on the Northern Pacific Railroad, and when railroad work was scarce he'd picked cherries and thinned apple trees in orchards throughout Washington state. And he had a mechanical touch, which led to a stint as a grease monkey—"lubrication technician," DeRyckere preferred—at a Montana service station. But before he'd joined the navy he'd rarely seen so much as a church steeple as tall as the breakers that now fashioned the liquid walls of the canyon engulfing the USS *Hull*.

The captain's paralysis bewildered DeRyckere. The chief was aware that "Bull" Halsey was so anxious for a fight with the Japanese that he had directed every vessel of the fleet to remain on station despite the high seas. The smart move, the seaman's move, would have been to allow them to run for their lives. And though it would later be made known that individual commanders throughout the fleet's task groups had disobeyed Halsey and taken the initiative to dog down for a typhoon, no official typhoon warning had yet emanated either from the CINCPAC weather station at Pearl Harbor or from Halsey's flag bridge on the battleship USS *New Jersey*.

The *Hull*'s job was to screen for enemy submarines as Halsey's fighting task forces rendezvoused and refueled, mid-ocean, from the bunkers of the lumbering oiler groups. Captain Marks's stubborn insistence on maintaining station may have had admirable motives but, given the circumstances, the skipper's fealty to duty in his first combat command did not instill in Chief Quartermaster Archie DeRyckere any great sense of confidence.

Just before 10:00 A.M. the largest wave yet, streaked with blue shadows, slammed into the *Hull*'s starboard quarter. The ship lurched awkwardly and heeled to port. There she remained, "as helpless as a cork in a river eddy," refusing to respond to any combination of rudder and engines. DeRyckere planted his feet on the bulkhead, the deck now at eye level. He was standing several paces behind Marks, who was staring straight ahead, wedged into the rear port corner of the pilothouse. The captain uttered not a word and refused to return DeRyckere's measured look, as though unable to acknowledge that he was losing control of his ship.

DeRyckere wondered over the fate of the other vessels in Admiral Halsey's flotilla.

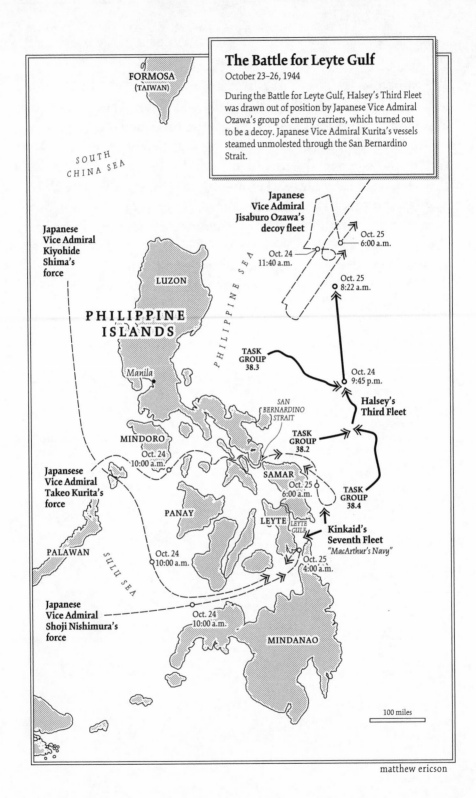

The Battle for Leyte Gulf
October 23–26, 1944

During the Battle for Leyte Gulf, Halsey's Third Fleet was drawn out of position by Japanese Vice Admiral Ozawa's group of enemy carriers, which turned out to be a decoy. Japanese Vice Admiral Kurita's vessels steamed unmolested through the San Bernardino Strait.

FORMOSA
(TAIWAN)

SOUTH CHINA SEA

Japanese
Vice Admiral
Kiyohide
Shima's
force

LUZON

PHILIPPINE SEA

PHILIPPINE ISLANDS

Manila

Japanese
Vice Admiral
Jisaburo Ozawa's
decoy fleet

Oct. 24
11:40 a.m.

Oct. 25
6:00 a.m.

Oct. 25
8:22 a.m.

TASK
GROUP
38.3

Oct. 24
9:45 p.m.

**Halsey's
Third Fleet**

SAN BERNARDINO STRAIT

MINDORO

Oct. 24
10:00 a.m.

Japansese
Vice Admiral
Takeo Kurita's
force

TASK
GROUP
38.2

SAMAR

Oct. 25
6:00 a.m.

TASK
GROUP
38.4

PANAY

LEYTE *LEYTE GULF*

**Kinkaid's
Seventh Fleet**
"MacArthur's Navy"

PALAWAN

SULU SEA

Oct. 24
10:00 a.m.

Oct. 25
4:00 a.m.

Japansese
Vice Admiral
Shoji Nishimura's
force

Oct. 24
10:00 a.m.

MINDANAO

100 miles

matthew ericson

HALSEY'S TYPHOON

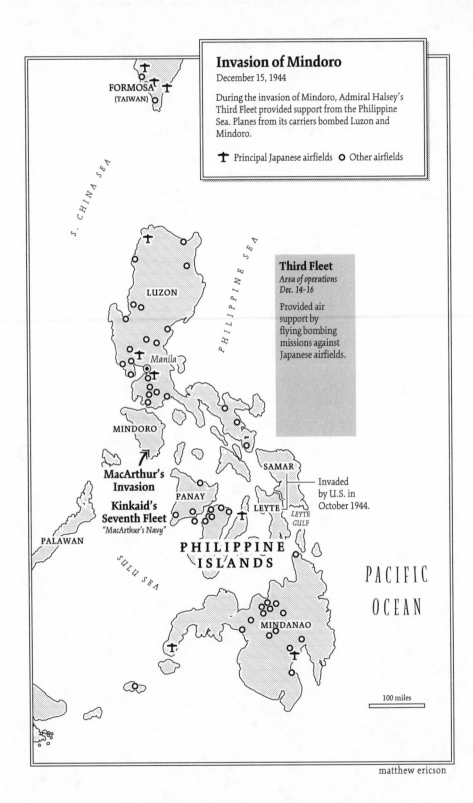

Invasion of Mindoro

December 15, 1944

During the invasion of Mindoro, Admiral Halsey's Third Fleet provided support from the Philippine Sea. Planes from its carriers bombed Luzon and Mindoro.

✝ Principal Japanese airfields ○ Other airfields

FORMOSA
(TAIWAN)

S. CHINA SEA

PHILIPPINE SEA

Third Fleet
Area of operations
Dec. 14–16

Provided air support by flying bombing missions against Japanese airfields.

LUZON

Manila

MINDORO

SAMAR

MacArthur's Invasion

Kinkaid's Seventh Fleet
"MacArthur's Navy"

PANAY

LEYTE

LEYTE GULF

Invaded by U.S. in October 1944.

PALAWAN

SULU SEA

PHILIPPINE ISLANDS

PACIFIC OCEAN

MINDANAO

100 miles

matthew ericson

BOOK ONE

THE FLEET

The sea—this truth must be confessed—has no generosity. No display of manly qualities—courage, hardihood, endurance, faithfulness—has ever been known to touch its irresponsible consciousness of power.

—JOSEPH CONRAD, *THE MIRROR OF THE SEA*

CHAPTER 1

The clipped words slid out of the judge advocate's mouth as if slipped through a mail slot: "Admiral, did you consider that you had timely warning or did you know that a severe storm was approaching around the sixteenth and seventeenth of December?"

William Frederick Halsey Jr. surveyed the wardroom of the destroyer tender USS *Cascade*. Seated in hardback chairs to his left were two vice admirals and a rear admiral, each clad in crisp, starched khakis, their postures erect as jackstaffs. The stenographers sat on his right, four chief yeomen with their backs to him, recording testimony as it was given. A Marine colonel occupied the table directly opposite Halsey, who undoubtedly noted the green felt cloth draped over it. A court-martial in the U.S. Navy had long been referred to as "sitting at the end of the long green table."

This, however, was no court-martial, merely a court of inquiry. Nearly eight hundred sailors from the United States Third Fleet had perished during a typhoon, almost three times the number of men who died at the Battle of Midway. The catastrophe was not, as some of Halsey's rivals suggested, Custer at the Little Bighorn, but, still, there were questions. The mood in the wardroom was somber, if polite. It was December 28, the dying wick of 1944, on a sun-splashed morning on Ulithi Atoll.

"I did not have timely warning," Halsey answered in a clear, resonant voice sharp enough to cut falling silk. "I'll put it another way. I had no warning."

The navy's judge advocate pressed on: "There has been testimony from other commanders that the local conditions indicated the approach of the storm. Was that evident to you?"

Although he was never to speak of it for the rest of his life, this could well have been the moment Admiral Halsey determined his need for legal counsel. Scuttlebutt had it that over dinner the previous evening he had joked to a friend, "Somebody ought to be court-martialed for this, either me or the Bureau of Ships." Yet now he answered the judge advocate's queries with a mixture of insouciance and ignorance. It was quite obvious, he said, that he'd needed his destroyers completely refueled in order to return as soon as possible to continue his strikes on Luzon, high seas be damned.

The implication was clear: There is a war on; General MacArthur was waiting. But Halsey also admitted to having no literal idea where the storm was heading, or whether, in fact, it was a severe storm or merely a local disturbance. "I am no weather expert," he said.

No, he was "Bull" Halsey, the U.S. Navy's Patton of the Pacific, the man who boasted he would ride the emperor's white horse into Tokyo. And this was humiliating.

Of all the naval heroes of World War II, none strode so large a stage as Adm. William Halsey. The self-proclaimed scion of "seafarers and adventurers, big, violent men, impatient of the law, and prone to strong drink and strong language," Halsey sailed determinedly in their wake. By December 1944 the obscure skipper, whose command of the destroyer USS *Shaw* during the First World War had merited the Navy Cross, was, at sixty-two years old, not only the most famous man in the United States Navy, but the most famous living naval officer in the world. He had borne the Allied cause on his shoulders during the war's first, flickering hours, and this would not soon be forgotten.

Halsey's raids on the enemy-held Marshall and Gilbert Islands less than two months after Pearl Harbor were America's first offensive assaults of the war. Twelve weeks later, in April 1942, his daring transport of Col. Jimmy Doolittle's bombers to within hailing distance of Tokyo—though but a tactical and strategic pinprick—was, as one newspaper correspondent wrote, a dose of vitamin B-25 for a nation still staggering under the trauma of the Japanese sneak attack.

Halsey's ascent was serendipitous. In the early miasma of World War II, America needed a hero. Halsey was it. His profile was as familiar to Americans as Clark Gable's or Gary Cooper's, and such was his fame that on a visit home to attend a Stateside reception a woman broke through the receiving line, clasped his arm, and cried, "I feel as if I were touching the hand of God."

A rawboned seaman of slender build, the hatchet-browed Halsey was an early riser who drank ten cups of coffee a day, smoked precisely forty cigarettes, and, like his forebears, was known to enjoy a glass of scotch whiskey. An early-eighteenth-century ancestor, Capt. John Halsey, had in fact been a privateer-turned-buccaneer, and Halsey's great-great-grandfather, Capt. Eliphalet Halsey, continued the tradition of sailing Halsey men by helming the first Sag Harbor whaler to round Cape Horn. Young "Willie" followed his father's path from his home in Elizabeth, New Jersey, to the U.S. Naval Academy as the nineteenth century turned. The caption under his 1904 graduation photo reads, "A real old salt (who) looks like a figurehead of Neptune." He was twenty-one years old.

Four years later, now an ensign, Halsey drew duty aboard the battleship USS *Kansas*, a ship of the line that famously circumnavigated the globe as part of Teddy Roosevelt's Great White Fleet. During the Great War he captained a destroyer, running convoys across the Atlantic. He was remembered by fellow officers as a stolid and able commander, possessing a conspicuous gift for handling men. The war experience left Halsey, he recalled, "as proud as a dog with two tails." In time his craggy face would come to reflect a map of the world's ports of call.

Between wars—early on, Halsey had foreseen the next one coming —he grew impatient with what Tennyson called "the long, long cancer of peace" and intuited the vital role airpower would play in the looming conflict against Japan and Germany. In 1934 he petitioned his superiors to be allowed to enroll in the Naval Air Corps flight school in Pensacola, Florida. He was persistent, and as a half measure he was granted transfer to Pensacola as an observer. Equally gifted with guile and celerity, he somehow, at age fifty-one, already a grandfather, wangled a change in his designation from "student observer" to "student pilot."

Competing against pilots half his age, and despite congenitally poor eyesight, he earned his wings. His flight instructor noted, "The worse the weather, the better he flew." By the eve of World War II he was one of only four flag-rank officers in the United States Navy who actually knew how to fly an airplane.

When the Japanese attacked Pearl Harbor, Halsey was two thousand miles away, commanding a carrier task group delivering fighter planes for the unsuccessful defense of Wake Island. He cursed fate for his failure to intercept the Imperial strike force, although military experts unanimously agree that had his ships challenged Adm. Isoroku Yamamoto's fleet, they would have been wiped out. Days later, when he witnessed the breadth of destruction at Pearl—his carriers sailed into the harbor through oil still seeping from the sunken vessels along Battleship Row—his reaction was emblematic. "Before we're through with 'em the Japanese language will be spoken only in hell," he said.

His carrier force refueled and immediately put to sea to hunt the Japanese, but more rotten luck followed. Halsey was laid up in the hospital with a severe case of dermatitis during the Battle of Midway. Powerless, sullen, itching, he was bedridden at Pearl Harbor's medical center, covered in emolument, when he received fragmented reports of Adm. Raymond Spruance's stunning victory. He considered missing this fight the worst break of his career.

In October 1942, by now a rear admiral, Halsey was plucked from his carrier task force by Adm. Chester A. Nimitz and charged with command of the South Pacific Theater. Nimitz, commander in chief of the U.S. Pacific Fleet (CINCPAC), realized he needed fighting sailors to relieve the "defeatist" U.S. Pacific commands. It annoyed Nimitz no end that his South Pacific commanders seemed to share General MacArthur's view that islands such as Guadalcanal could not be held. In the face of this pessimism, Halsey's "devil-may-care" reputation of being at his best when things seemed most desperate appealed to CINCPAC.

Nimitz wrote that he was looking for someone unafraid to sail west into Asia, north to Japan, "to sail into hell itself if need be," to spread destruction among enemy-held island chains and disrupt Japan's vital ocean supply lines. Halsey himself could hardly wait "to begin throwing punches," and eight days after his promotion he defeated the Japanese at the Battle of the Santa Cruz Islands. One month later, after inflicting severe damage on a huge enemy armada during a three-day shoot-out in the waters off Guadalcanal, he was promoted to full admiral.

There were whispers in Washington about Halsey's rough edges, his pneumatic temper, his vocabulary's profanity-laced default setting. But, to Nimitz, Halsey's transgression, like Adm. Horatio Nelson's admission before sailing to his death in Trafalgar, had not been that great. "If it be a sin to covet glory," Nelson admitted to his mistress, Lady Emma Hamilton, "I am the most offending soul alive." Moreover, he fit precisely the profile Secretary of the Navy Frank Knox had sent to fleet headquarters at Pearl Harbor.

"Men of the aggressive fighting type must be preferred over men of more judicial, thoughtful, but less aggressive characteristics," Knox wrote Nimitz in a concise, frank memo whose prose limned the edge of poetry. "I presume most of us, if we had been required to choose at the beginning of the war between the brilliant, polished, socially attractive McClellan and the rough, rather uncouth, unsocial Grant, would have chosen McClellan, just as Lincoln did."

Nimitz was not about to repeat the error. A different historical analogy may also have played into the selection. It was proverbial in military circles that the one question Napoleon asked his commanders prior to bestowing the field marshal's baton was, "Are you lucky?" The techniques of war fighting may have changed in the decades since Austerlitz, but command instincts had not, and Halsey was acknowledged to possess deep reserves of good luck.

Not long after taking over the South Pacific Command, he demonstrated just this by ordering a feeder airfield hacked out of the jungles of Guadalcanal on terrain totally unsuited to the task. The ensuing, disastrous attempt at construction marooned a battalion of Marine Raiders. Trapped behind enemy lines, the Marines flanked the Japanese and broke through with a striking victory. As one Halsey biographer noted, "Even his mistakes turned out well."

When Halsey received his promotion orders, he exclaimed, "Jesus Christ and General Jackson, this is the hottest potato they ever handed me!" When the announcement was officially posted, cheers resonated from the mess rooms of the lowliest scows tethered at Pearl to the muddy trenches encircling beleaguered Henderson Field on Guadalcanal. Said one air combat intelligence officer stationed on Guadalcanal, "I'll never forget it. One minute we were too limp with malaria to crawl out of our foxholes; the next we were running around whooping like kids."

Like many sailors, Halsey was a superstitious man. He had a life-long dread of the thirteenth day of every month, and he carried or wore his totems proudly, in particular a tiki greenstone bracelet from New Zealand and a Hawaiian "good luck" strip of white linen. He was also something of a neat freak, to the point of obsession, and once had his steward follow the notoriously disheveled Vice Adm. John Sidney "Slew" McCain around his flag bridge with a dustpan and brush to sweep up McCain's cigarette ashes. His junior officers suspected him of being a "bathroom dawdler," for at each staff briefing his shoes were invariably shined to a brown mirror, his tuft of hoar-gray hair meticulously slicked and parted, his fingernails clipped, cleaned, and buffed. And such was his reputation as an epicure that when he hosted a contingent of visiting army dignitaries aboard his flagship with a meal as sumptuous as a condemned man's, one officer was heard to remark afterward, "Good God, why didn't we join the navy?"

Despite this personal fastidiousness, ordinary seamen instinctively felt a special camaraderie with the admiral, sensing that he was willing to face their perils, able to bear their hardships. When Halsey's twenty-seven-year-old son, Lt. (j.g.) William F. Halsey III, an aviation supply officer on the carrier USS *Saratoga*, went missing in the South Pacific in the summer of 1943, the admiral explicitly ordered that the search for him be conducted by the book. "My son is the same as every other son in the combat zone," he told his operations officer. "Look for him just as you'd look for anybody else."

Young Halsey and several crewmates were recovered four days later from a life raft floating near New Caledonia. But the admiral's evenhandedness, and equanimity, in the face of personal privation was noted by U.S. sailors across the fleet. It was common knowledge throughout the Pacific Theater that Halsey enjoyed forgoing flag-country tradition to watch the regular shipboard movies with the enlisted men in the hangar deck, and he was known to complain loudly to Nimitz about the lousy films being shipped from Stateside. Once, when a sudden squall interrupted his regular afternoon game of deck tennis, he grabbed a mop and joined the maintenance crew in swabbing the teakwood weather deck.

Navy Secretary Knox often repeated a story that symbolized Halsey's rapport with his enlisted men. One day, two sailors walking across the deck of the repair ship USS *Argonne* were discussing Halsey.

"I'd go through hell for that old son of a bitch," said one.

The seaman was slapped on the back, and turned to find himself face-to-face with the admiral. "Young man," said Halsey, "I'm not that old."

The anecdote could be taken for apocryphal—Knox recognized the value of good advertising—were it not for dozens of similar tales. A Marine sentry assigned to Halsey's cabin, for instance, once had the occasion to mention to the admiral that he hailed from the Bronx in New York City.

"Oh, yeah?" replied Halsey, who had been a gridiron star at the Naval Academy. "I'm from Elizabeth, New Jersey. You're a big guy. You play football?"

The two then bantered for some time about sports—an exceptional, upstairs-downstairs exchange that rapidly made the rounds of mess decks throughout the fleet.

Ordinary sailors and Marines were not the only men who carried a special fondness for the "fighting admiral." War correspondents loved Halsey, and he loved them back. Along with Patton in Europe, he was the closest thing Americans had to the mythic sinner-saint warrior, and he held lusty, detailed press conferences that composed, for the newspapermen, contemporary history.

Not only was he given to salty epithets deriding the Japanese as "yellow-bellied sons of bitches" and "fish-eating yellow bastards," he knew what actions made good copy. In January 1942, when an enemy reconnaissance plane passing overhead inexplicably failed to spot his carrier task force steaming toward the surprise raid on the Marshalls, Halsey summoned his language officer to translate a message. "From the American admiral in charge of the striking force, to the Japanese admiral on the Marshall Islands," he dictated. "It is a pleasure to thank you for having your patrol plane not sight my force."

The next morning bombers from his carrier flagship USS *Enterprise* dropped copies of the leaflet along with their payloads. The flamboyant stunt was the talk of the Pacific Theater.

On occasion, however, Halsey's spark-plug persona lapped itself. He was of the opinion that political language was the ability to give an appearance of solidity to pure wind, and during a summit in Auckland with New Zealand's prime minister Peter Fraser in January 1943, he guaranteed reporters that the war would be won within a year. The forecast, wildly off base, not only infuriated the War and Navy Departments but embarrassed President Franklin D. Roosevelt. Tokyo Rose began cataloging the tortures Japan would inflict upon Halsey when he was captured, and even MacArthur, whose vanity brooked no competition, perceived in the banty admiral what the writer Ambrose Bierce called "a person of low taste, more interested in himself than in me."

But to moms and pops and wives and sweethearts back home, newspaper dispatches filed from Halsey's vicinity reflected a can-do American buoyancy that civilians yearned for. He often signed off correspondence with what came to be known as his slogan—

"Kill Japs, kill Japs, and keep on killing Japs." As one contemporary noted, "No one in the South Pacific forgot it."

Two months after Halsey took command in the South Pacific, U.S. Marines drove the last of the Japanese from Guadalcanal. It was America's first land triumph in the Pacific Theater—more important, it was seemingly impregnable Japan's first defeat. It was left to an Englishman, commenting on a simultaneous Allied landing half a world away in North Africa, to frame what Americans back home felt upon receiving the news of the Marine victory on the Bloody 'Canal. "Now is not the end," said Winston Churchill. "It is not even the beginning. But it is, perhaps, the end of the beginning."

In April 1943, Halsey achieved a measure of revenge for his "failure" to engage the brilliant Yamamoto off Pearl Harbor. Naval intelligence code breakers decrypted a message from the Japanese Imperial Staff revealing Yamamoto's plan to make a morale-boosting inspection tour of his air squadrons in the upper Solomon Islands. The Japanese admiral was renowned as a punctilious officer, and the decoded communiqué helpfully listed his itinerary down to the minute. Nimitz studied his maps and determined that the first leg of Yamamoto's flight would bring him to within three hundred miles of Guadalcanal, the very periphery of the range of U.S. fighter planes at Henderson Field. If they flew with supplementary belly gas tanks, they just might reach him and make it back alive.

But a decision to assassinate the Japanese admiral was well beyond Nimitz's pay grade. He contacted Washington, where Secretary Knox consulted with a group of religious leaders about the morality of targeting a specific enemy commander, even one whose prominence in Japan was second only to that of the emperor. The churchmen gave the attack their blessing, and President Roosevelt signed off on the plot. Nimitz handed Operation Vengeance to Halsey with the message, "Good Luck and Good Hunting."

Halsey and his staff devised their plan, and at first light on April 18 a flight of seventeen P-38 Lightnings fitted with belly tanks launched from Henderson Field. Two hours later they intercepted Yamamoto's squadron of two Mitsubishi bombers and its escort Zeros near the southern coast of Bougainville. Eight of the American fighters engaged the Zeros. The rest sped after the two Mitsubishis, now diving for the treetops. The U.S. squad leader had not expected two bombers. Which one carried Yamamoto? Taking no chances, American cannon and machine gun fire sent one flaming into the jungle canopy. The other, also hit, pancaked into the sea.

The next morning Japanese troops hacked through the overgrowth and recovered the remains of Yamamoto. The admiral's body was still strapped into its seat, unblemished except for the two tidy holes, crusted with dried blood, left by the bullet that passed through his jaw and exited his temple. He was still gripping his samurai sword. The Japanese navy never won another major sea battle.

"Pop goes the weasel" was the prearranged radio signal confirming Yamamoto's death. When it was flashed from Henderson Field to Halsey, who was meeting with MacArthur in Brisbane, Australia, an aide in the room began hooting and applauding. Halsey silenced him with a wave and a scowl. "What's good about it?" he demanded. "I'd hoped to lead that scoundrel up Pennsylvania Avenue in chains, with the rest of you kicking him where it would do the most good."

A Stateside headline writer had christened Halsey "Bull," and newsmen the world over invariably picked it up. Though he disliked the epithet—"I got that name from some drunken newspaper correspondent who punched the letter 'u' instead of 'i' writing Bill"—he tolerated it, and among his admirers he certainly lived up to the nickname's snorting connotation. It was "Bull" Halsey's lust for a good fight, anywhere, anytime, that secured his reputation. Once, aboard the destroyer *Hull*, Chief Quartermaster Archie DeRyckere was asked by a new sailor to describe the Third Fleet's commander in one word. DeRyckere stroked his chin. "Attack," he finally said.

In August 1944, Halsey took over the rotating command of the Pearl Harbor–based Pacific, or Big Blue, Fleet from his good friend, sometimes rival, and future in-law Vice Adm. Raymond A. Spruance. If, as was held, every ship of the U.S. Navy was stamped with the personality of its skipper, Halsey's imprint loomed large over the entire fleet. In contrast to the buttoned-down Spruance, Halsey rarely stood on ceremony. A British Royal Navy liaison officer once skiffed ashore to introduce himself to the American admiral. The prim, proper Englishman found the usually fastidious Halsey larking about barefoot on his veranda, wearing only shorts and a khaki shirt with no insignia. Halsey mixed cocktails as the two settled in to swat mosquitoes, converse, and watch the sun set.

Later, the Brit recalled that out of uniform Halsey might have been mistaken for "Long John Silver." But, he added, "When I left him and thought of what he had said, I realized I had been listening to one of the great admirals of the war."

Halsey was also blessed with an appreciation that the wheel of fortune is oiled by whiskey—or, as he put it, "A bottle of Scotch on the table always bore fruit in our dealings with other commands." He often said that "as a general rule I never trust a fighting man who doesn't smoke or drink." And his favorite toast soon became a staple in Pacific tiki bars frequented by American servicemen: "I've drunk your health in company; I've drunk your health alone; I've drunk your health so many times, I've damned near ruined my own." This liquid diplomacy proved particularly felicitous in smoothing over simmering rivalries between Nimitz's staff and army units under MacArthur's command. Further, whenever an army outfit assisted the navy by any manner or means, Halsey went out of his way to ensure that the ground-pounders received full credit in the newspapers.

Though a newspaper reporter once made note of the close "affinity between [Halsey's] foot and his mouth," and sticklers may have found his humor too ribald and his references to the Japanese as "monkey meat" somewhat crude (given even the racial dictates of the age), the admiral's loyalists rightly argued that the U.S. Navy was not a debating society. If Spruance, unencumbered with charisma, was a master of cautious planning and seemed to speak in italics, Halsey's instinctive, seat-of-the-pants audacity inspired partisanship.

In a sense, the two admirals' personalities, and their respective importance in spearheading America's Pacific campaign, mirrored the personal disparity GIs observed between two warfighters on the other side of the globe, Dwight D. Eisenhower and George S. Patton. A fellow naval officer who worked with both Spruance and Halsey may as well have been writing about the two U.S. generals on the European front when he noted, "When Admiral Spruance was in command you knew precisely what he was going to do. But when Admiral Halsey was in command, you never knew what he was going to do." At the end of the day, however, it was the swabbies who kept score. In their respective battles against Japanese fleets, Spruance, who was not an aviator, had sunk three of the nine enemy carriers he'd faced; Halsey had dispatched four of four.

It was against this backdrop that Admiral Halsey now found himself sitting in the dock at the end of the long green table on Ulithi Atoll, trying to explain the perfect storm that had just decimated his fleet.

U.S. naval courts of inquiry were common during World War II, as regulations required that a formal investigation be held whenever a vessel was lost. Known throughout the officer corps as "captain-breakers," their purpose was to examine in depth the circumstances that led to a ship's sinking, to establish responsibility, to determine if any offense was committed, and to fix blame if necessary. But today's was no routine hearing. Among the observers in the makeshift courtroom aboard the destroyer tender *Cascade* was CINCPAC himself, Adm. Chester A. Nimitz.

Tall, courtly, and strikingly handsome, with a patrician mien that lent an air of confident gravitas to his office, Nimitz was a map hobbyist whose profound interest in military literature contrasted starkly with Halsey's preference for the *Police Gazette*. He had arrived on Ulithi from Pearl Harbor on Christmas Eve accompanied by Vice Admirals George D. Murray and John Howard Hoover, the latter a prickly officer with the hard look of a man who didn't mind being known as a place where trouble started. Hoover and Murray, along with Rear Adm. Glenn B. Davis, would comprise the three-man court of inquiry.

On Ulithi, Nimitz "broke flag" on the *New Jersey*—navy slang for an officer of higher rank bunking on another officer's flagship—and presented Halsey with a miniature Christmas tree complete with ornaments. He appeared miffed that Halsey and his staff noticeably preferred the nuts-and-bolts metal "tree" fashioned by the battleship's engine room gang. The next morning, Christmas Day 1944, Nimitz formally convened the court. He appointed Admiral Hoover its presiding officer and named forty-three-year-old Capt. Herbert K. Gates, an expert in mechanical and marine engineering, as judge advocate. The position was equal parts prosecutor and legal adviser to the sitting admirals.

The hearing was closed to all but court officers, stenographers, witnesses, defendants, and "interested parties." The record of its proceedings, classified "Secret," was kept so for over half a century. This not only shut out any casual observers, but left the frustrated war correspondents prowling Ulithi—several of whom had barely survived the typhoon themselves—on the outside looking in.

Naval courts of inquiry followed a fairly straightforward formula. The court determined if an officer or enlisted man should be classified as a defendant—"A person whose conduct is the subject of this investigation"—or an interested party—"Any person, not a complainant or defendant, who has an interest in the subject matter of the inquiry." The proceedings would begin with the commanding officer of a lost vessel—or, as the case may be, her highest-ranking survivor—dictating in private a narrative of the circumstances under which the ship sank.

That narrative would then be read aloud in court in the presence of all the surviving officers and crew. The court would ask the officer if he had any objections to the narrative's content and, if not, whether he had any charges to make against a fellow officer or enlisted man with regard to the ship's destruction. If again the answer was no, the process was reversed, with each surviving seaman granted the opportunity to bring a complaint against any officer or fellow crewman. The court then followed up with questions of its own. Some hearings were perfunctory. Others were tense.

Before Halsey was sworn in on December 28, the court had been sitting for three days and had already heard the testimony of close to half of the fifty-four witnesses it would call over its eight-day session. When Halsey's star turn arrived, Judge Advocate Gates was relentless.

"When fueling had to be stopped on the seventeenth of December due to increasing bad weather, what were your considerations?" he asked.

"The general picture was sour," Halsey replied, and so by this point was the admiral's mood. In his own defense Halsey again fell back upon his obligation to support MacArthur's amphibious landings on the Philippine island of Mindoro. He told the court of his experiences encountering, and successfully riding out, previous Pacific typhoons. He also mentioned as a mitigating factor a warning weather report from a reconnaissance seaplane that, having reached his flagship, the battleship New Jersey, in plenty of time, was not decoded and read for another forty-eight hours. Judge Advocate Gates was unimpressed. Seven hundred and ninety-three men were lost. Three ships rested on the ocean floor. The Third Fleet was decimated.

"At what time did the storm considerations begin to govern the disposition of the fleet, if at all?" It was the "if at all" that blistered.

So it went. The judge advocate thrusting; Halsey parrying. This was not the admiral's strength. By temperament and training he was accustomed to playing offense. As the questioning wore on, Halsey's answers seemed to become more frustrated at the direction of the hearings. At the end of the day he requested the court to officially designate him an "interested party," and asked to be represented by counsel. His appeal was granted.

The inquiry was the talk of Ulithi, if not the Pacific Theater. It was a story that was not only developing legs, but tentacles that might take down America's most famous naval hero. Throughout engine rooms and mess halls, Halsey's loyalists argued that the typhoon was an unfathomable act of God, tempered by a combination of shoddy staff work and miscommunication. Battered survivors, most especially the sailors who had floated for days or watched their crewmates be torn apart by sharks, may have held a different view, but all remained too awestruck, overwhelmed by the presence of so much brass, to speak for the record.

Admiral Hoover, the court's president, quietly let it be known that he believed Halsey should be court-martialed. Sailing the fleet into that storm, he thought, losing those men and ships, was a severe dereliction of duty.

Nimitz was more circumspect, at least in public. His admiration and friendship toward Halsey ran deep, and changing an admiral's mind is akin to reversing a carrier's course. It takes a lot of tack and persuasion. In private, however, CINCPAC seethed. The retaking of the Philippines was the most important American offensive of the Pacific war to date, the last stepping-stone before bringing the fight to the Japanese mainland, and Nimitz considered the debacle during the storm "a totally unnecessary disaster."

He also feared that Halsey's political enemies, both Stateside and in-theater, had finally the ammunition to sink him. Nimitz personally knew most of these sailors, and to a man he considered them respected officers of the line.

These were seamen who remembered—and still resented—Halsey's performance during the largest naval engagement in history, the Battle for Leyte Gulf.

CHAPTER 2

*That the fleet movements directed by Commander THIRD
Fleet after bad weather conditions set in on the forenoon of
17 December were logical in view of his war commitments
and the manner in which he evaluated the meager weather data
he received or had.*

—GENERAL OPINION #1 IN THE REPORT ISSUED BY THE
COURT OF INQUIRY INVESTIGATING "HALSEY'S TYPHOON."

Often overlooked in the distant fog of World War II is the fact that
the Japanese attacked the northern Philippine island of Luzon five
hours after Admiral Yamamoto's strike force bombed Pearl Harbor five thousand miles to the east. The Imperial War Department's
primary goal was the capture of the country's capital, Manila, a
chocolate-box colonial city that rises from the eastern shore of
Manila Bay, the most excellent natural anchorage in the Pacific.
Control of Manila Bay meant control of the South China Sea and
the sea-lanes to the oil-rich Dutch East Indies.

Geography is destiny, and within weeks of Manila's fall, the banner of the Rising Sun—"the flaming red asshole" American troops
called it—would be hoisted not only on flagstaffs across the Dutch
East Indies, but across French Indochina and British Malaysia as well,
until the Japanese were knocking on the back door to India. The
"Kimigayo," the Japanese national anthem, reverberated from Manchuria in the north to New Guinea in the south as the isles of
Micronesia and Oceania fell. For a brief spell Imperial troops even

garrisoned Attu and Kiska, the two most westerly of Alaska's Aleutian Islands.

And though the Japanese invasion of the Philippines inflicted nowhere near the psychological blow of Pearl Harbor, it was, arguably, strategically more important. Because America's aircraft carriers were at sea, the sneak attack on Pearl, for all its devastation, was in the end a debilitating hit-and-run. In the Philippines and elsewhere across the Pacific, however, the enemy would have to be dislodged. Given the Philippines' cultural relationship with the United States, the Imperial Army's capture of the islands was as close as Japan would come to occupying contiguous American soil.

Of all the United States' overseas holdings, the U.S.-Filipino dynamic was the most complex. In essence, by the onset of World War II the U.S. had been the country's colonial ruler for over four decades, since Spain ceded the territory in the Treaty of Paris following the 1898 Spanish-American War. Having acquired this sprawling archipelago halfway around the world, America didn't quite know what to do with it, and U.S. occupation forces viciously eradicated more than 200,000 Filipinos in the Orwellian-named Philippine Insurrection. American military commanders directing this operation against the "gugus" tended, in the words of one analyst, "to see the conflict as an extension of the Indian extermination campaigns for which they had been trained."

When the U.S. military finally subdued the rebellion and gained nominal control of the more than seven thousand islands that constituted the nation, "enlightened colonialism" became the order of the day. American bureaucrats, ministers, and teachers set out to Westernize the indigenous population of 19 million—"our little brown brothers," as one U.S. governor of Manila, the future American president William Howard Taft, referred to the Filipinos.

Over time, Spanish influence gradually faded as a modern infrastructure of schools, roads, and bridges sprouted, and an American-style market economy took root. If English was not the official lingua franca, it ran a close second to Tagalog. And urban Filipinos, regarded

in some quarters as the Irish of Asia for their toughness and voracious appetite for life, gradually grew accustomed to attending movies
filmed on America's West Coast, driving cars constructed in her
heartland, and listening to music recorded on her East Coast.

It was against this backdrop that Japan invaded under the pre-
tense of its "Asia for Asiatics" campaign. Although President
Roosevelt had promised the Philippines independence by 1946, the
Japanese propagandized their landings as an effort "to free you from
the bonds of Western colonialism." They proceeded to plunder the
islands' natural resources, most especially its rubber plantations, and
treat the Filipinos as serfs at best, slaves at worst.

Despite warnings of an imminent invasion, the grandiloquent and
histrionic Gen. Douglas MacArthur, field marshal of the combined
American-Filipino army, was caught unawares when the Japanese
landed. (Due to the country's location across the International
Date Line, the invasion is officially listed as having occurred on December 8, 1941, east longitude date.) The son of a Civil War general who became the first military governor of the Philippines,
MacArthur had amassed a sterling service record since graduating
West Point in 1903 at the head of his class and was destined to
become the most decorated officer in the history of the United
States military.

MacArthur had been sent to the Philippines by Roosevelt in 1935
to organize the country's defense and stayed on after retiring in 1937
to become military adviser to President Manuel Quezon. Recalled
to active duty just months before the war, he felt betrayed by Washington, and Roosevelt in particular, when no American reinforce-
ments arrived to stave off the invading Japanese.

Within three days of Japan's initial strike, Imperial Navy bombers and fighter planes destroyed most of the U.S. aircraft stationed
on Luzon, the country's largest island. As forty-three thousand
troops from the Fourteenth Imperial Army rolled south, American and Filipino soldiers fought a rearguard action, awaiting the
arrival of the U.S. Fleet at Pearl Harbor. This, needless to say,
would not occur. MacArthur despaired as he holed up in his

Manila hotel, the shock of events leaving him unable or unwilling to react. He fled finally to a bunker on Corregidor, "The Rock," at the mouth of Manila Bay.

Issuing directives from his bombproof stronghold deep beneath the earth, "Dashing Doug" became "Dugout Doug," complete with mocking limericks composed by embittered American troops. Notwithstanding his much-publicized vow to return, MacArthur's vaunted "swaggerstick style" was nowhere in evidence when, in March 1942, he was evacuated by PT boat and submarine to Australia. One month later, their backs to the sea at the southern tip of Luzon's Bataan Peninsula, the largest surrender in American history occurred. Seventy-six thousand soldiers, including close to 12,000 Americans, laid down their arms.

The Philippines was merely the first of the domino tiles to fall before the advancing forces of Dai Nippon. Years of complacency strewn with contempt by the Western powers for Japanese fighting men—thought to be stunted, nearsighted, and generally frail—now brought a cruel reckoning of defeat after defeat. Hong Kong. Singapore. Kuala Lumpur. Rangoon. Port Moresby. Rabaul. All felt the lash of the whip from a nation no larger than the state of California. With the U.S. Pacific Fleet crippled at Pearl Harbor, Japan ruled the seas.

Worse, to their horror, Allied military commanders realized that the Mitsubishi A6M1 fighter plane, the fearsome, agile Zero, was faster and more maneuverable than anything the United States could throw into the sky. With bitter irony, U.S. Army Air Force pilots noted that the Zero's design had largely followed specs first developed by the American pioneer aviator Howard Hughes.

On December 8, 1941, President Roosevelt addressed the nation in a radio broadcast, vowing, "No matter how long it may take us to overcome this premeditated invasion, the American people in their righteous might will win through to absolute victory." Considering the speed and ease with which the Japanese empire was expanding, this struck Roosevelt's staggered countrymen as an overly optimistic assessment. More citizens tended to agree when he added, "There is no blinking at the fact that our people, our territory, and our interests are in grave danger."

Yet despite Japan's seeming invincibility, as early as October 1942, while U.S. Marines and Japanese soldiers were still fighting to exterminate one another on Guadalcanal, CINCPAC Nimitz sensed that the U.S. was already winning a grinding war of attrition across the Pacific. Japan had a robust, if limited, manufacturing capability, and its capture of the resource-rich territories enveloping the South China Sea certainly upgraded that facility. But within a year of the attack on Pearl Harbor the United States was simply outproducing the rest of the combined world in ships, planes, weapons—and martial ideas.

A writer once observed that war is God's way of teaching Americans geography, and certainly the ensuing rolling D-days on unpronounceable specks of coral and sand from Tarawa to Kwajalein to Eniwetok to Tinian to Peleliu left every U.S. sailor, soldier, and airman fighting across these alien shores with a map of the Pacific embossed in his psyche. At bottom, however, the island-hopping raids and landings had one common goal: the retaking of the Philippines as a springboard from which to launch the invasion of Japan.

Moreover, unlike the great land battles being fought against the Nazis in Africa and Europe, the Pacific Theater was and would remain primarily a naval and air campaign. The Japanese may have occupied far-flung islands, but they still needed to supply them. Without realizing it, the enemy had disastrously exceeded its bite/chew ratio. As such, Nimitz exhorted his admirals never to shy from taking the "calculated risks" that would decimate the enemy's land, sea, and air forces.

These daring forays had already resulted in stunning victories at the Battles of the Coral Sea and Midway as well as a humiliating American defeat at the Battle of Savo Island. One fact was clear: The age of the dreadnought had given way to the epoch of the aircraft carrier, and the era when battleships were cheaper than battles was over. The continuing, if bloody, U.S. advances across the Pacific were thus marked by recurring carrier attacks in conjunction with amphibious Marine Corps landings on an ever-widening range of targets.

To that end, a two-pronged series of U.S. land, sea, and air attacks inexorably began to sap both Imperial manpower and material. In the south, MacArthur was planning to jump from Australia to New Guinea, and send his Sixth Army through dense jungle over the Owen Stanley Mountains to the island's northern coast, thus freeing Australia from the threat of invasion. In the Central Pacific, Nimitz had already successfully landed his Marines on Tarawa in the Gilberts chain, providing—despite the carnage that horrified an American public—valuable lessons for future amphibious landings.

Moreover, as America scrambled to get its armaments factories up and running, it instinctively drew upon its own pioneering military history, increasingly utilizing a hit-and-run strategy that had worked splendidly a century and a half earlier, when a ragtag collection of eastern seaboard colonials had overthrown the professional armies of a monolithic British crown. These bold strokes ranged from Burma—where Brig. Gen. Frank Merrill's aptly named Marauders emulated the guerrilla tactics of the Revolutionary War's Rogers' Rangers—to New Guinea, where MacArthur's army commanders transformed a rough-hewn battalion of mule skinners made redundant by mechanized warfare into the 6th Ranger Battalion, the first American Rangers in the Pacific Theater.

This concept of guerrilla warfare was not limited to land. On the high seas, Nimitz's agenda of "calculated risks" resulted in the formation of fast, stealthy destroyer squadrons that were designed to not only surprise and confuse the enemy, but overburden the Imperial Navy's ability to protect its supply lines and shipping lanes. And no group was to transform the concept of destroyer tactics in a more dramatic fashion than the notorious "Little Beavers" of Destroyer Squadron 23, placed under Halsey's command in June 1943.

Within six months of arriving at Halsey's headquarters at Noumea, on New Caledonia, the eight destroyers of DesRon 23—consisting of the newer and faster *Fletcher*-class vessels—delighted Halsey with their ability to "Kill more Japs." Sailing under the command of the innovative naval strategist and tactician Capt. Arleigh "31-Knot" Burke, the Little Beavers were the only destroyer squadron in World War II awarded a group Presidential Unit Citation for "extraordinary heroism."

Burke managed to fuse the individual vessels and their crews into an offensive unit that took the preconceived notions of destroyer capability—patrol, escort, and submarine screening—beyond the ken of most navy brass. (Burke personally adopted the insignia of the bow and arrow–wielding Little Beaver, sidekick to the popular comic strip character Red Ryder, after noticing a torpedo man's artwork decorating his tin fish tubes aboard the destroyer USS *Claxton*.)

As their ghostly attacks mounted—off the Carolines, off Truk, off Guam—to the Japanese it must have appeared that the aggressive Little Beavers were everywhere and nowhere. Typical was their encounter with a Japanese troop transport squadron, a Tokyo Express out of Rabaul delivering soldiers to defend Buka Island in the Solomons.

"Thirty-One-Knot Burke, get athwart the Buka-Rabaul evacuation line," came Halsey's orders. "If enemy contacted, you know what to do." He did. The Little Beavers sank three destroyers, including a troop transport, in a battle Halsey deemed "the Trafalgar of the Pacific." The engagement is studied to this day at the U.S. Naval War College.

The forty-three-year-old Burke—whose nickname indicated his desire and ability to lead his ships in spectacular dashes at boiler-bursting speed—was an Academy graduate whose doctrine of independent destroyer actions not only baffled the enemy, but laid foundation to the idea of the "Tin Can Navy," a "destroyer service" physically and metaphorically distinct from the U.S. Navy. This notion was captured in the esprit de corps depicted in a letter written by Ens. Vincent McClelland, a twenty-three-year-old assistant gunnery officer aboard the DD USS *Spence*, a member of DesRon 23. Admiral Nimitz had personally awarded the square-jawed

McClelland, recently the captain of the Yale football team, a citation for "meritorious and efficient" actions off Kavieng in February 1944. But the tribute seemed to embarrass the officer.

"I am enclosing the commendation," McClelland wrote his parents matter-of-factly at the end of the letter. "I feel badly about it because it was not deserved. If I rated one, everybody on board did, too."

If McClelland was the kind of fighting man the United States was turning out to throw against the Japanese, then typical of the new machines America was also producing was his ship, the destroyer *Spence*, a vessel destined to play a major role in the most devastating natural disaster the United States Navy was ever to suffer.

Commissioned in early 1943 and named after a nineteenth-century master commandant from Portsmouth, New Hampshire, who had chased pirates from the Caribbean Sea to the Barbary Coast, the 2,050-ton *Spence* had been attached early in the war to the Atlantic Fleet to run convoys to Casablanca. In July she was reassigned to the Pacific, where she joined the Little Beavers. Her service record was striking. Awarded eight battle stars in addition to the Presidential Unit Citation, she was the flagship of a destroyer division that sank twenty Japanese landing barges during the invasion of the Solomons; a month later with the rest of the Little Beavers she'd covered the landings on the Treasury Islands and at Bougainville.

It was during the Bougainville invasion that a case of mistaken identity on a starless night provided one of the classic ripostes of the war. After being sideswiped by fellow DesRon 23 member USS *Thatcher* during the heat of the Battle of Empress Augusta Bay, the *Spence* was limping home under blackout conditions when her crew was rattled by a shower of shells falling about her from the direction of her own picket lines. Her skipper, Comdr. Bernard L. Austin, raced for the TBS phone and shouted frantically to Arleigh Burke, "We've just had a close miss! Hope you are not shooting at us!"

"Sorry," came Burke's reply. "But you'll have to excuse the next four salvos already on their way."

Burke's second bombardment narrowly missed the *Spence*, and in her haste to take evasive action she happened upon the wounded Japanese destroyer *Hatsukaze*. Her gunners ran out of ammunition pouring shells and torpedoes into the flaming wreck. Several days later her battle-hardened crew bore witness to one of the more grisly acts of the war, a telling indication of the lengths to which the Japanese were willing to go in the furtherance of their samurai cause.

Sighting a makeshift raft that appeared to have several dead men strewn across it, the *Spence* closed to investigate. Her lookouts counted seven enemy soldiers, and as the destroyer neared, suddenly they all stood and began shouting in Japanese. One, apparently an officer, produced a machine pistol. He passed it in quick succession to each man, who put the barrel in his mouth and pulled the trigger. One man seemed reluctant, and two others held him down while the officer shot him. Now only the officer remained. After a brief, passionate speech directed toward the Americans, he, too, blew his brains out of the back of his skull and tumbled into the now-shark-infested waters. The entire event took five minutes.

In March 1944 the gallant Little Beavers of DesRon 23, the only destroyers granted the honor of flying the swallow-tailed blue, yellow, and red burgee signifying their Presidential Unit Citation, were disbanded and reassigned to Halsey's carrier fleet. Although Commodore Burke was appointed chief of staff to Vice Adm. Marc Mitscher's carrier division, a step along the path that would eventually lead him to his postwar position as America's chief of naval operations, he complained bitterly that "somebody was trying to railroad me out of these lovely destroyers."

Not long after the Little Beavers were reassigned, the near-simultaneous U.S. invasions of Saipan, Tinian, and Guam in the Marianas chain—dubbed Operation Forager—opened a new phase in American warfighting. The island chain lay just twelve hundred miles southeast of Tokyo, and as one U.S. infantry general predicted prior to the assaults, "We are through with flat atolls. . . . Now we're up against mountains and caves where Japs can dig in. A week from now there will be a lot of dead Marines."

His words proved prescient. Such was the slaughter on both sides—22,000 Japanese civilians on Saipan committed suicide after the island's fall—that Japan's prime minister Hideki Tojo was replaced by Kuniaki Koiso, considered a "moderate" politician. It did not go unnoticed in Tokyo that in addition to landing 127,000 Americans in the Marianas, the United States possessed the manpower to fight on concurrent fronts ranging from Italy to China to France to New Guinea.

More important, the Marianas were close enough to the Japanese mainland to draw out a probing Imperial Fleet. The subsequent engagement—known in history books as the Battle of the Philippine Sea but remembered by the American sailors and airmen who fought it as the "Marianas Turkey Shoot"—resulted in a stupendous U.S. victory as well as one of the great controversies to this point in the war. When American sailors took Admiral Halsey's side in the ongoing, intramural Halsey-Spruance debate, it was often Spruance's actions during the Marianas Turkey Shoot to which they pointed. (Months later, of course, Spruance's defenders would only have to mention the Battle for Leyte Gulf to impugn Halsey.)

On June 17 scout planes from Spruance's Fifth Fleet spotted the Japanese Mobile Fleet of five separate flotillas, each anchored by an aircraft carrier, 350 miles west of the Marianas chain. Spruance's carrier commander, Vice Admiral Mitscher, argued that to attack was the only reasonable recourse. The enemy's Mobile Fleet accounted for 90 percent of Japan's combined naval forces. America could put the Japanese navy out of commission then and there. But Spruance demurred, citing his orders from Nimitz to protect the men and vessels taking part in the landings on Saipan.

The next day the Japanese commander, Adm. Jisaburo Ozawa, sent four waves of assault planes against Spruance's task force. In perhaps the most lopsided victory of the war, American pilots destroyed 243 of the 373 bogeys, and U.S. submarines sank two Japanese carriers. Two days later Mitscher finally prevailed upon

Spruance to be allowed to hunt down what was left of the enemy's ships. His four carrier groups launched 216 planes in eleven minutes, which destroyed another 150 enemy aircraft and sank a third Japanese carrier.

Though a stunning tactical victory—despite the fact that eighty of Mitscher's returning planes crashed during a risky night carrier landing—in strategic terms the Battle of the Philippine Sea proved alarming. Though Imperial naval power had suffered irreparable damage, most especially to its experienced carrier pilots, the bulk of Ozawa's vessels, including six crucial carriers, managed to escape Mitscher's airmen. In addition, Japan now realized that the noose was tightening and that its conventional air strength would never recover. Its leaders began to contemplate far more desperate measures of defense. To this point in the war, few if any Americans were familiar with the word *kamikaze*.

Meanwhile, one of the ships taking part in the Marianas Turkey Shoot had been the destroyer *Spence*, whose crew by now was as well traveled as any of Cook's or Magellan's. For her actions during the battle the *Spence* received her eighth battle star and subsequently sailed on to bombard the Mariana Islands themselves. In August she was sent to San Francisco's Hunters Point Naval Shipyard for overhaul, from which she returned to the Pacific Theater with a new captain and an almost completely remanned crew to spend the next ten weeks screening Halsey's carriers.

Just prior to her brief dry dock, one of the holdover crewmen, Assistant Gunnery Officer Ens. Vincent McClelland, again took pen in hand, this time to write to his brother, a U.S. Army Air Force officer.

"We have seen every kind of action there is and come through unscathed," he wrote. "The machine guns have a couple of planes to their credit now. The past two weeks are sort of a long blur to me. We have stood so many nights at General Quarters that we are about done in. To start it off—in the space of 24 hours we made two shore bombardments, took part in the longest night surface action of the war, and underwent an all-out air attack. Oh—I forgot—we also had a collision during the same spell and had a five-inch shell hit us just below the water line. I guess it all sounds unbelievable, and it certainly seems so to me. All in all life isn't too bad. Bird men such as you really have the life. . . . Still I wouldn't swap. The fightin' Spence is plenty good enough for me. I really think she is one of the best cans afloat."

With sailors such as Vincent McClelland under his command, Halsey's confidence in America's ultimate victory comes into sharper focus. The invasion of the Philippine Island of Luzon, and the recapture of Manila, loomed. For that success to be realized, however, the United States would not only need to overcome a fanatical human enemy, but also face the voracious natural phenomena of the Pacific's vast, uncharted seas.

This was not lost on Ensign McClelland's family, who noted that the poignant remarks in the final letter they would ever receive from him were postmarked November 15, 1944—one month before he would drown off the coast of Mindoro during what was soon to become known as "Halsey's Typhoon."

CHAPTER 3

That action be taken to impress upon commanders the necessity of giving full consideration to adverse weather likely to be encountered in Western Pacific.

—RECOMMENDATION #3 IN THE REPORT ISSUED BY THE
COURT OF INQUIRY INVESTIGATING "HALSEY'S TYPHOON."

Despite great leaps in technology, by 1944 not much more was known about the provenance or mechanics of tropical cyclones than had been understood a millennium earlier. What was certain, however, was that the word "typhoon"—from the Greek *typhon*, Aristotle's mythical "whirlwind" monster with one hundred heads—remained a navigator's nightmare.

Called *baguios* in Manila, *tufans* in Muscat, and *taai fungs* in Hong Kong, these annual tempests have ravaged Oceania from time immemorial, shaping the culture and commerce of Asian societies as surely as the hard winter breakup determined the rhythms of Inuit civilization, or the screaming Boreas winds influenced the religious sacrifices of the ancient Athenians. And to the U.S. Navy during World War II, nowhere was this more apparent than in the funnel-shaped channel of water in the Northwestern Pacific known as the Luzon Strait, through which more typhoons sweep than anywhere else on the planet.

To greatly simplify, a typhoon or hurricane is a tightly organized storm system of furious energy in which a warm center of low barometric pressure is surrounded by gale-force winds rotating counterclockwise in the Northern Hemisphere, and clockwise in the Southern Hemisphere. Typhoons, like hurricanes, are elliptical in shape and generally cover an average area of about three hundred miles in diameter, with the curving cloud bands forming their eye walls extending anywhere from three to sixty-five miles in circumference. The blinding rains and furious winds of a Pacific typhoon's eye wall are the fiercest on the planet—some have been measured in excess of 250 knots, more than half the speed of the winds whipped up by the atomic bomb dropped on Hiroshima. Yet it is within the still, humid eye where the air pressure is lowest and the domed, "upswelling" storm surge most violent.

Pacific typhoons, which travel in a general westerly direction at between five and twelve miles per hour, occur far more frequently than either Atlantic hurricanes or Indian Ocean cyclones. And such is their enormity that some of the lowest barometric pressures ever recorded have been observed in their vortexes. In the Philippines the official "typhoon season" runs nine months, from April to December, and the weight on the earth's crust shifting under a large storm's rapidly plunging barometric pressure has been known to cause earthquakes through the archipelago's active tectonic zones.

Born as tropical disturbances on one of the 120-odd low-pressure "tropical waves" that develop annually on the broad band of eastern trade winds that gird the planet near the equator, the storms are spun into a circular motion by the earth's rotation and migrate westward between the latitudes 6 degrees North and 12 degrees South toward the North Pacific basin. Called tropical depressions in their embryonic state, they ride the heated, sun-swollen ocean in a roughly westerly direction along the equatorial trough. In a typical rainy season, somewhere between 15 and 20 actual typhoons evolve to lash toward the Philippines, Japan, and China before eventually recurving northeast toward the Aleutian Islands or the American Pacific Northwest.

Given the Pacific's vast swaths of watery distances—the world's largest ocean covers 32.4 percent of the earth's surface, 3.2 percent more than the total land mass of the entire planet—these storms often remain potent for several weeks and roam over thousands of miles of sea. Their dense, gray cumulonimbus clouds can rise fifty thousand feet into the troposphere and, on rare occasions, their plateau-shaped canopies have actually penetrated the tropopause, the barrier that separates the earth's atmosphere from the stratosphere.

Throwing out winds a considerable distance through the dual processes of convection and advection—the vertical and horizontal eggbeater-like movement of heat and moisture within the eye—it is not unusual for a typhoon's "wind spread" to extend 200 miles from its core, and for hurricane-strength winds to be felt 75 miles distant.

Approaching gales, precipitous drops in barometric pressure, and long, lazy cross-swells arriving at the rate of about eight per minute are all indicators of a typhoon's imminent emergence. On his second voyage to the New World, in 1494, Christopher Columbus noticed these swells and ordered his caravels to take refuge off the southeastern tip of Hispaniola. There he rode out a tropical storm—classified according to the British admiral Francis Beaufort's wind-force scale as any disturbance whose sustained (one-minute mean) surface wind speed falls between 34 and 63 knots.

Though Columbus's caravels suffered no damage, the experience proved valuable. For on his fourth, "High Voyage" nine years later, his high-sided *naos* sailed before a full-blown Atlantic hurricane in the Mona Passage between Puerto Rico and the present-day Dominican Republic. Columbus read the signs of the "canvas-ripper" at the first appearance of a southeasterly swell, and despite sailing beneath a blue-domed sky, instructed his ships to run for shelter. The Portuguese commander of a hard by *flota* of galleons and caravels, unfamiliar with the warning indicators and buoyed by the benign weather conditions, lost 26 of his 30 vessels and over 500 men.

Long before the Dutch meteorologist Christopher Buys-Ballot posited, in 1860, his eponymous premise for locating typhoons at sea, captains of Chinese junks and Micronesian outriggers alike were passing down to younger generations of seamen their age-old version of "Buys-Ballot's Law" for finding, and fleeing, the eye of a storm. That is, face the wind head-on and extend a right arm at an angle between 90 and 135 degrees. The storm center will fall somewhere within that 45-degree arc. Buys-Ballot's Law dictates that vessels to the right of the storm's path—"the dangerous semicircle" —should put the wind to their starboard bow and attempt to outrun it. Ships in a direct path or to the left of the storm's track— "the navigable semicircle"—should place the wind to the starboard quarter and run.

Ancient Polynesian mariners learned to race for the lee side of a typhoon once its oncoming warning signals were identified, particularly the rolling swells and the wispy veiling of advancing high-level cirrus and cirrostratus clouds, like bony white fingers, far off to the east or southeast.

By the eighteenth century the 30-million-square-mile expanse of the North Pacific Ocean was already being referred to as "Typhoon Alley" by American navigators. The nautical pioneer Nathaniel Bowditch, in his encyclopedic *The American Practical Navigator*, cautioned whalers and merchant ships sailing these sea-lanes to beware of "the largest and most intense tropical cyclones in the world; circulations covering more than 600 miles in diameter are not uncommon." Yet long before the "golden age" of sail, the myth of the tropical typhoon had also acquired a spiritual semblance.

It was, in fact, out of an ancient religious awe that the Imperial Japanese War Department "venerated" the suicide pilots that wreaked havoc on the U.S. Navy during World War II by naming them after the furious kamikazes that scattered the Mongol emperor Kublai Khan's two invasion fleets in the thirteenth century. The Japanese honorific "kamikaze" translates roughly as "divine wind," and in the Middle Ages it was only such a wind that twice prevented Japan from becoming a Chinese vassal state.

Although Japan's squabbling feudal lords united in 1274 under the Kamakura shogunate to defend their country against Kublai Khan's first armada of 900 Chinese ships carrying more than 40,000 troops, they proved no match for the Khan's cavalry with its terrifying gunpowder bombs. Japanese nobles fled to temples and shrines to pray for divine intervention, and the civilian populace—as they would seven hundred years later on Saipan—prepared to commit mass suicide. After overrunning the islands of Tsushima and Iki, however, the Chinese fleet was demolished in Hakata Bay by a freak gale that shifted course overnight. More than 200 ships were lost, and 13,000 Mongol soldiers drowned. The result was not only the retreat of the Khan's landing force, but the spawning of the belief among Japanese that their islands had been rescued by a miraculous wind directed by the Shinto gods.

Seven years later, in 1281, when a thunderous typhoon ravaged another, larger invasion fleet of more than 4,400 Chinese vessels, this conviction was cemented. These failed offensives remained the only severe threat to the Japanese mainland prior to World War II. And despite the rapacious destruction and loss of life wreaked by the Great Tokyo Typhoon of 1918, the ethos and spirit of the kamikazes remained a key component of Japan's homeland myth, a sort of inverse Manifest Destiny.

But it wasn't until the British adventurer and circumnavigator William Dampier published his sublime *A New Voyage Round the World*, in 1697, that Europeans became acquainted with the "violent whirlwinds" of what Dampier referred to as a Pacific "tufoon."

"Before these whirlwinds come on there appears a heavy cloud to the northeast which is very black near the horizon," reported Dampier, describing the wall of cumulus and cumulonimbus clouds that has since come to be referred to as the "bar" of a tropical cyclone. "But toward the upper part is a dull reddish color. The tempest came with great violence, but after a while, the winds ceased all at once and a calm succeeded. This lasted . . . an hour, more or less, then the gales were turned around, blowing with great fury from the southwest."

Ironically, in the late nineteenth century a Pacific typhoon may have played the odd role of peacemaker in preventing another conflict that presaged the twentieth century's two world wars. This occurred in the spring of 1889, when three German men o' war dropped anchor in the bottle-shaped Samoan port of Apia. They were on a mission that U.S. president Benjamin Harrison adroitly, and correctly, viewed as a colonial probe by Germany's empire-hungry "Iron Chancellor," Prince Otto von Bismarck. Harrison dispatched three U.S. warships to intimidate the Prussian flotilla. Joining the American vessels was a British corvette.

In the ensuing standoff, a state of war was narrowly averted when, on March 16, a typhoon struck the island and raged for three days. Warships and merchantmen alike anchored in the harbor were wiped out. German and American sailors even worked together to help keep the fatalities to about 150 men—a cooperative effort that lasted only as long as the storm raged. As it was, however, the typhoon not only obliterated the two miniature fleets, but also destroyed Germany's Pacific territorial ambitions.

Following the Samoan cyclone, European powers were forced to begin factoring the Pacific's violent weather into their colonial equations. Toward the end of the nineteenth century the British Royal Navy even attempted to thwart nature, or at least warn of her approach, by positioning a large cannon capable of firing 48-pounders near the entrance to Hong Kong's harbor. The firing of this "Typhoon Gun" served as not only the first alert of a forthcoming storm to both the island's residents and vessels at anchorage, but also the last. It was better than nothing, if not by much. On September 18, 1906, the cannon was fired less than an hour before the eye of a powerful typhoon, with its pounding rain, shrieking winds, rising seawater, and terrific streaks of lightning, swept through the harbor. Ten thousand people were killed.

As the British experience in Hong Kong illustrated, foreknowledge of a Pacific typhoon was woeful prior to the invention of rudimentary long-distance radar, much less our current satellite-borne radiometer systems and Doppler radar stations. Mariners and islanders were familiar with the approximate months of a storm's arrival, the peak season of July through October. But this was often deceptive, as a good 30 percent of Pacific typhoons also form in the preceding and succeeding months.

As merchant vessels were gradually equipped with radios in the early twentieth century, typhoon notices could be forwarded to fellow merchantmen and populated islands. These wireless communications ended, however, with the onset of World War II. Not only did merchant shipping virtually cease during the war, but both combatants enforced strict radio blackout rules. Great blank stretches of ocean returned to spawning giant, heat-seeking atmospheric engines of which no sailor was ever aware. Between 1941 and 1945, maps of Pacific typhoon lanes may as well have been marked "Here Be Dragons."

But, in the autumn of 1944, with America's invasion plans for the Philippines pumping at full throttle, not many sailors among the U.S. Pacific Fleet's high command, and certainly not the voracious "Bull" Halsey, were of an inclination to be distracted by dragons.

CHAPTER 4

Communications in the fleet are in my opinion still not adequate for handling weather. Various attempts have been and still are being made to improve them and to provide weather with priority and OP [operational priority] classification, that is, to get weather messages from the bottom of the heap of messages in the communications center up to the top of the heap.

—TESTIMONY OF WILBUR M. LOCKHART, CAPTAIN, U.S. NAVY, AEROLOGICAL OFFICE STAFF, COMMANDER IN CHIEF, PACIFIC, TO THE COURT OF INQUIRY INVESTIGATING *"HALSEY'S TYPHOON."*

When General MacArthur fled Corregidor in 1942, he'd carried with him the new title of U.S. Army Commander in the Far East as well as the new burden of defending Australia and New Zealand. "Hold Hawaii; Support Australia; Drive Northward" became the War Department's slogan. The soldier whom William Manchester would famously dub *American Caesar* had set up headquarters in Melbourne's Menzies Hotel. But with as yet no troops to lead—"A Hero on Ice" *Time* magazine called him—MacArthur was left with little to occupy his time. He thus took to swanning about the southern continent holding press conferences, making speeches to the Australian Parliament, and giving numerous radio broadcasts.

MacArthur was a prolix man, and in each of his famously polished communiqués he invariably portrayed himself as the last best hope standing between the United States and the yellow scourge, a virtual Leonidas at Thermopylae. It was this relentless self-promotion that inspired Congress to award him the Medal of Honor (thus making the MacArthurs the only father and son to have both received the nation's highest military award). Gratifying as this commendation was, however, MacArthur stewed incessantly over his failure to be appointed supreme commander of the Pacific Theater.

As early as October 1941, prior to Pearl Harbor, there had been intramural skirmishing among the Joint Chiefs as to who would be promoted to Allied supreme commander when war inevitably arrived. This "Eastern Ike" would be awarded overall authority of American land, sea, and air forces in the Pacific, and Army Chief of Staff Gen. George C. Marshall recommended to Secretary of War Henry L. Stimson that MacArthur be that officer.

Marshall's proposal was rejected outright by the bluff and ornery Adm. Ernest J. King, Chief of U.S. Naval Operations. No general would dictate orders to his admirals, King argued, adding that the navy had been preparing for twenty years to fight a war against Japan. It was King's belief that naval warfare would determine the course of the Pacific campaign, and Admiral Nimitz deserved to be in charge.

This raised an immediate concern: MacArthur outranked Nimitz. Thus, in Washington a compromise was struck. Nimitz was designated commander in chief of the Pacific Ocean Areas east of the east 160th meridian of longitude, a region that included the South Pacific, New Zealand, Samoa, Fiji, and most of Oceania. The area west of the east 160th meridian, incorporating Australia, New Guinea, and the Philippines, would be ceded to MacArthur. (Although Sumatra, Malaya, Burma, and the Indian Ocean would remain under British control.)

In military shorthand, Nimitz's command was referred to as the Central Pacific Force, MacArthur's as the Southwest Pacific Force. MacArthur was also vaguely promised his own small fleet, its vessels to be siphoned from various task forces. Thus, following the attack on Pearl Harbor, the war against Japan became a divided responsibility, and MacArthur never forgave the "Navy cabal" for depriving him of the unified authority he was certain he deserved.

MacArthur's rivalry with Nimitz—and Nimitz's subordinates such as Halsey—blossomed straightaway. The general vociferously and publicly derogated U.S. sea power, arguing that the defense of Australia as well as future offensive campaigns required an amphibious army supported by a concentration of land-based bombers and fighter aircraft. In other words, aircraft earmarked for him. He even advocated the abolishment of the Marine Corps, arguing that its troops could better serve his army—a viewpoint not forgotten, nor forgiven, by Marine Corps veterans to this day.

In turn, navy brass, specifically King, allowed it to be known that they considered MacArthur an unhinged megalomaniac with a corncob pipe. When in July 1942 MacArthur demanded that Nimitz cede him two carrier task groups for a daftly conceived invasion of Rabaul in the northern Solomons—technically in MacArthur's Southwest Pacific Command zone—Admiral King objected so vehemently to Marshall that their boundary of authority was "adjusted" in order to transfer supervision of that island chain to Nimitz.

Halsey had never met MacArthur, although in 1901 the two had stood at attention on opposite sides of Pennsylvania Avenue—Halsey as a plebe at Annapolis, MacArthur a third-class cadet at West Point—as President William McKinley delivered his second inaugural address. Now, forty-one years later, Halsey initially shared his superiors' lack of esteem for the general, tagging him an arrogant fraud more than worthy of the "Dugout Doug" appellation. Each time Halsey, as commander of the South Pacific Theater, sent something or someone to Australia—ships for repair, combat-weary Marines for a few days of R&R—he feared that MacArthur would swallow them up. And when Halsey requested a "loan" of several bombers from MacArthur's Australia-based army air wing in February 1943, the general first demanded to know for what use Halsey intended them.

Halsey fumed that MacArthur had insulted his competence and wrote to Nimitz, "I refuse to get into controversy with him or any other self-advertising Son of a Bitch."

To the navy men, reasoning with MacArthur proved tougher than boning a marlin. Thus Halsey valued, and came to rely upon, the diplomatic skills of his chief of staff, Rear Adm. Robert "Mick" Carney. Carney, whose son was married to the daughter of MacArthur's chief of staff, was the officer he dispatched to kowtow to MacArthur whenever his carrier raids crossed the demarcation line into the general's Southwest Pacific domain. But even Carney's golden tongue could accomplish only so much. So it was that in April 1943, three months after his famous "guarantee" of imminent victory over Japan, Halsey decided a personal introduction was in order and set off for Brisbane.

The encounter did not start well. MacArthur and several of his aides greeted Halsey's cortege on the wharf as they climbed from their seaplane. The general and the admiral clasped hands warmly and began leading the group to parked cars. One of MacArthur's officers fell in next to Halsey's flag secretary, Comdr. Douglas Moulton. "Say, Doug . . ." he said.

MacArthur spun on his heels and leveled his patented hard stare. Even Mrs. MacArthur was forbidden to address her husband as anything other than "General."

Back at MacArthur's headquarters, the general immediately began lecturing Halsey and his staff on a matter that "galled" him, that is, the jurisdiction of a small island base under construction in the Admiralties. MacArthur told Halsey he had no intention of tamely submitting to CINCPAC's every whim, reviewed in detail the reasons why his Southwest Pacific Command should control the island, and finally pointed his pipe stem at Halsey and demanded, "Am I not right, Bill?"

Halsey and his staff answered with one voice. "No, sir!"

The general's staff gaped at the impertinence. Halsey wasn't through. "General," he said, "I disagree with you entirely." Then he told him why.

Halsey thought he had won the argument over what he considered a petty, jurisdictional dispute. MacArthur would not let it go. Three times over the next three days he summoned Halsey back to his offices to restate his case, and three times Halsey told him he was wrong. When the misunderstanding was cleared up, however, Halsey found his bias toward the general dissolving. MacArthur was charismatic and solicitous, the very model of a modern major general. "Five minutes after I reported I felt as if we were lifelong friends," he wrote. "I have seldom seen a man who makes a quicker, stronger, more favorable impression. If he had been wearing civilian clothes, I would have known at once that he was a soldier."

The Bull, as one biographer noted, also lived up to the American Caesar's expectations. "Blunt, outspoken, dynamic," is how MacArthur, unsurprisingly, described Halsey. Provided the admiral did not compete with the general too vigorously for press attention and glory, MacArthur could live with that.

Nevertheless, the entire problem of a divided Pacific command could be massaged by conferences in Brisbane and concessions in Washington, but it could never be truly overcome. As the United States moved closer to retaking the Philippines, the rivalry over whether the Southwest Pacific or the Central Pacific commands would lead the offensive against Japan began to take on the form of a war within a war.

In time, however, as the general fought his way north with tactical support from Halsey's South Pacific Fleet, his rancor toward the navy did not prohibit him from coming to regard as his own the admiral's battleships, carriers, and cruisers. And so it was that in late November 1943, during yet another summit to hammer out a single line of attack strategy against the Imperial Empire, MacArthur approached Halsey with a discreet offer.

"I'll tell you something you may not know," he said, and confided to Halsey that the War Department and the British planned to place a combined fleet at his disposal, and he wanted, he said, an American to lead it.

"How about you, Bill?" MacArthur said. "If you come with me, I'll make you a greater man than Nelson ever dreamed of being."

A flustered Halsey, who knew full well that the last thing Admiral King wanted was MacArthur in command of his own armada, replied that he was flattered, but in no position to commit himself.

But despite this newfound amity with Admiral Halsey, MacArthur continued to press his case to the War Department for a succession of Philippine landings aimed at establishing air bases that would lead to the ultimate recapture of the island of Luzon, and the prize of Manila. He had, after all, promised to return. Admiral King failed to see the advantage of this strategy. Luzon, he maintained, was too heavily fortified, the enemy too well dug in. King instead advocated bypassing Luzon, with Nimitz thrusting toward the Japanese mainland via Formosa and various ports on the Chinese coast. This meant first securing the several enemy-held island chains between Pearl Harbor and Tokyo.

MacArthur refused to give way. In a letter to General Marshall, army chief of staff, he cited the Japanese defeat at Midway as an example of the result of attempting to take enemy-held islands. He also noted the number of casualties incurred during the recent amphibious landings on Tarawa, in November 1943. King's island-hopping strategy, he wrote, constituted "tragic and unnecessary massacres of American lives." He complained that "the Navy fails to understand the strategy of the Pacific." To several admirals, this argument brought to mind the old Arab proverb: *Too soft and you will be squeezed; too hard and you will be broken.* The navy feared that MacArthur's forces would be broken on Luzon.

In March 1944 the Joint Chiefs negotiated yet another compromise in hopes of quelling this festering feud. Nimitz's Central Pacific Command would begin its drive west, hopscotching from the Marianas to the Palaus while keeping Formosa in its long-range sights. MacArthur, meanwhile, would start slugging his way up the northern coast of New Guinea in preparation for a landing in the central Philippines. It was also around this time that the title U.S. Fifth Fleet, previously used to designate only ships of Nimitz's Central Pacific Force, was changed to also include amphibious troops and land-based aircraft. The name Central Pacific Force was dropped. In essence, Nimitz now commanded the Pacific Fleet, and a smaller Seventh Fleet was cobbled together for MacArthur's use.

In June 1944, Nimitz relieved Halsey of his South Pacific duties, summoned him to Pearl, and promoted him to co-commander, with Spruance, of the Pacific, or Big Blue, Fleet. He and Spruance would share rotating commands, the theory being that this alternating, double-echelon arrangement would speed up the war. While one admiral fought, the other and his staff would be planning the next campaign. The arrangement had the added bonus of confusing the Japanese (as well as many Americans, who marveled at their navy's ability to field two Big Blue Fleets). When it sailed under Spruance it would continue to be called the Fifth Fleet. When it steamed under Halsey it would be known as the Third Fleet. Similarly, Spruance's carrier Task Force 58 would become Halsey's carrier Task Force 38. Nimitz informed Halsey that he would take fleet command when Spruance finished his Marianas campaign to secure Saipan, Tinian, and Guam. This meant Halsey had caught the Philippines invasions.

For the sequential landings on a series of Philippine islands, MacArthur would sail with his own Seventh Fleet, commanded by Vice Adm. Thomas C. Kinkaid, and receive support from Halsey's Third Fleet. This, naturally, did not meet with the general's satisfaction. He wanted Halsey under his outright command, not acting as a mere adjunct. And he continued to interpret almost any directive emanating from CINCPAC as an unjustifiable impugning of his "personal honor." But at least he was returning to the Philippines.

By October 1944 the United States was a step closer to that goal. MacArthur's Sixth Army, buttressed by his new Seventh Fleet under Kinkaid, prepared to make the jump from New Guinea to the small central Philippine island of Leyte, situated midway between the larger, more strategic islands of Luzon to the north and Mindanao to the south. As MacArthur's troops arranged to secure airfields on Leyte capable of accommodating his heavy bombers "preparatory to a further advance to Formosa, either directly or via Luzon," so it occurred that Japan was gearing up for its own Battle of the Bulge, a last-gasp attempt to smash two American fleets at once and repel MacArthur's invaders at the flash point of Leyte Gulf.

Meanwhile, when Admiral Halsey received his orders for the Third Fleet's Leyte Gulf operations, his eyes alighted on one subordinate clause included in Admiral Nimitz's directives that was to hover like Banquo's ghost over his reputation for the remainder of his life.

"In case opportunity for destruction of a major portion of the enemy fleet is offered or can be created, such destruction becomes the primary task."

Twenty-five words. Simple. Direct. Disarmingly to the point. That sentence was, of course, part of the more comprehensive command from CINCPAC Nimitz to Halsey on the eve of MacArthur's Leyte invasion. But to Halsey those twenty-five words carried more weight than the rest of the U.S. Navy's Operations Plan 8-44 combined. To wit, as MacArthur's amphibious Sixth Army, sailing north from New Guinea, was put ashore in Leyte Gulf by Kinkaid's Seventh Fleet, Halsey's Third Fleet was ordered to:

COVER AND SUPPORT FORCES OF THE SOUTHWEST PACIFIC IN ORDER TO ASSIST IN THE SEIZURE AND OCCUPATION IN THE CENTRAL PHILIPPINES;

DESTROY ENEMY NAVAL AND AIR FORCES IN OR THREATENING THE PHILIPPINE AREA;

IN CASE OPPORTUNITY FOR DESTRUCTION OF A MAJOR POR-
TION OF THE ENEMY FLEET IS OFFERED OR CAN BE CREATED,
SUCH DESTRUCTION BECOMES THE PRIMARY TASK.

In other words, Halsey's Task Force 38, steaming west from recently captured Ulithi Atoll, had been ordered to stand sentry over
MacArthur's northern flank against any Japanese naval attempt to
scuttle the landings. Yet, upon deeper reflection, CINCPAC's orders
were confounding, ambiguous. Which was it? Protect MacArthur,
or hunt the enemy? As it happened, Halsey's interpretation of this
directive transformed what should have been an unfettered American landing on Leyte into, as Wellington said of Waterloo, "a damned
close-run thing." To this day military historians and World War II
veterans debate, often acrimoniously, whether Halsey recklessly
abandoned his station at Leyte Gulf and should be held responsible
for the deaths of over one thousand American sailors.

Yet with that twenty-five-word proviso in Operations Plan
8-44, Nimitz had specifically directed the admiral that—MacArthur's
landings notwithstanding—his "primary task" was to annihilate the
Japanese carrier fleet should he encounter it, or should he have the
opportunity to "create" such an encounter. The order, a variation
of the Jesuit concept of freedom within discipline, was in keeping
with the general-quarters flexibility Nimitz consistently granted his
on-site fleet commanders.

There is a back story. Following his friend and co-commander
Adm. Raymond Spruance's failure to engage the Japanese fleet during
the Marianas Turkey Shoot, Halsey had vowed to his staff that any
enemy ships venturing that close to his task force would not escape
his guns. Nimitz's contradictory Operations Plan 8-44 only buttressed
his resolve. So it was that when MacArthur put his Sixth Army ashore
at Leyte Gulf on October 20, 1944, Halsey, despite sending the general congratulations for his "return," chafed at having nothing more
to do than "babysit" MacArthur's right flank.

Halsey's three carrier task forces were charged with shielding
a specific point of the eastern exit into the Philippine Sea of the

San Bernardino Strait, a narrow cut separating the islands of Samar and southernmost Luzon, northeast of MacArthur's 120,000 amphibious troops and 100,000 tons of supplies landing on Leyte. At 8:20 on the morning of October 24, American submarines and scout planes indeed observed a small Japanese fleet of battleships, cruisers, and destroyers under the command of Adm. Takeo Kurita making for the strait. But Halsey's jubilation at having the enemy in his gun sights was tempered by his disquiet over the lack of enemy aircraft carriers sailing with Kurita.

If left to his own devices, Halsey would have steamed west into the San Bernardino Strait to meet the Japanese ships head-on. But Nimitz feared the channel might be mined, so Halsey instead ordered air strikes. By the end of the day the Third Fleet's Helldiver dive bombers, Avenger torpedo bombers, and Hellcat fighters would fly over 259 sorties, and what was left of Kurita's ravaged vessels were retreating at flank speed back through the strait.

Halsey was overjoyed, for this left him free to concentrate on the Japanese carriers. His gut told him that they were somewhere in the area. But where? Lurking west of Luzon? Steaming south from Japan? No one could find them.

That afternoon, as his Hellcats were still strafing Kurita's fleeing ships, Halsey drew up a contingency order carving up pieces of his Task Force 38 carrier groups to create a separate Task Force 34, to be anchored by four fast, new battleships. If Kurita's undamaged ships should attempt another breakout—however unlikely that scenario—his battlewagons would eviscerate them while his carriers hunted the Japanese flattops.

In a radio message monitored by Kinkaid in Leyte Gulf, CINCPAC Nimitz at Pearl, and Admiral King in Washington, D.C., Halsey specifically maintained, "If enemy sorties, Task Force 34 will be formed when directed by me." The three admirals all took this to mean the battleship-led Task Force 34 had already been established and dispatched. It was to prove a crucial misunderstanding. For Admiral Kurita, with prodding from Tokyo, was already experiencing second thoughts about his withdrawal.

Two hours after sending his radio message, Halsey's reconnaissance pilots finally sighted the Japanese carrier force—the Imperial Navy's last four attack flattops and their supporting vessels —maneuvering some one hundred miles north of his task groups. This was the grail Halsey had been hunting since missing the Battle of Midway. To a fighting admiral like Halsey, "it seemed childish," he wrote, to idly stand guard over MacArthur when such big game was afoot. Further, by devastating Kurita's fleet, hadn't he already fulfilled Nimitz's orders to "Destroy enemy naval and air forces in or threatening the Philippine area"?

As the naval historian Samuel Eliot Morison was to observe, "Halsey was no man to watch a rathole from which the rat might never emerge."

Sensing the opportunity to knock the last of the Japanese carriers out of the war, the same chance Spruance had passed up in the Marianas, he directed each of the Third Fleet's three task groups, 16 carriers and 78 combat vessels in all, to give chase. In his van were the battleships ostensibly set aside to guard the San Bernardino Strait. Never divide your strength in a combat zone. It is one of the first precepts taught at the Naval War College. Halsey knew it well, and was not about to tempt fate.

His design on the Japanese was elegant in its simplicity. He would find the Japanese vessels in the night and slaughter them at first light.

Halsey fired off a message to Kinkaid giving the last known coordinates of what was left of Kurita's battered force in the Sibuyan Sea. It concluded, "Strike reports indicate enemy heavily damaged. Am proceeding north with three groups to attack enemy carrier force at dawn." By the time Kinkaid read the communiqué, Halsey was asleep in his bunk. Kinkaid, preparing to attack a second Japanese force approaching from the south, assumed that Halsey had left his battleships—the newly formed Task Force 34— to guard the exit of the strait. He saw no need to send his own scout planes north to make certain.

Halsey had no way of knowing that the enemy carriers, commanded by Adm. Jisaburo Ozawa, were a magnificent decoy embarked on a suicide mission to lure him away. Once Ozawa's scout planes confirmed that Halsey had taken his bait, he reversed course. Halsey, still under the impression that Kurita's strike force was mortally wounded, chased Ozawa all night. Dawn found the Third Fleet three hundred miles from the San Bernardino Strait, through which Kurita's remaining vessels were now steaming unmolested. MacArthur's flank had been left wide open, with only three of Kinkaid's small, backup task groups standing between the Japanese and MacArthur's certain destruction.

The determined heroism and reckless gallantry Kinkaid's outnumbered and outgunned sailors subsequently displayed during the victorious Battle of Samar stands in the American pantheon with Crockett at the Alamo, Chamberlain at Little Round Top, and York at Argonne. Every single one of the ships battling Kurita suffered devastating hits, over one thousand sailors were killed, and an escort carrier, two destroyers, and one destroyer escort were sent to the bottom of the Philippine Sea.

But the Americans had managed to make Kurita turn and run once again. Kinkaid, MacArthur, and Nimitz gave rapt attention to real-time radio reports from the running fight, and the sea battle also attracted the notice in Washington, D.C., of Admiral King, Navy Secretary James Forrestal (who had replaced Frank Knox, recently dead from a heart attack), and even the White House. Roosevelt himself requested hourly updates.

Meanwhile, as Halsey's fliers engaged the Japanese carriers, he received a message from Nimitz demanding to know his whereabouts. In a bitter misunderstanding, the communiqué from the usually laconic CINCPAC contained an encryption snafu that enraged the exhausted Halsey. The original dispatch Nimitz had dictated to Halsey—"Where is Task Force 34?"—had for some reason been encrypted to read, "Where is rept where is Task Force 34 RR The world wonders."

Double letters in encrypted navy dispatches, called "nulls," were signals to the intelligence officer decoding a message that all the letters following these nulls were mere padding to confound any enemy intercepts. Normally this padding was a gibberish string of letters. But for reasons never determined, perhaps out of sheer whimsy, after the "RR" nulls, the dispatcher at Pearl had appended that morning's front-page headline from the *Honolulu Advertiser* as the padding. To compound the error, the *New Jersey*'s decoding officer delivered the entire message to Halsey.

The admiral, believing that Nimitz was chiding him with the sarcastic "The world wonders," was enraged. His gnarled face turned red with fury. He whipped off his baseball cap and stomped the message tape into the deck. "What right has Chester to send me a goddamn message like that?" he shouted. Then he broke into sobs and stormed off to his flag quarters. Although his strike force had managed to decimate Ozawa's Japanese carriers, his vaunted battle-ship line had never fired a shot.

The American victory in the Battle for Leyte Gulf was, and remains to this day, the largest naval engagement in the history of the world. Yet despite the outcome, feelings were mixed and criticism was sharp. Had Kurita, who came within forty miles of MacArthur's landing force, managed to reach and attack the American beachhead, the result could well have signaled not only the deferment of the Philippines campaign but, as Nimitz estimated, a six-month setback for America's long-range war plans. Halsey's actions left such a bitter taste that his mad dash north was soon etched in navy lore as the "Battle of Bull's Run," a play off the humiliating rout of the Union Army in the opening days of the Civil War.

Yet the one soldier whose opinion may have carried the most weight refused to condemn the admiral. Shortly after securing the Leyte beachhead, MacArthur sat down to dinner with his staff and overheard an officer criticizing Halsey for "abandoning us while he went after the Jap decoy fleet." Another was said to have made an allusion to Churchill's scathing remark about Admiral Jellicoe's performance at the 1916 Battle of Jutland—"He was the only man who could have lost the war in an afternoon."

MacArthur slammed his fist on the table. "That's enough!" he roared. "Leave the Bull alone. He's still a fighting admiral in my book."

In late November, following the successful landings on Leyte, MacArthur's personal staff, prodded by back-channel pressure from Nimitz, persuaded the general to push back the next step of his Philippine island hop—the invasion of Mindoro—by ten days, to December 15. The navy's high command breathed a sigh of relief. Despite the overwhelming victory at Leyte, like Pyrrhus surveying the victorious field at Asculum, Nimitz was uneasy. The Battle for Leyte Gulf had introduced something new and macabre into the war's equation, a tactic that CINCPAC realized Halsey needed time to countermand. After seven hundred years, swirling kamikazes had once again blackened the skies.

Over the last year America's grinding war machine had so depleted the Japanese naval and air forces that the Philippine Sea had come to be referred to as an "American lake." The destruction of Adm. Jisaburo Ozawa's carrier fleet during the three-day Battle for Leyte Gulf appeared to apply the coup de grace. But the Allies' undisputed mastery of the Pacific suffered a serious psychological setback during the Leyte campaign. The inauguration of the Kamikaze Special Attack Corps caught Halsey and the United States military completely by surprise.

Five months earlier, following their loss of the Marianas, the Japanese high command had secretly devised the kamikaze strategy to ratchet its homeland defense to another level. Now, in October, with their territorial holdings shrinking daily, MacArthur gaining a toehold in the Philippines, and down to a handful of experienced pilots, the Imperial War Ministry put its plan into effect. The kamikazes were, one historian notes, the world's first guided missiles, "with human pilots as the guidance system."

The airmen who volunteered for these missions of no return thought of themselves as modern-day samurais. They were, on average, between eighteen and twenty years old, and pitifully undertrained. When they launched, they were accompanied, when possible, by trailing wingmen to bear witness in order that their warriors' sacrifice could be reported personally to the emperor. "We were bubbling with eagerness," wrote one pilot prior to his final mission. "I thought of my age, nineteen, and of the saying, 'To die while people still lament your death, to die while you are pure and fresh, this is truly Bushido.' Yes, I was following the way of the Samurai."

But it was not ancient Japanese Bushido—the "way of the warrior" code of conduct and moral principles—that concerned Halsey. It was this bomb-laden steel hurtling from the skies and sending his vessels to the bottom of the sea. The depth of the kamikazes' desperation countered everything that American soldiers and sailors held "fair." The concept of pilots standing at attention in their ritual silk scarves, drinking in both the "Kimigayo" and ceremonial cups of sake before taking to the air to immolate themselves, was alien to American sensibilities. Even the Marines charging into the meat grinders at Guadalcanal and Tarawa believed they had a fighting chance to come out alive.

Yet despite the American contempt for their means, the kamikazes briefly achieved their ends. They had succeeded in virtually stopping in its tracks the Allied advance across the Pacific. Halsey realized that his navy's complete mastery of the air was seriously threatened for the first time since the deadly night battles in the Solomons two years before. On October 29, during mop-up operations at Leyte, the admiral got his first, personal taste of the "divine wind," watching from the flag bridge of the *New Jersey* as a suicide bomber glided at a 45-degree angle through a chiaroscuro of antiaircraft fire and dived into the USS *Intrepid*, a thousand yards away. The bandit struck only a glancing blow to the carrier's aft gun emplacements, but killed ten seamen and wounded six others.

Halsey was staggered. He had been on the bridge of the *Enterprise* during the raid on the Marshalls in February 1942 when a Japanese pilot, his plane mortally wounded, crashed into the carrier and skidded across its flight deck. The Zero's fuel tanks had ruptured, causing only minor damage. But that plane had been on fire, its pilot's fate already sealed. The idea of this new combat-by-suicide sat in his gut like a broken bottle.

"We could not believe that even the Japanese, for all their hara-kiri traditions, could muster enough recruits to make such a corps really effective," he wrote. He was wrong. The day after the attack on the *Intrepid*, her sister carriers USS *Franklin* and USS *Belleau Wood* were struck; 148 Americans were killed, another 68 seriously wounded. Both vessels were put out of commission by what U.S. sailors quickly took to calling the "Green Hornets," after the Sunday funny-papers character.

In the month after the kamikaze strike on the *Intrepid*, suicide planes slamming into the Third Fleet killed 328 men, sank 8 ships, destroyed over 90 planes, and sent numerous vessels—including the three aircraft carriers—limping back to Pearl for major repairs. Before the war concluded, over 2,550 kamikaze attacks would take more than 12,000 American lives, wound another 36,000, and sink or damage 74 ships. The *Intrepid*, on its way to acquiring the black-humored nickname "*Decrepit*," was hit again on November 25, with the loss of another 69 men.

Halsey had seen enough. That very day, as MacArthur's Sixth Army continued to grind across Leyte, he ordered Third Fleet's withdrawal to Ulithi Atoll in order to refuel, reprovision, and—of paramount importance—pursue a plan to scrub the skies of the "kami boys." The suicide attacks had inflicted an unacceptable level of damage, to both ships and morale. He was determined to find a way to stop them.

CHAPTER 5

All commanding officers and most of the officers and men of the squadron who have been in the ships any length of time were very much aware of the lack of stability of the ships.

—TESTIMONY OF CAPT. PRESTON V. MERCER, U.S.
NAVY, COMMANDING DESTROYER SQUADRON 1,
FLAGSHIP USS DEWEY, TO THE COURT OF INQUIRY
INVESTIGATING "HALSEY'S TYPHOON."

Ulithi had been captured by American forces less than two months earlier and proved an ideal staging area for the navy's push west and north. The tiny atoll, sitting forlorn at the rump end of the Caroline Islands about midway between the Philippines and the great Mariana Trench, is shaped like an inverted horseshoe broken by a string of channels, its axis extending twenty miles from north to south. The central lagoon, sheltered by coral reefs and sandy beaches, formed a natural harbor deep and expansive enough to moor the entire Third Fleet, and the largest cay, measuring almost a mile across, accommodated an air base with a twelve-hundred-yard landing strip. Although the island of Yap, less than 150 miles to the southwest, was still under Japanese control, its decimated air squadrons had been virtually abandoned by the Imperial War Department and were not considered a major threat.

It was on Ulithi that Halsey and his inner core of confidants, which he famously dubbed his "Dirty Tricks Department," would hatch their Boy's Own schemes to bedevil the enemy during the upcoming Mindoro landings, in particular their successful nullification of the kamikaze threat. But they also had fresh "toys" to learn how to deploy in the form of brand-new navy ships called destroyer escorts.

These trim, sturdy vessels were another innovation in America's burgeoning military-industrial complex. The prewar Lend-Lease Act passed by Congress had enabled the British Royal Navy to procure merchant vessels and munitions designed and built in the United States. The act also stipulated the manufacture of an escort vessel specifically intended for deepwater, anti–U-boat screening patrols, or ASW duty—antisubmarine warfare. Drawing upon the blueprints and schematics of the smaller British and Canadian destroyers called corvettes, the navy's Bureau of Ships ordered development of the destroyer escort, or DE.

Traditional American destroyers had been built to accentuate speed and firepower, but they could not match the agility of the German U-boat. The DE's maneuverability, in contrast, was more than up to the task. Her narrow turning circle of 440 yards nearly halved the turning radius of the conventional destroyer, and with her rounded "bubble" hull and wider stern and bow, she was perfectly suited for the stormy North Atlantic. Destroyer escorts were rough-riding ships, and it took time for sailors posted to them to accustom themselves to the constant plunging, lurching, and rolling, even in placid seas. Lt. Comdr. Henry Lee Plage, skipper of the DE USS *Tabberer*, jokingly complained to friends that in every photo of him taken aboard his ship, it appeared as if he were about to topple over. But the little destroyer escorts were harder to sink than cork.

Although the average DE was nearly ten knots slower and, at 306 feet long and 36 feet abeam, slightly smaller than a destroyer, she sailed with nearly the same payload, albeit with a smaller crew and a lesser caliber of long- and short-range deck cannon. Naval engineers had compensated for this shortfall with an impressive battery of underwater weaponry that included three torpedo tubes, two depth charge racks, eight depth charge projectors (called

K-guns), and the menacing hedgehog, a cluster of twenty-four mortars that could fire forward at an undersea target.

The first destroyer escort made its deepwater debut for the British Royal Navy in 1941. Equipped with the latest radar and sonar technology, these tidy "Sea Dwarfs" soon became the bane of German submarine commanders. Monitoring the progress of these little subchasers, the Navy Department became so enamored with their efficiency that it determined to incorporate them into its own Atlantic and Pacific fleets. DEs proved not only invaluable for screening convoys and coast-watching, but, as the navy discovered, they were also particularly adept as long-range, "first alert" radar picket ships for island-hopping in the Pacific. Although the first U.S. Navy destroyer escort was not commissioned until January 1943, nearly one hundred more followed shortly.

Halsey was delighted to incorporate them into his task forces, and on Ulithi he tasked his Dirty Tricksters with deciding how best to use them. He had it in his mind that using the DEs as outlying submarine screeners would free up his destroyers for shore bombardment duty, but wanted to see what other strategy his staff could cook up for them.

Meanwhile, the fleet's exhausted sailors and airmen looked forward to two weeks of deserved R&R. They had steamed over thirty-six thousand miles since departing Pearl Harbor in August, fighting up and down the Philippine coasts in "unprecedented intensity and scope." Resting heavy on their minds and nerves, heavier perhaps than the combat itself, was the tension inherent in the constant expectation of combat, and Halsey knew that tension bred fatigue. Indicative of this notion was a report sent from the flight surgeon on the carrier USS *Wasp*. He informed Halsey that only 30 of his 131 pilots were fit for immediate duty. Everyone needed to blow off some steam.

Fortunately, on the small sandbank of Mog Mog in the middle of Ulithi's lagoon, the Seabees had constructed a thatched-hut recreation area and bar. Although trapped under a baking sun where, at dusk, the temperature dropped from the infernal to the merely intolerable, to Halsey's thousands of battle-weary sailors, Mog Mog may as well have been The Ritz. Officers chowed down on barbecued steaks and scotch whiskey at picnic tables, tossed horseshoes, and swam. Enlisted men played volleyball, baseball, and football. Each swabbie was also issued chits to exchange for two bottles of Iron City beer per day. Word quickly spread that the suds, shipped all the way from Pittsburgh, were laced with the preservative formaldehyde. The rumor discouraged few men.

"Hot sun, beer, formaldehyde, not a good mix," the destroyer *Hull*'s chief quartermaster Archie DeRyckere warned new arrivals. "I mean, it really gets to you after you drink a couple dozen. Beyond that, well, at least you go to your grave with a smile on your face."

Moreover, if one were clever enough, shore leave presented manifold opportunities to "impound" certain provisions difficult to obtain at sea. Ship's Cook 1st Class Paul "Cookie" Phillips, of the USS *Tabberer*, was one such enterprising sailor.

Phillips, a butcher from Texarkana, Texas, had honed his scrounging skills while serving for nearly a year on Atlantic convoy duty. His talents blossomed upon his transfer to the destroyer escort *Tabberer*. Phillips readily volunteered to his skipper, Lieutenant Commander Plage, that he wasn't much of a chef. "I guess I'm pretty much best at S.O.S.," he admitted, referring to the chipped beef on toast dish universally reviled among sailors as "shit on a shingle." But what Phillips lacked in culinary talent he made up for in creativity.

Phillips was an expert at "relieving" fellow Allied vessels of precious stores, and the fruits of his labor ranged from sacks of potatoes to cases of toilet tissue. "You just got to have a good nose, a feel for when another ship's stuff will be left just laying there on the dock, and not be afraid to sneak around in the middle of the night," he instructed his *Tabberer* messmates.

But his pièce de résistance occurred one afternoon when he noticed a crew of dockworkers delivering an ice cream freezer and crates of ice cream mix to a "heavy" vessel berthed at Ulithi beside the *Tabberer*. The galley of an undersized, no-nonsense destroyer escort was considered too cramped to sail with such extraneous bulk. Moreover, she was not authorized to possess one. To Cookie Phillips, however, the U.S. Navy's rules were made to be broken.

Eyeing his prize, he gathered about him a dozen deckhands, including several from his kitchen staff, and laid out his plan. Phillips and his crewmates would stage a fistfight among themselves on the wharf, not a terribly difficult bit of playacting for men who had just spent forty-nine straight days in close quarters at sea. When the brawl escalated into a donnybrook, the Shore Patrol would arrive, rendering the scene even more confusing.

As all hell broke loose among the *Tabberer*'s crew, the dockworkers, and the Shore Patrol, the *Tabberer*'s assistant cook would spring into action. "You get two men and grab that ice cream freezer and the ice cream mix and carry it back aboard ship," Phillips instructed. "Don't look back, don't stop for no one, and look official."

To the *Tabberer*'s skipper, his ship's cook's accomplishments were all in a sailor's day's work, for by all accounts the charismatic Lieutenant Commander Plage was a special commander, and a special man. Tall, slender, and athletic, he was not only one of the most beloved skippers in the Pacific Theater, but circumstances were to prove him one of the bravest. He and his ship were, in fact, destined to employ what one senior officer called Plage's "peculiar magic" and play an outsized role in an impending drama that was to change the nature of seafaring navies forever.

The Plage family had emigrated to the United States from the bitterly contested Alsace-Lorraine area of Europe in the nineteenth century, and Plage often joked that his forebears "could be French or German, depending on the historical era." Both his grandfather and father were engineers, and one of the family's prized possessions was a White House ashtray personally inscribed by President Theodore Roosevelt and sent to the elder Plage as a token of appreciation for helping to design and construct the living quarters of American workers building the Panama Canal. Plage's father had moved his family from Oklahoma City, where Henry was born in 1915, to Atlanta when Plage was a toddler, and young Henry was reared in an upper-middle-class environment redolent of Southern gentility.

As a teenager, Plage honed his knack for leadership as a summer counselor at the exclusive Camp Tate for Boys in the Stone Mountain area of northern Georgia. The camp, a sort of finishing school for young men, offered among its sundry programs daily exercise regimens, nature studies, swimming and sailing lessons, rifle practice, and war games. At Camp Tate, Plage proved a natural sailor, and in a group photo of counselors in its 1934 brochure an athletic and arrestingly handsome nineteen-year-old "Hank" stares back at the camera wearing an unruly shock of black hair and a look of confident determination. In fact, with his square jaw, high cheekbones, and thick dark hair, Henry Plage was as striking as a Roman bust. Not a few seamen destined to sail under his command remarked upon his resemblance to the actor Cary Grant.

In 1933, Plage enrolled at Georgia Tech, where he majored in engineering and indulged his love of the sea in the school's naval ROTC program. It was also at Georgia Tech where he met his future wife, Marjorie Armstrong, daughter of the university's faculty director of athletics. Plage excelled at school as an honor roll student and as a member of the Honor Society, the president of his fraternity (Chi Phi), the captain of the swimming team, and a member of the golf team. When he graduated in 1937, he carried not only an ensign's commission in the Naval Reserve, but the responsibility of a new bride, which meant placing his engineering career on hold. A job as an insurance claims investigator opened up in Pensacola, Florida, and Henry and Marjorie moved south, where he remained on inactive Naval Reserve duty for three years.

In late 1940, sensing war's approach, Plage wrote the navy asking to be transferred to active duty. He had conferred with Marjorie and was considering making the service his calling. He also concluded that the request, at this point in time, would give him a career jump on the generation of men who he was certain would shortly be called up or drafted. The navy acquiesced and, still in the Reserves, he graduated from officer candidate school in 1941 as a lieutenant commander.

In May 1942 he was posted to the Charleston, South Carolina, navy yard, where his first sea duty was as skipper of a 173-foot subchaser. Plage made several patrols through the Caribbean, sometimes skirting hurricanes, aboard the frigate, and ten months later he was bumped up the command chain to destroyer escorts.

One of the earliest of these agile new ships was the Pacific-based USS *LeHardy*, and it was to this unhappy vessel Lieutenant Commander Plage was assigned as executive officer in late 1943. The regular navy crew took immediately to this stately Reserve XO with the ramrod posture and slight Southern drawl; word quickly spread belowdecks, "Them crumbum Japs have had it now. Cary Grant's come aboard."

"Cary Grant" did not disappoint. Her crew, predominantly young Southern boys, considered the *LeHardy*'s skipper a pompous and aloof "by-the-book" martinet who seemed more intent on enforcing petty regulations than in fighting a war. "Just a foul pole," one seaman called him. Most nettling, he issued strict orders forbidding any social contact, including conversation, between his officers and the ship's enlisted men.

Yet from the day of his arrival Plage blithely ignored this directive. He announced that his door "is open to any sailor," and once, when a ship's electrician took him up on the offer and barged into his cabin while he was showering, Plage turned to the sailor, smiled, and said, "Come on in, the water's fine."

On deck rounds he would stop and speak to any enlisted man he met, and during shore leave he made it a point to join the crew's dockside sandlot baseball games, albeit as the umpire. His seamanship was obvious, and enlisted men and officers alike commented upon the "mother's love" with which the young Plage would sail the little DE into her mooring. He formed lifelong friendships with several of his crew, and sailors lined the ship's rail to bid him a fond, if bittersweet, farewell when he was transferred to command of his own vessel, the DE USS *Donaldson*.

In June 1944, Plage was skippering the *Donaldson* through the Marianas campaign when he received a radio message ordering his immediate return to Pacific Fleet headquarters at Pearl. From there he was flown to Houston, Texas, where, on May 23, 1944, the destroyer escort *Tabberer*, having just rolled off the line at the Brown Shipbuilding Yard, was commissioned. The vessel—named for Charles Arthur Tabberer, an American fighter pilot awarded a posthumous Distinguished Flying Cross after being killed in action two years earlier—carried 12 officers and 124 enlisted men. Plage's orders were to steam the *"Tabby"* back to the Pacific via the Panama Canal and join a hunter-killer DE squadron anchored by the escort carrier USS *Anzio*. Plage was thankful for the long shakedown cruise.

Of the *Tabby*'s officers, only four had ever been to sea, and close to 90 percent of her enlisted crew were teenagers with an average service record barely exceeding three months.

"They were boys when they came into the navy," Plage told his new executive officer, twenty-seven-year-old Lt. Bob Surdam, himself a navy reservist who until recently had been an industrial analyst for a commercial bank in upstate New York. "A few months active duty on this ship and they'll become men in a hurry."

Before weighing anchor for Pearl, Plage ran the *Tabby* through dock trials and underway maneuvers in the Gulf of Mexico, steamed her through shakedown training exercises to Bermuda, and put into the Boston navy yards for her final overhaul. Along the way Plage and Surdam instituted a backbreaking regimen of seamanship drills designed to shape the crew into fighting trim. The skipper exuded a quiet authority that did not go unnoticed by his men. They not only admired his obviously exceptional seamanship, but sensed that he was as much concerned for their safety and well-being as he was for his own. "A fine gentleman, a man among men," one subordinate described him, not, it turned out, without good reason.

To nineteen-year-old Mailman 3rd Class William McClain, Plage was the antithesis of everything he had expected from a navy commander. Before joining the service, McClain had been out of his home state of Tennessee precisely once, and when he joined the *Tabby*'s crew in Houston for her maiden voyage, he was unsure what to expect from the ship's officers. Plage quickly set him straight. He played no favorites and pulled no rank.

"The one thing that stands out about the Cap'n is his evenhandedness," McClain told new arrivals to the *Tabberer*. "We're a small ship, and when we load stores, everybody loads stores, the Cap'n makes sure of that." In fact, Plage would drag a chair to the fantail of the *Tabberer* when it came time to take on provisions, and sit there throughout the entire process making sure none of his enlisted men worked any harder than his officers. McClain was not the only sailor who noticed that Plage, though but twenty-nine himself, was wont to take an inordinate paternal interest in every member of his crew.

Two months out of port, a twenty-five-year-old shipfitter named Leonard Glaser caught Plage's eye. Glaser was pale and drawn, bordering on emaciated. He looked, a crewmate observed, "like he was walking around just to save funeral expenses." In fact, he had lost a pound a day in the sixty days the *Tabby* had been at sea. Plage found Glaser alone one day and pulled him aside. "What's wrong with you?" he said. "You look like you're wasting away."

Glaser explained that he had been raised in a kosher household and could not eat much of the galley's mess, including the copious servings of bacon and ham.

"This is war, son," Plage told him. "I know your religious decrees, but I also know your rabbi says you can eat anything and everything."

Faith had nothing to do with it, Glaser said. His stomach just couldn't hold down the food to which his system was so unaccustomed. Plage placed his hand on Glaser's shoulder and marched him straightaway to the galley. There he instructed "Cookie" Phillips that Shipfitter 3rd Class Leonard Glaser hereby had the run of the galley. He turned back to Glaser. "Anytime there's food served you don't think you can eat, you come up here and find yourself something you can," he said.

Shortly thereafter, as the *Tabby* steamed for the Panama Canal, she made another brief port of call in the Caribbean. The crew was given one-day shore leave. When Glaser returned to the ship, he found a carton of sardines, peanuts, and other kosher foods on his bunk, compliments of the captain.

It was true, the skipper could be a stern disciplinarian when necessary, but just as the crew felt they had reached their breaking point during, say, one of his relentless crash-course drills, he would relent. He had an innate feel for just how much stress the men could take, and he even looked the other way when several sailors, against regulations, adopted and smuggled aboard a mascot, a scruffy abandoned terrier they christened, naturally enough, Tabby. Plage could often be spotted on the fantail donning gloves and competing in the ship's intramural boxing matches, or eschewing meals in officers' country in order to dine in the enlisted men's mess. By late 1944 the *Tabberer* boasted one of the most efficient crews in the U.S. Navy to complement her beloved skipper.

After Cookie Phillips installed his new ice cream freezer on the DE, it was Plage's habit to ensure that all hands had been served dessert before he appeared at the galley door, late at night, eager to see if any might be left. Of course Phillips always put some aside, and "the Cap'n," Cookie, and the galley staff, sometimes joined by an officer or two, would often talk well into the night over bowls of ice cream, their topics ranging from Hollywood movies to their postwar plans.

It was on one such visit belowdecks, on December 8, 1944, that Lt. Comdr. Henry Lee Plage notified several of his crew that the *Tabby* would be sailing with her hunter-killer Task Group 30.7 squadron early the next morning. Her mission: to conduct long-range submarine sweeps in preparation for the invasion of Mindoro.

CHAPTER 6

A tropical cyclone is a cyclone originating in the tropics or sub-tropics. Although it generally resembles the extratropical cyclone of higher latitudes, there are important differences, the principal one being the concentration of a large amount of energy into a relatively small area. Tropical cyclones are infrequent in compari-son to middle and high latitude storms, but they have a record of destruction far exceeding that of any other type of storm. Because of their fury, and because they are predominantly oceanic, they merit special attention by mariners. A tropical storm may have a deceptively small size, and beautiful weather may be experienced only a few hundred miles from the center. The rapidity with which the weather can deteriorate with the approach of the storm, and the violence of the fully developed tropical cyclone, are difficult to imagine if they have not been experienced.

—Nathaniel Bowditch

That warning was written over two centuries ago. Nathaniel Bowditch, an autodidact and mathematical savant, was the first American to compile and accurately record every element essential to navigation in his compendious *The American Practical Naviga-tor*, a thick, heavy tome first published in 1802 that has subse-quently been updated in over fifty editions. *The American Practical Navigator* has sailed with U.S. merchantmen in an unbroken chain for those two hundred years, and U.S. warships have carried it from Tripoli to Havana Harbor to the Persian Gulf. To sailors, the phrase "according to Bowditch" evokes the same resonance as does Hoyle for contract bridge grandmasters. It remains to this day the bible of the United States Navy.

Bowditch was born in 1773 in the seafaring town of Salem, Massachusetts, the fourth of the Revolutionary War shipmaster Habakkuk Bowditch's seven children. When he was an infant, his father left the sea to seek his fortune as a coopersmith, a profession at which he failed miserably. By the time Nathaniel was ten years old, his family faced such poverty that he was forced to leave school to join his father in the cooper's trade. But the young Bowditch's skill at fashioning wooden tubs also proved negligible, and two years later he found employment as a clerk with a local ship chandlery firm. The barrel-making industry's loss was the nascent U.S. Navy's gain.

By his mid-teens, Bowditch's remarkable mind was celebrated throughout New England and beyond. He taught himself French, Spanish, German, and Greek in order to better comprehend the nuances of the finest scientific sourcebooks of the era in their original languages, and at thirteen he began studying the rudiments of navigation. A year later he assisted local Salem authorities in surveying his hometown, by fifteen he had published an almanac and constructed a crude barometer, and at sixteen years old the international scientific community credited Bowditch with discovering a mathematical error in Sir Isaac Newton's classic *The Principia*, which he had read in the original Latin.

When Bowditch was twenty-one, he went to sea for the first time as a sort of scholar-in-residence on the Salem merchant ship *Henry*, circumnavigating the globe from Reunion Island in the Indian Ocean and back. During four subsequent sea voyages over the next decade, the last as master and part owner of his own three-master, he compiled his timeless text through firsthand observation and analysis of all aspects of the planet's seas, tides, currents, winds, and stars.

Bowditch's official portrait depicts a pinched, scrivener-like visage from the pages of Dickens, and this is fitting: He was just as prolific as the English novelist, all the while never forgetting that he was writing for the learner. Aware that most seamen of his era were poorly educated, if not illiterate, his stated purpose in publishing *The American Practical Navigator* was, above all, functionality—"to put down in this book nothing I cannot teach the crew."

During World War II his encyclopedia remained the premier reference work for seafaring fundamentals. It was from their "Bowditches" that ship commanders such as Lt. Comdr. James A. Marks of the destroyer *Hull* administered promotion examinations to enlisted men such as Chief Quartermaster Archie DeRyckere. And during an earlier naval court of inquiry investigating losses from a separate, devastating storm, a restless admiral sitting in judgment was overheard to mutter, "The whole matter certainly is a mess, and indicates that nobody ever heard of a guy named Bowditch."

In December 1944 a well-thumbed "Bowditch" took center place in the small library in the ship's quarters of Comdr. George F. Kosco, chief aerologist of the Third Pacific Fleet.

In essence and utility, Kosco was Admiral Halsey's head weatherman. A handsome, athletic six-footer, Kosco's relationship with the admiral stretched back to the late 1920s, when as a midshipman he'd boxed at the Naval Academy under the guidance of the team's supervisor, then-captain William F. Halsey. After graduation, Kosco earned a master's degree in weather aerology from the Massachusetts Institute of Technology and began his career as a seagoing officer of the line.

He spent much of the 1930s in the Caribbean helping to pioneer the nascent science of "hurricane hunting"—hazardous duty in the early era of flight—and he acquired a reputation as an authority on navigation and meteorology. When war broke out, he served as the aerological officer aboard several carriers before being assigned to Halsey's Third Fleet in early October 1944. Following two months of special weather indoctrination at Pearl Harbor, he was billeted aboard the *New Jersey* in early December.

From his office on the battleship's navigation bridge, one deck above flag plot, Kosco rapidly became a member of Halsey's inner circle. He was charged with overseeing a staff of seven—a chief aerographer's mate and six rated enlisted men—when Task Force

38 was to weigh anchor in Ulithi and steam for Mindoro on December 11.

Unknown to Halsey and Kosco, on that very day a small, invisible mass of air, calved from the atmosphere like an iceberg from a glacier, had begun churning in one of the most volatile corners of the earth. This meteorological disturbance had been seeded in the natural hothouse climate of the intertropical convergence zone, an equatorial trough of warm, sticky air known to mariners as the doldrums. The storm proceeded to incubate just north of the equator, over six hundred miles southeast of Ulithi, midway between the coast of New Guinea and the Caroline Islands.

In what sounds suspiciously like an apocryphal report, three Japanese soldiers stationed on an enemy-held island in the Carolines later claimed to have been fishing not far from shore in a small dugout canoe that very morning. They recalled that the sky was cloudless, the air still, the water as smooth as polished mica. Abruptly, one of the soldiers nudged his sergeant and pointed at what appeared to be a small whirlpool developing some twenty feet from their bow.

Just as they dipped oars to paddle closer and investigate, a sudden and powerful gust of wind lifted the canoe and dumped the men into the sea. They scrambled to right the vessel, climbed back aboard, and turned the craft to run for the beach. By the time they reached land, the sea before them had turned choppy and dirty in a great circle around the vortex, and a stiff breeze was already causing the palm trees about them to rustle and sway.

Simply put, cyclonic winds are the result of a complex interaction of air temperature, atmospheric pressure, and the topography of an ocean's surface. They have been long recognized as a Pacific typhoon's most destructive meteorological feature. It is these powerful, low-altitude streams of air that birth both the long swells that radiate outward from a storm's inverse barometer—the domed mound of seawater in the eye—as well as the huge, deadly waves that ensue. Moreover, it is wind that allows a typhoon to grow by, in a sense, cannibalizing itself. The spindrift and spray sheared off the tops of these great gouts of water by slicing gales combine with solid sheets of falling rain to feed a typhoon engine's constant demand for evaporation.

The synchronous horizontal and vertical winds of a typhoon, fashioned by the dual kinetic processes of advection and convection, can best be imagined as a haphazardly tiered meteorological layer cake. Moving outward from the center, the soft, humid, 15-mile-per-hour breezes that waft through the eye of a storm give way to the violent "gust zones" of the thick eye wall, whose air speeds can average a ship-scuttling 155 miles per hour. Further removed, the eye wall's sustained gusts gradually cede to heavy gales that extend 150 to 250 miles from the eye. These, in turn, devolve into the windy rain bands that dominate a typhoon's fringe.

Similarly, this gentle-voracious-rapid-slower pattern of moving air also applies to a vertical cross section of a tropical cyclone's circulation. Once free from the friction created by the earth's surface, a typhoon's winds become more violent as they rise until, finally cooling and decelerating, they dissipate in the upper atmosphere of the storm system's outflow layer.

Winds and seafarers share an ancient, symbiotic narrative in which the hand of God, or the gods, is manifestly present. The medieval Japanese who perceived a benevolent celestial purpose behind the kamikazes that destroyed the Great Khan's invasion fleets in the thirteenth century do not stand alone. From Zeus's breath instigating Odysseus's windblown adventures across Homer's "salty waste" to the hallowed "Protestant Wind" that scattered the remnants of the Spanish Armada about the west coast of Ireland in 1588, sailors and landsmen alike have come to associate their confluence with divine providence. Early Americans were no less immune to the myth.

Following a particularly violent hurricane that struck the Outer Banks in the early 1700s, a humbled North Carolina colonist noted in his journal that the gusts were a form of heavenly punishment. "Then the Lord sent a great rain and a horrible wind," he wrote, "whereby much hurt was done." A century later the editor of South Carolina's *Winyaw Intelligencer* detected in a vicious, two-day storm that spanned several high tides "none other than a ringing condemnation of the ironies of intellectual hubris of an overconfident town."

"[The] inhabitants apprehended no danger from the tide, as, from the violence of the gale," the *Intelligencer* thundered. "It was presumed that it could not continue until the period of the succeeding high water. In this expectation, however, it pleased the Almighty to disappoint them and, by the awful result, to prove how fallacious are all human calculations."

But for men working upon the sea, the Lord apparently saves his worst, in the form of giant, cyclonic, wind-spawned walls of water that can reach heights of one hundred feet and have washed an ocean clean of all who sail before them. Moreover, the intricate collision of surface and subsurface ocean currents set in motion by a typhoon's winds run with the ferocity of a swollen river. These wind-driven tides have been known to shatter coral reefs, snap sunken airplanes in two, send schools of sharks into feeding frenzies, and crumple sunken ships resting on the seabed as if they were aluminum toys.

Before the dawn of modern meteorology, fleets trapped in a typhoon often assumed that because the winds blew from two directions—northwesterly from the storm's upper left corner and southeasterly from the lower right—they were actually caught between two storms, with the calm eye the barrier separating them.

Now, by 1944, the United States had amassed the greatest naval forces in the history of warfare. The sailors of this contemporary armada had no way of knowing that theirs would be the last world war to ever employ such sea power. Nor, like the Spanish and Mongol cohorts who had sailed before them, could they guess at the forces of nature soon to be arrayed against them.

In fact, if they are to be believed, the only humans to sense that nature would again interfere with the destiny of fighting men upon the sea were three lonely Japanese soldiers, fishing off a forlorn Pacific atoll. If their story is true, they remain perhaps the only humans in history to witness the birthing of a typhoon. Their exact conversation on this momentous occasion is not reliably recorded. What is chronicled, however, is that as they watched the sea turn into a maelstrom before their eyes, they were convinced of one thing: Whatever this force of nature before them was, it was unquestionably growing.

CHAPTER 7

Planes were flying through it normally, patrol planes, making it look like a normal storm. On the same night, Pearl Harbor coded reports to me that gave us storm indications in about the same location, a tropical storm, very weak, and I didn't think it would amount to much so I just took it under advisement. And I told the Admiral and Chief of Staff that I didn't think it would amount to anything serious and that from present indications it wouldn't give us much trouble.

—Testimony of Comdr. George F. Kosco, U.S. Navy, Aerologist and Navigator, Commander, Third Fleet staff aboard the USS New Jersey, to the court of inquiry investigating "Halsey's Typhoon."

Positioning and utilizing his new destroyer escorts such as Lt. Comdr. Henry Lee Plage's *Tabberer* was only one of the several strategies Halsey addressed before his Third Fleet sailed from Ulithi. There was also the dilemma of the kamikazes, compounded by a nettlesome mystery. After the Battle for Leyte Gulf, land-based Japanese aircraft from Luzon to Formosa had seemed to intuit the exact location of his carrier task forces each time he positioned them for air strikes. The admiral who claimed to favor the *Police Gazette* knew he needed sharp minds to help him solve this mystery. None, in Halsey's opinion, came sharper than Vice Adm. John Sidney "Slew" McCain's.

War is the best teacher of war, Clausewitz said, and McCain was an apt student. Thus when the Third Fleet steamed home from Leyte, Halsey rotated an exhausted Marc Mitscher out of the command of carrier Task Force 38 and replaced him with McCain.

Skinny and wrinkled, his face as pinched as a hatchet blade—"an ugly old aviator," his friend the author James Michener called him—McCain looked as if he had been run over by a freight train and not fully reassembled. Wherever he went, he sported a drab and threadbare green fatigue cap upon which his wife had sewn an old "scrambled eggs" visor encrusted with verdigris. Even the tolerant Halsey found McCain's hat "revolting." But McCain's subordinates knew to race as if their lives depended on it to retrieve the combat talisman should it blow off the admiral's head at sea.

McCain looked as if he shaved with a blowtorch, and walked with a gait described as a "series of jerks," a shambling pace that earned him the nickname "Popeye the Sailor Man" among enlisted men. He scattered tobacco to the winds as he rolled his own Bull Durham cigarettes with one hand, and was prone to uttering strings of muttered oaths through false teeth so ill fitting that his mouth inadvertently clicked and whistled as he spoke. Slightly stooped, and weighing no more than 140 pounds dripping wet, McCain, in short, did not look the part of a master tactical planner. But that is precisely what he was.

Although two years younger than Halsey, the two could have been separated at birth such were their common interests—not the least of which included their mutual fondness for a dram of spirits, in McCain's case three fingers of Kentucky bourbon and water. A wartime magazine profile of McCain noted that the admiral preferred to work in his flag quarters in his stocking feet, and was "one of the Navy's best plain and fancy cussers." Once, when his wife suggested a new, expensive treatment for his congenital ulcers, McCain pounded his fist on the table and exploded, "Not one penny of my money for doctors—I'm spending it all on riotous living."

McCain was of Scottish descent, the scion of illustrious military forebears who reached back through American history nearly as far as the Halseys. A maternal ancestor had served on Gen. George Washington's Revolutionary War staff; two more on his father's side had fought in the War of 1812 and the Civil War (for the Confederacy). He in turn would become the father to a future commander of the United States Pacific Fleet, and grandfather to a future Vietnam prisoner of war turned Arizona senator and Republican presidential candidate.

The McCains were an army clan, and Camp McCain, in Grenada, Mississippi, was named after an uncle. "Slew" became the first McCain to eschew West Point, and graduated from the Naval Academy in 1906. His initial post-Annapolis assignment was to the Philippines, where he acquired a lifelong love of gambling, and he was eventually posted as executive officer to the gunboat USS *Panay*, captained by Ens. Chester Nimitz—a vessel destined to be bombed to the bottom of the Yangtze River in 1937 during the infamous Japanese Rape of Nanking.

In another eerie similarity to his old friend and superior officer, following McCain's service aboard an armored cruiser during the Great War, he had hectored his way into navy flight school and, like Halsey, earned his wings past his fiftieth birthday. Promoted to vice admiral, he had served with "Bull" in the South Pacific, commanding all land-based aircraft during the Battle for Guadalcanal. One evening, while he, Nimitz, and Halsey were touring Henderson Field, the Japanese attempted to assassinate the three admirals with a lightning air raid. As bombs fell about him, McCain dived into what he thought was a drainage ditch, and spent the night in an active latrine. None the worse for his usual wear, he was awarded the Distinguished Service Medal and transferred to Washington, D.C., where he ran the Bureau of Naval Aeronautics with tactical brilliance.

McCain's experiences on Guadalcanal taught him one overriding lesson: In the Pacific the navy had too few planes, too few pilots to fly them, and too few crews to service and maintain them. In

Washington he lobbied, bullied, and brayed about the corridors of the War Department until he convinced the Joint Chiefs not only to accelerate production of the stubby, stubborn Wildcat fighter planes and Avenger torpedo bombers, but also to train and assign two separate crews for every aircraft in the theater. That mission accomplished, in the summer of 1944 he was reassigned to the Third Fleet, where Halsey referred to him as "not much more than my right arm."

On Ulithi, Halsey maintained a deliberately casual routine, and it was his habit to refrain from discussing military tactics at dinner with his staff in flag mess. But as soon as the table was cleared, abiding by his war credo that too much is never enough, he schemed well into the night with his inner circle of Dirty Tricksters, now including McCain, who skiffed across the harbor from his berth on the carrier USS *Hancock*.

The *New Jersey* was a floating city, with a complement of 1,800 enlisted men and close to 100 officers. Halsey preferred the big battlewagon as his flagship—as opposed to a carrier—because his penchant for obtaining as many creative opinions as possible required space for a large staff. Flag country was in the tower's superstructure, with the admiral's bridge below it, and the chart-laden flag plot below that. Halsey slept in quarters beneath flag plot, and it was around the large oval table in the cabin next to his bedroom where the Dirty Tricksters argued into the night.

On Ulithi they approached the Japanese defenses on the Philippines in much the manner that a skilled boxer takes on a plodding puncher—with a lot of cape, and then the sword. Mindoro, a small, isolated island 250 miles north of Leyte, was tucked under the shadow of Luzon. Strategically worthless in and of itself as a military objective, it would, however, provide air bases within striking distance of Manila for MacArthur's bombers.

The Japanese War Ministry had positioned 250,000 seasoned troops of the Fourteenth Imperial Army on Luzon for a last stand, and its radio propagandists labeled the coming battle the war's "most decisive." Even taking into account Radio Tokyo's dependable hyperbole, MacArthur and Nimitz held little doubt that Tokyo Rose was deadly serious when she promised the invading American Sixth Army "the hottest reception in the history of warfare."

With this phalanx of defenders facing him on the ground, MacArthur needed to be sure that America owned the skies when the Luzon landings finally occurred. Nimitz and MacArthur agreed that the Third Fleet's responsibility, meaning Halsey's responsibility, during the Mindoro invasion would be to suppress and destroy as much enemy land-based airpower as possible on Luzon and a few smaller, surrounding islands. It was left to Halsey and his staff to figure out how, all the while avoiding kamikazes.

As the carriers *Intrepid, Belleau Wood,* and *Franklin* had all retired to Pearl Harbor for repairs, McCain suggested that for the Mindoro campaign Halsey downsize his carrier groups, from four to three. This would not only retain ample space for air operations, but the compressed task groups would be more effective at concentrating defensive antiaircraft fire against suicide attacks. Halsey also directed that a substantial increase be made in the fighter aircraft complement aboard his attack carriers.

But before tackling the problem of how to negate the kamikazes, however, he first fretted over the apparent Japanese foreknowledge of the movements of Third Fleet's carrier groups. Several of the Dirty Tricksters blamed MacArthur, whose communications staff was suspected of lax discipline and loose lips. But Halsey had another idea. One day, while he treated his senior officers to a picnic on Mog Mog, he put it to the test.

Studying the Third Fleet's post-Leyte after-action reports, the admiral noted that on numerous occasions his carriers had launched air raids from virtually the same coordinates in the Philippine Sea. They had also employed similar, fleetwide radio traffic patterns prior to the launches. To check his theory, Halsey ordered his radio operators to broadcast a series of bogus messages mimicking his previous transmissions. Sure enough, scout planes reported that after each broadcast, kamikazes mobilized and Japanese merchant

vessels ran for cover from Luzon to the far side of the South China
Sea. Despite the seriousness of the intelligence breach, Halsey had
to laugh at the irony. He knew he was denigrated in certain navy
quarters for "never doing the same thing twice."

Following what he called his "picnic launch," Halsey sent the
antiaircraft cruiser USS *San Juan* to a remote position in the
Western Pacific, where it began transmitting "urgent" dummy
messages that he hoped would create the impression that the Third
Fleet was already at sea. To further confuse the Japanese, on the
advice of his Dirty Tricksters he directed all vessels remaining at
Ulithi after the fleet's departure three days hence to begin broadcasting communications of the same urgency and type. He hoped
that any enemy code breakers would think the fleet was in two
places at the same time.

Halsey and McCain next turned their attention to another ruse
the Japanese had perfected, which was to tuck individual kamikazes
close in behind returning American carrier-bound squadrons. "Tail-
End Charlies" they were called, and to thwart them McCain suggested
deploying a number of "Tom Cat" picket destroyers sixty miles off
the attack carrier's flanks. Each destroyer would be specially equipped
with modern "bedspring" radar antennae as well as homing devices
to act as buoy markers for the returning American planes.

As navy pilots made tight turns around these Tom Cats on their
way home to their carriers, regular combat air patrols, or CAPs,
protecting the destroyers would weed out and pick off these trailing bogeys—"delouse them," as McCain had it—as well as alert the
"Jack Patrols" flying low cover for the main body of the carrier fleet.
Any aircraft failing to follow this procedure was automatically assumed to be a bandit.

Finally, at the end of the day it was McCain who deserved the
lion's share of credit for lifting the cloud that had darkened Halsey's
mood since the morning he had watched the suicide bandit slam
into the *Intrepid*. For it was "Popeye" who spearheaded the plan
for the preemptive "Big Blue Blanket," an audacious strategy to
completely nullify any kamikazes emanating from Luzon.

Named after the Naval Academy's football team, the Big Blue Blanket gambit consisted of putting up a twenty-four-hour screen, or blanket, over every Japanese airfield on Luzon. To accomplish this, not only would Marine Corps fighter squadrons be incorporated for the first time ever into navy carrier air groups, but aboard each flattop the complement of fighter planes would be doubled, from 36 to 72, while dive bombers were halved. The number of torpedo planes, the two decided, would remain about the same.

The fighting component of the Third Fleet, Halsey's carrier Task Force 38, was scheduled to weigh anchor for Mindoro on December 11. But the fleet's undertaking was far from a one-day operation. Long-range picket destroyer escorts such as the *Tabberer* had departed December 9, and on December 10 the fleet's oiler logistics group, dubbed Task Group 30.8, steamed from Ulithi.

TG 30.8 was a "unique and new refueling-at-sea organization" commanded by Capt. Jasper T. Acuff, a former submariner. Prior to the war, midocean refueling was as laborious as it was rare, accomplished one ship at a time by transferring oil by a lengthy hose that ran from fantail to bow. But innovations in refueling engineering now permitted two ships to take on oil simultaneously, not only hastening the procedure, but allowing carrier task groups to remain at sea for weeks while conducting air strikes.

Nimitz went out of his way to praise "the utmost skill in seamanship" of the unsung tanker crews who risked life and limb for little glory. As CINCPAC noted, "Not many an oiler will ever be able to paint a Jap flag, for planes downed or ships sunk, upon her bridge—but every man in the task force is aware of the importance of the contribution of these service ships."

As oil hoses stretched no farther than 100 feet, this new technique of open-ocean refueling required attaching the hoses to ships pulling abreast of each other, to within 40 or 50 feet on either side. Sometimes a third vessel could even be refueled astern. This was no mean task even in calm waters: too slack and the hoses washed into the sea; too taut and they broke. Destroyers "drank" from the larger carriers, battlewagons, and cruisers, which in turn filled their own bunkers from the oilers. These piggyback assemblies steamed together like moving gas stations for up to four hours at a time at between five to twelve knots, which left them sitting ducks for enemy aircraft.

During refueling operations all captains personally assumed the conn, and only the most experienced helmsmen were allowed to maneuver the vessels. Further, the ship's most qualified watch officer and a second helmsman were stationed aft in the emergency manual steering gear compartment, ready to assume control in the event of a malfunction on the bridge.

Acuff's task group consisted of 27 oilers, 7 ammunition ships, 8 escort aircraft carriers, and 7 oceangoing tugs, with a combined 40 DDs and DEs assigned to screen them. Sailors had taken to calling the tough little escort carriers, with their flat tops laid over a tanker's hull, "jeeps," after the small but mighty creature Eugene the Jeep from the Popeye comic strip.

In addition to fuel oil and aviation gasoline, the task group was also charged with replenishing Task Force 38's depleted stocks of aircraft replacement parts, food, ammunition, and—most important to sailors stranded at sea for weeks—mail. These underway replenishment operations, or "unreps," proved vital to morale, although a moment's inattention during these transfers could also spell disaster.

As one warning put it, "Aside from collisions, a parted line can cut men down like a scythe, a shattered block can be as lethal as a cannon shell, and unwary soldiers have been crushed to death by pallets of ammunition, food, and even bags of mail." As Acuff well knew, unfavorable weather conditions only rendered the procedure all the more hazardous.

On December 10, as Acuff breached Ulithi harbor and shaped his task group west, he chewed over a particular dilemma. He was charged with not only locating coordinates in the Philippine Sea that would provide some cloud cover for the vulnerable refueling process, but at the same time finding a placid enough stretch of ocean to accomplish the delicate task. Moreover, as Halsey had reorganized his task force into three task groups, it was now Acuff's mission to also trisect his oiler groups accordingly and plan a rendezvous for three predetermined sites.

Poring over his own weather charts, and consulting frequently with the Third Fleet's chief aerologist, Comdr. George F. Kosco aboard the *New Jersey*, Acuff pinned down three locations to "top off" the battleships and large carriers of Task Force 38 along the thousand-mile path between Ulithi and Mindoro. Each of these behemoths held nearly 7,000 tons of thick, black oil, as opposed to the 500 to 600 tons required by the destroyers and destroyer escorts.

Halsey quickly signed off on Acuff's coordinates, and the transfer of oil, aviation gas for the planes, and some diesel fuel was scheduled for December 13. Because Task Force 38 would be only two days out of Ulithi, more stores and ammo transfers weren't necessary. But Halsey knew that those conveyances—by way of cargo nets, breeches buoys, canvas bags, and temporary trolleys—would be sorely needed after three days and two nights of constant combat from Mindoro to Luzon. He scheduled another rendezvous with Acuff's oiler fleet for 6:00 A.M. on December 17. They were to meet about 450 miles east of Luzon.

While MacArthur's army stormed Mindoro's beaches and Halsey's task force threw its Big Blue Blanket over Luzon, Acuff's task group was to mark time and remain cruising at sea, within hailing distance at all times. The entire Mindoro operation could conceivably take weeks, and Acuff issued orders that any of his oilers less than half full should transfer their cargo to other tankers and return to Ulithi for replenishment. Every three days or so, three newly filled oilers would join Acuff's group while three others would be sent back in ballast.

No matter how long the Mindoro assault lasted, Halsey would never lack for replenishment stores. At least, such was the plan.

At daybreak on December 11, Ulithi harbor was a whorl of activity. Gangs brought anchors to short stay and battle guidons whipped in the breeze as the ninety-odd ships of Task Force 38 steamed

Indian-file at five-hundred-yard intervals through Ulithi's Mugai Pass, the only navigable passage into and out of the vast anchorage.

On either side of this nautical parade, sailors cheered from the rails of the hundreds of Third Fleet auxiliaries remaining behind—the hotel barges and distillery ships, the refrigerator vessels and reserve fuel tankers, the dry docks and hospital ships. Overhead, land-based combat patrols formed a two-tiered umbrella guarding against stray bandits from Yap Island. Yet despite the "sortie fever," it was a tranquil, almost idyllic morning, with the sunlight sending flickers and flashes of reflections glancing up from the mirrored sea; one sailor remarked upon "the caps of silvery filigree topping the cresting waves" of the long line of breakers on the reef. Beyond them lay blue water.

The core of Halsey's flotilla, the three carrier groups that formed Task Force 38, were his floating airfields, consisting of seven heavy carriers of the huge *Essex* class and six *Independence*-class light aircraft carriers. It was their payload of about 540 fighter planes, 150 dive bombers, and 140 torpedo bombers with which Halsey would execute Slew McCain's Big Blue Blanket strategy. Escorting and screening the carriers were 9 battleships and 16 cruisers, a mix of heavy and light, their guns glistening in the rising sun. Finally came the destroyers, numbering close to 60, skimming the surface like a disciplined school of porpoises.

No eyewitnesses to the procession could refute the naval historian Samuel Eliot Morison's description of this contemporary armada as "representing the last word in the energy and ingenuity of man on the ocean."

The previous night Halsey had hosted a farewell dinner on the beach, and as one attendee put it, "There was more, but less formal, shoptalk, but no ringing fight talk by the admiral." Now, alternately pacing and seated in an armchair on the flag bridge of the hulking battleship *New Jersey*, he watched as the greatest naval force in the history of warfare shaped course beneath him. He had been on the bridge two days before as his DEs steamed away, and again a day earlier as the oiler Task Group 30.8 set sail. With the departure of Task Force 38, the chessboard was complete.

It was, all told, a magnificent enterprise. Despite the threat of kamikazes, despite the enemy buildup on Luzon, despite the certainty of the countless more American deaths and casualties that stood between Mindoro and Tokyo, there was a sense on the tiny atoll that morning that the United States had finally broken the back of the Japanese; that a war-ravaged nation had come full circle since the dark days following December 7, 1941.

As Halsey stood upon his towering bridge inspecting his departing vessels below, he surely noticed the slender forward stacks of the destroyer USS *Monaghan* as she departed with the oiler task group. There was no more fitting representative of the war's circle being squared than the plucky *Monaghan*. For, in a sense, the *Monaghan*'s World War II narrative not only encapsulated the conflict as a whole, but embodied all that American sailors thought right and true with America's collective military effort.

Named in honor of a twenty-six-year-old ensign who had been killed defending a wounded fellow officer against a native uprising in Samoa in 1899, the *Monaghan* was the last of the *Farragut*-class "gold-platers" constructed at the Boston Navy Yard. Commissioned in 1935, she'd spent her early years as a training vessel in the Atlantic before being transferred to the Pacific Fleet in the closing months of 1939.

During the attack on Pearl Harbor the *Monaghan* had been the port's ready-duty destroyer, and was preparing to slip her cables just as the first Japanese aircraft appeared overhead. Her guns filled the sky with ack-ack as she steamed toward the mouth of the harbor less than thirty minutes after the initial bombs fell. Just inside the entrance, one of her lookouts sighted a periscope pointed toward Battleship Row. Heeling about, the *Monaghan* struck an enemy midget submarine a glancing blow before perilously dropping two depth charges that sank the sub in the harbor's shallow waters. A week later she was steaming with Halsey's carrier task force in the failed attempt to relieve Wake Island.

She subsequently earned two of her twelve battle stars for actions during the Battles of the Coral Sea and Midway, where she was cited for distinguished service after retrieving several downed pilots. And when a Japanese submarine fired three torpedoes into the carrier USS *Yorktown* two days after that heraldic victory, she helped rescue its crew before the flattop disappeared beneath the waves. From Midway she sailed for the Aleutians, and in March 1943 had the unique "honor" of taking part in the war's only old-fashioned, slug-it-out, surface gun duel with a Japanese task group off Siberia's Komandorski Islands.

No submarines or aircraft were involved in the fight, just the *Monaghan*'s outgunned and outnumbered cruiser task group trading shell and torpedo, shot-for-shot and brace-for-brace, for four breathtaking hours. The *Monaghan* and two sister destroyers led the charge, and the enemy eventually withdrew. After the war, a Japanese commander who fought in the engagement remarked, "I do not know how a ship could live through the concentration of firepower that was brought to bear upon the leading destroyer. All three ships were literally smothered with shell splashes." Three months later the *Monaghan* capped a one-on-one night shoot-out with a surfaced submarine by driving the vessel onto the shoals surrounding Kiska Island.

Recalled to Pearl, she covered the landings at Tarawa and ran patrols near the Marshalls. But by this stage of the war the *Monaghan*, as well as the remaining *Farraguts* such as her sister ship the *Hull*, had become desperately outdated. Beloved by their crews, particularly the veteran hands who'd served on the old "China Station," the ships were nonetheless unable to match the newer and more sophisticated destroyers of the *Fletcher* and *Sumner* classes in armament payload or communications technology. Worse, the somewhat haphazard attempt to modernize the *Farraguts* had inadvertently served to make them less seaworthy.

The *Hull*, for instance, now steamed at over 2,000 tons, more than 500 tons over what she had been designed to carry. Her topside bristled with four 5-inch deck guns, a full complement of depth charges and racks, two centerline-mounted clusters of four torpedo tubes each, and several antiaircraft machine guns. This additional deck weight combined with her two stacks to form "sails" just waiting to be caught by heavy winds. If a wave knocked her over, a gale would keep her heeled, fighting her return to an even keel.

The *Hull*'s chief quartermaster, Archie DeRyckere, was well aware of this hazardous anomaly as the destroyer prepared to steam from Ulithi. Eighteen months earlier, in June 1943, he'd been at the helm when the destroyer had joined a task group bombarding Wake Island. On approach to the fire zone, the wake from a cruiser sailing on her port beam—"A cruiser's wake, for Lord's sakes!"— had laid the ship so far over that the coppers in the galley dumped the midday mess and her starboard whaleboat dipped into the sea. More disturbing yet, during the *Hull*'s most recent Stateside refitting in Washington State's Bremerton Navy Yard, Captain Marks had ordered a test power run at 28 knots at 50,000 horsepower in the calm waters of the Strait of Juan de Fuca. When he called for left full rudder, she'd laid over like a beached whale and had to be coaxed back up, oh so slowly, with an immediate countermanding right full rudder. DeRyckere was not surprised.

And even when older vessels like the *Hull* or *Monaghan* had been jury-rigged as best as possible with modern radar systems, there still remained a dearth of seamen who had any experience in operating the new technology. Sometimes, however, a ship got lucky. Such was the *Monaghan*'s case in May 1944, when radar expert Keith Abbott was unexpectedly billeted aboard the fabled vessel and assigned to her new Combat Information Center.

A rawboned lad, as a teen Abbott had taken to "fooling around" with radios, breaking them down and reassembling their component parts. He had also done some electrical work on construction sites before enlisting a year ago, in March. When the navy learned of his mechanical bent, it had sent him through the Point Loma training school for radar operation and maintenance in San Diego before assigning him to the destroyer escort USS *Emery*.

Abbott had been blooded early, joining the *Emery* just as she'd been assigned patrol duty on the waters in and around the Japanese-held Palau Islands. Soon after his berthing, an enemy PT boat had darted out from a cove and raked the destroyer escort with machine gun fire, killing a crewmate. And once, while serving night raft-boarding duty, he'd recovered the samurai sword with which he'd witnessed a Japanese soldier commit hara-kiri rather than be taken prisoner.

The highlight of his service had occurred while the *Emery* was escorting a troop transport to the Ellice Islands (now Tuvalu) deep in the South Pacific. Abbott had tracked several returns, what the sonar men called pings, on his radarscope. He was certain that a Japanese submarine had surfaced nearby. The *Emery* and the enemy sub played a cat-and-mouse game for the next twenty-four hours, culminating with the destroyer escort's launching depth charges that sank the sub.

But three months ago, just as he'd received a message that he was the father of a beautiful baby girl, Abbott had been transferred from the *Emery* to teach a radar maintenance course at Pearl. Abbott had been anxious to return to his original berth on the destroyer escort *Emery*, but by the time the curriculum was complete the *Emery* was thousands of miles away, patrolling the deep South Pacific. His new orders directed him to pull temporary duty on the *Monaghan*—the first American vessel to draw enemy blood after the attack on December 7, 1941—"until such time as [Abbott] can come in contact with and be transferred back to DE 28 Emery." As it happened, such time did not arrive until Abbott had fought with the *Monaghan* through the Marianas Turkey Shoot and the invasion of Peleliu, one of the bloodiest battles of the Pacific.

During her approach to Peleliu, the destroyer had plowed through the tail end of an unnamed typhoon, and Abbott was duly impressed. Once, aboard his former ship the *Emery*, he had been ordered to climb the ninety feet to the tip of the DE's mast in the middle of a violent squall to repair a malfunctioning radar connector. Yet he had never encountered a storm as furious as the one the *Monaghan* faced off Peleliu. The waves were so large that the huge aircraft carriers she was assigned to escort completely disappeared from view. But, to Abbott's astonishment, no major damage was recorded in the ship's log.

It occurred that not long after the Peleliu landings, both the *Emery* and the *Monaghan* found themselves reprovisioning together at Manus Island, in the Admiralties off New Zealand. Abbott had already transferred his seabag, hammock, and prized samurai sword from the destroyer to his old cabin on the DE when he was summoned to the *Emery*'s bridge.

"I've had a request from the *Monaghan* to keep you aboard," the *Emery*'s skipper, Lt. Comdr. R. G. Coburn, informed him. Coburn explained that the *Monaghan* had been slotted to take part in the Third Fleet's upcoming support of MacArthur's Philippine invasions, and her captain was loath to sail without an experienced radar technician. The choice, he said, was completely Abbott's, as his orders explicitly stated. But he added that the *Emery* was scheduled for no more than to continue her fairly routine South Pacific patrols, an unsubtle hint that the radarman could much better serve the war effort aboard the *Monaghan*.

Abbott was conflicted. He peered out over the bridge wing as small swells lapped against the *Emery*'s hull. Vessels of every shape and size bobbed across Manus Island's harbor. He considered his wife, Hannah, who had recently delivered the couple's first child, a baby girl they'd named Sherran. "I'm no thrill-seeker," he thought. Still. This was a war. He was a patriot.

"Of course I'll do it," he told his skipper. He saluted, turned, and left to retrieve his seabag.

Unfortunately, no one ever filed the paperwork recording this transfer. So it was that Radar Maintenance Technician Keith Abbott found himself a ghost sailor lost in the U.S. Navy's vast bureaucracy as he sailed with the *Monaghan* out of Ulithi harbor on December 10, 1944, as part of the destroyer screen for the oilers of Task Group 30.8.

*   *   *

As the several components of Halsey's fleet sailed west toward the Philippines, seamen busied themselves as they had for centuries. Enlisted men swabbed, chipped, and painted. Chiefs plotted charts and readied battle stations. And officers caught up with the mountainous tide of official directives that flow up and down the chain of command of any enterprise as large as an entire fleet on war footing.

One of the most recent of these directives, sent from the Navy Department in Washington, D.C., was a Pacific Theater–wide warning to all vessels regarding typhoons, specifically declaring the storms as great a threat to Allied shipping as the Japanese. The notification carried an ominous addendum: "All the scientific methods available to modern meteorology are not sufficient to forecast accurately the movement and intensity of the frequent typhoons of this area."

Nevertheless, as the invasion of Mindoro loomed large, the divine winds that most concerned Halsey and his sailors had the blazing orange fireball of the rising sun stenciled upon their wings.

CHAPTER 8

That the northeasterly courses steered by the fleet from about 0700 December 16 in an attempt to fuel certain destroyers contributed to the disaster since this maneuver held the fleet in or near the path of the storm center, and was an error in judgment on the part of Commander Task Force 38 who directed it and of Commander THIRD Fleet who permitted it.

—General Opinion #10 in the report of the Court of Inquiry investigating "Halsey's Typhoon."

Comdr. George Kosco had read the Navy Department's recent weather warning. Yet he knew well from both research and personal experience that most Pacific typhoons are stillborn, smothered and buried in their infancy by the very doldrums that conceive them. American sailors, deconstructing ancient rumors through a kind of mariners' osmosis, may have dubbed this stretch of the ocean "Typhoon Alley," but Kosco understood that of all the thousands of embryonic squalls that raced across the Northwestern Pacific, it was the rare thunderstorm that made the triple leap from tropical disturbance to tropical depression to tropical storm.

Moreover, those few that managed to mature into tropical storms blew themselves out in even greater numbers before reaching typhoon status. This high mortality rate reassured the fleet aerologist.

There was, however, a flaw to Kosco's reasoning. Meteorology was not high on the U.S. Navy's list of wartime priorities. It was, in essence, treated as small-bore intelligence. In the summer of

1944, to take one example, several army meteorological officers recently posted to Fleet Weather Central at Pearl were asked to provide a weather forecast for a carrier-based strike the following day against Marcus Island, an isolated speck of rock midway between Tokyo and Wake Island. They stared blankly at the weather map, at each other, and back at the weather map. There were seven areas on the map larger than the United States that contained no weather data whatsoever.

With so little to base any forecast upon, they fell into a philosophical discussion regarding Magellan's thoughts upon setting out into the boundless western sea. Finally, their deadline looming, they processed what little data they could glean from the weather reports of surface ships and submarines near the coordinates. After much head-scratching, they finally determined that a nearby storm system would curve north and collide with the carrier task force set to bombard Marcus Island, and so reported. Their senior commander, however, rejected the analysis.

"Typhoons don't recurve at that longitude at this season," he told his weathermen. "They move straight west. Change that forecast!"

The forecast was duly changed, and off the shores of Marcus Island the following morning planes were lost and brave men died when the cyclone struck the task force.

There were various reasons for this lack of institutional awareness. For one, even by 1944 the rudimentary weather-forecasting radar installed aboard each American aircraft carrier was not designed for making long-range projections. Kosco's staff, who maintained a round-the-clock weather watch on the navigation deck of the *New Jersey*, realized that the meteorological equipment on Halsey's flagship was not that much more efficient than that which sailors of Bowditch's era had carried on sea voyages—a good barometer, a thermometer, and a seasoned "weather nose."

For another, America did not have enough planes in the Pacific Theater to devote to secondary missions such as weather reconnaissance flights. Even if search crews flying out of the U.S. bases from the Marianas to Ulithi to the Palaus had been trained to differentiate commonplace Pacific storms from incipient ty-phoons, which they were not, their aircraft were ill equipped to track them.

When American recon pilots had the time and the fuel, they tried to box a large storm's coordinates; if not, they simply marked its general location on their maps. In any event, even these efforts often fell short. Radio silence prevented scout planes from reporting their sightings until they returned to base, typically hours later. And, un-like their Caribbean counterparts, Pacific typhoons frequently fol-low no directional pattern.

Although the preponderance of Pacific typhoons travel in a west-northwesterly direction, on occasion they have been known to abruptly turn in on themselves and reverse course in a phenome-non known as recurvature. This occurs when the storm falls under the influence of the upper-level, high-pressure anticyclones that dominate circulation patterns aloft in the atmosphere over the North Pacific.

Before the age of weather satellites, it was any navigator's guess as to whether a typhoon would collide with the Philippine archi-pelago and continue west into the South China Sea, or turn sharply and blow nearly due north before slamming into Japan. This held especially true for late-season storms. Even Bowditch notes that De-cember typhoons in the Western Pacific are the most unpredictable.

Despite these forecasting obstacles, Kosco and his staff did their best to analyze the myriad reports coming in from Allied weather posts and surface ships scattered about the Pacific. They knew some-thing was out there. Fleet Weather Station at Pearl had been tracking and collating tantalizing hints of a brewing storm since De-cember 11. But, lacking a Ouija board, the exact nature of the cy-clone the U.S. Navy was shortly to dub Typhoon Cobra remained hidden from their view.

In her embryonic stage she glided west along the trade winds through the doldrums, leisurely, invisible, avoiding any contact with men, or at least men with radios. When she collided with areas of highly favorable warmth and moisture, she nearly came to a halt while sucking up energy from surface water whose temperature was 78 degrees or higher. As her barometric pressure fell, nearby cumulus and nimbus cloud systems moved in to fill her low-pressure center, at first gently gathering around her vortex, then swirling in ever-tightening coils that generated thunderous rumbles and bold strokes of lightning.

Like a massive pump sucking in humid, sea-level air and sending it spiraling upward, her convection cells progressively flourished as her cloud towers, bound for the troposphere, climbed to 10,000, 15,000, 20,000, 25,000 feet. It was at one of these points that she evolved into a tropical depression, defined by sustained wind gusts up to 33 knots. As noted, these squalls are as common in the Pacific as coral reefs. Cobra, however, continued to engulf more and more warm air masses, accruing weight and size as her core became more clearly defined.

When she neared the equator, where the earth's rotational force is weakest, she turned and began moving at 15 knots in a north-northwest direction toward Ulithi. Somewhere around 175 miles east-northeast of the atoll she again loitered, her pressure gradient dropping steeply and her circumference elongating to the west and bulging to the north. Here she drew in enough heat and moisture to mature into a tropical storm, releasing torrential rains and hurling winds of 30 to 40 knots, with gusts as high as 64 knots.

It was at this place and time, on December 15, that army meteorologists stationed on Saipan found her. She had passed south of their Guam weather station, where the foul conditions had turned what sailors call spitty. Kosco, collating all his information, spread his charts across a table on the *New Jersey*'s navigating bridge and placed the storm eight hundred miles southeast of the Third Fleet's position in the Philippine Sea, moving due west.

The question was raised: Would she continue on her straight westward course, or take a northwest turn toward Halsey and his Mindoro task force as the pilot charts for December advised?

Like most naval officers, Kosco was not unaware of the destructive potential of a Pacific typhoon, particularly the late-season

variety that, since the beginning of the war, U.S. military meteorologists had begun to dramatically classify as "super typhoons" (as
opposed to the rainy, relatively mild "bean" or "midget" typhoons
that form earlier in the year). Kosco had flown through hurricanes
in the Caribbean, and officers of the line were steeped in storm lore,
which was as old as the service itself. The story of the Continental
Army sloop *Saratoga*, destroyed off the Bahamas with all eighteen
hands aboard in March 1781, was still told at the Naval Academy.
And prior to the Civil War, the U.S. War Department officially
counted at least fourteen ships lost to storms on open oceans around
the world.

During the Spanish-American War, President William C.
McKinley had deftly delineated the debate between military necessity and weather hazards when he admitted to being "more afraid
of a West Indian hurricane than I am of the entire Spanish Navy."
And despite the echoes of the fate of the Spanish Armada the
president's words evoked, the Navy Department was also aware that
bad weather and high seas could strike anywhere water rippled, as
evidenced by the three gunboats that sank in Chesapeake Bay and
the schooner lost beneath frigid Lake Ontario in the early 1800s.

Moreover, by the onset of World War II, weather officers such
as Kosco had taken a special interest in the fifty-year-old face-off,
and subsequent devastation, of the American and German naval
squadrons in Samoa's Apia Harbor. Although over 450 American
sailors had perished in Atlantic storms since the commencement
of the war, the Samoan storm, being a Pacific phenomenon, seemed
more raw in the collective memory of the men fighting the Japanese, as did the powerful Pacific typhoon that nearly destroyed
Adm. Matthew C. Perry's flagship frigate USS *Mississippi* as he
sailed home from his historic "opening" of Japan in 1853.

Given the advances in naval engineering over the past century,
however, Kosco was not overly concerned. Only three months earlier, in September, Third Fleet had safely ridden out the outer
fringes of a typhoon on open water near Peleliu, the same storm
that had buffeted Radar Technician Keith Abbott. And in early

October, Halsey had even used a typhoon that limned Ulithi as cover to deliver surprise attacks on Okinawa and other outlying Japanese islands. (In appreciation of its efficacy, this "good guy" typhoon had been dubbed "Task Force Zero-Zero," the first time a typhoon or hurricane was ever informally named.)

And despite being one of nature's most impregnable forces, a typhoon does have innate meteorological enemies at sea. Cold water, dry air aloft, and most especially the massive cold fronts that scream out of the arctic and extend across the Pacific like invisible cordilleras will rapidly sap a tropical storm of its energy. For the past forty-eight hours Kosco had been tracking just such a high-pressure area pushing an enormous mass of cold air down from Siberia and across the eastern contours of Asia.

He knew from intelligence sources that this near-freezing bloc of air had already collided with the warm water of the Japan Current and spawned a series of violent frontal storms now tearing across the Japanese islands and riding the current toward the Aleutians. The storms had pulled the cold front down behind them, and he saw that it had begun to bulge as far south as the Philippine Sea. This front, Kosco was certain, would devour any tropical disturbance in its path.

Given the circumstances and Commander Kosco's academic training, it should be said that he was sure he'd done the best he could. He'd studied every weather forecast sent to him; there had been no portents. He had no idea that by the evening of December 16, as Halsey's carrier planes were raking Japanese installations on the Philippines, Typhoon Cobra was already a churning maelstrom covering several hundred square miles of ocean and rising thousands of feet into the atmosphere. The storm was also the ideal distance from the equator to have the deflective sources of the earth's rotation set her counterclockwise cyclonic winds in motion. A small eye, probably no more than six miles in diameter, appeared in her core, producing winds in excess of 64 knots.

That night—her now clearly delineated circular eye swiftly organizing itself into an efficient airshaft, "an umbilical cord through which the storm will grow from the inside out"—she officially became a typhoon. But Cobra, as tightly coiled as a DNA helix, was maturing so slowly that she was not yet throwing out to her periphery the massive gusts and swells that would typically herald the arrival of a full-blown typhoon.

Halsey was busy coordinating his attacks against Luzon, Mindoro, and beyond when Kosco interrupted him in flag plot to inform him that a tropical disturbance, "not necessarily a typhoon," was developing some five hundred miles east of the fleet. He further informed the admiral that he had been following what he would later call this "evil thing dedicated to death and destruction," moving north-northwest at about nine knots. Kosco predicted that the storm would collide with the cold front bearing down across Japan and rebound toward the northeast. Away from the fleet.

Satisfied, Halsey returned his attention to the Japanese.

BOOK TWO

THE STORM

Bursts as a wave from the clouds impends,
And swell'd with tempests on the ships descends;
White are the decks with foam; the winds aloud
Howl o'er the masts, and sing through every shroud:
Pale, trembling, tir'd, the sailors freeze with fear;
And instant death on every wave appears

—HOMER, *THE ILIAD*

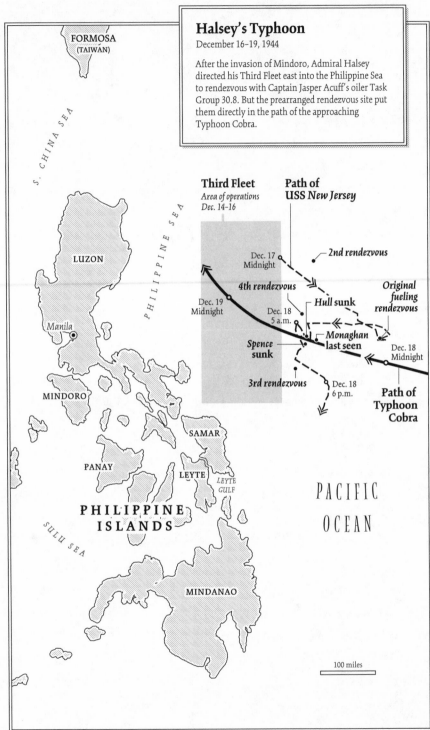

Halsey's Typhoon
December 16–19, 1944

After the invasion of Mindoro, Admiral Halsey directed his Third Fleet east into the Philippine Sea to rendezvous with Captain Jasper Acuff's oiler Task Group 30.8. But the prearranged rendezvous site put them directly in the path of the approaching Typhoon Cobra.

FORMOSA
(TAIWAN)

S. CHINA SEA

PHILIPPINE SEA

LUZON

Manila

MINDORO

SAMAR

PANAY

LEYTE

LEYTE GULF

PHILIPPINE ISLANDS

SULU SEA

MINDANAO

PACIFIC OCEAN

Third Fleet
Area of operations
Dec. 14–16

Path of USS New Jersey

Dec. 17
Midnight

2nd rendezvous

4th rendezvous

Original fueling rendezvous

Dec. 19
Midnight

Dec. 18
5 a.m.

Hull sunk

Spence sunk

Monaghan last seen

Dec. 18
Midnight

3rd rendezvous

Dec. 18
6 p.m.

Path of Typhoon Cobra

100 miles

matthew ericson

CHAPTER 9

I received warnings continuously for 24 hours before I got into the storm, from my aerographer, from the action of the ship, and the condition of the sea. I was fully aware of the storm, and that it was going to be severe.

—TESTIMONY OF CAPT. MICHAEL H. KERNODLE,
COMMANDING OFFICER, USS SAN JACINTO, TO THE
COURT OF INQUIRY INVESTIGATING "HALSEY'S TYPHOON."

Moments before first light on December 14, from a launch point several hundred miles northeast of Manila, Task Force 38 struck the Japanese with what one seaman called "God's own hammer."

Gouts of sand and shredded coconut palms erupted from the beaches of Mindoro as the big guns of battleships and cruisers cleared landing zones for MacArthur's Sixth Army. Carriers turned into the wind and released deckloads of deafening aircraft that vanished over the western horizon, their targets the one hundred–odd Japanese-held airfields mapped by naval intelligence on Luzon. Low-altitude fighter squadrons from the "Jack Patrol," scanning the wavetops for incoming kamikazes, flitted in formation like flocks of gulls three thousand feet above Halsey's task groups.

Because the Imperial Fleet had lost all of its carrier-based air strike capability during the Battle for Leyte Gulf, there was no concern that an enemy flattop might flank the strike force. But midget submarines with their *Kaiten* payloads—manned suicide torpedoes—were reported prowling the area. Admiral Halsey relied upon his screen of picket destroyers and destroyer escorts to counter the threat.

As was his seagoing routine, the admiral had been awake since 5:00 A.M., seated in his high steel chair on the *New Jersey*'s flag bridge, watching his air squadrons lift off. There he would remain for three consecutive days as navy and Marine fighter pilots screamed low over the canefields and nipa shacks of the Philippine archipelago, flying in overlapping intervals, clamping an iron lid on enemy airfields. Between these round-the-clock "shifts," U.S. Helldiver dive bombers and Avenger torpedo bombers ravaged Japanese runways, barracks, warehouses, and ships as far north as Formosa.

In central Luzon's notorious Camp Cabanatuan, the largest American prisoner-of-war camp ever established on foreign soil, emaciated GIs who almost three years earlier had endured the Bataan Death March reacted to the planes streaking overhead with wonder and disbelief. Twenty-four hours earlier they had been hollow-eyed POWs without expression, as if coming from no past and having no future. Now small strands of hope rippled through their ranks as, above them, so close you could hit them with a rock, U.S. pilots, their leather helmets worn at cocky angles, waggled their wings.

Hardly a sailor or an aviator in Halsey's fleet was not aware of the deprivations American prisoners had suffered at the hands of the Japanese. (It was an American chaplain who, during the retreat down the Bataan Peninsula, had coined the lasting phrase, "There are no atheists in foxholes.") Since the surrender of Bataan and the Rock of Corregidor in April 1942, Cabanatuan had housed over nine thousand American POWs, nearly a third of whom now lay rotting in shallow graves beside the camp's barracks. Those who survived had been degraded to living skeletons constructing a Japanese landing strip adjacent to the encampment. It was destroyed in an instant.

"All of us were watching through barbed wire when the planes came and turned it into a big hole," said one prisoner. "I can't tell you how ecstatic we were to see our own work go up in smoke."

Another American was "filled with joy" to see the panic in his sadistic jailers' eyes.

Not all POWs were as fortunate. Just past daybreak on December 14, a Japanese reconnaissance seaplane spotted MacArthur's invasion convoy steaming up the Sulu Sea toward Mindoro. A report was relayed to the commander of the small Puerto Princesa prison camp on the neighboring island of Palawan, who ordered 150 bewildered Americans herded into covered trenches that served as crude bomb shelters. They were doused with gasoline and set afire. The few who broke free were machine-gunned as they fled.

MacArthur and Halsey had expected atrocities, well aware that the enemy deemed foreign prisoners subhuman. The Allies also knew that five months earlier the Japanese War Ministry in Tokyo had fashioned a secret guideline for the "final disposition" of prisoners of war. The policy came to be known as the "August 1 Kill-All Order." But neither American commander became cognizant of the specifics of the prisoners' fate until weeks later.

For Halsey especially, the air strikes on Luzon were the most important foray any American fleet had made against a land-based enemy to this point in the war. He was ecstatic. The "Big Blue Blanket" had paralyzed Japanese airpower, breaking the kamikazes' eight-week hold over the American navy. Only after MacArthur's landing force had established a beachhead on Mindoro, on December 15, did enemy sorties swoop in to strike the expeditionary force. The belated Japanese counterattacks cost the general but two tank-landing ships and four LSTs.

Moreover, McCain's "Tom Cat" strategy worked so well that not one enemy aircraft made it to within twenty miles of Third Fleet's carriers. On the second day of fighting, a squadron of eight Zeros approaching "off the grid" was detected and blasted from the sky. The grizzled McCain glowed as if polished.

Halsey and his Dirty Tricksters had disproved the battlefield bromide that no military plan survives first contact with the enemy. Their strategy and tactics had worked to perfection. Halsey, in triumph, radioed Nimitz that every one of the Japanese planes thrown against MacArthur's Sixth Army and Kinkaid's Seventh Fleet had originated from airfields on either Formosa or the central Philippines; none had come from his areas of coverage on Luzon. As one eyewitness wrote, "What the toll would have been had Luzon not been covered by a huge and hostile air umbrella is easy to guess but impossible to define."

It was, in fact, a shooting gallery. American aviators destroyed over 270 enemy aircraft, most of which never got off the ground. They reported sinking 18 Japanese ships, mostly small and medium-sized oilers, and crippling 37 more. (Unknown to Halsey's pilots, one vessel struck by navy dive bombers on December 14 and 15 was the *Oryoku Maru*, a freighter moored on the west coast of Luzon in whose fetid hold were crammed sixteen hundred American prisoners of war. The POWs, most of them also survivors of the Death March, had been hastily evacuated from Camp Cabanatuan and were awaiting shipment to Japan as slave labor. Two hundred died in the bombardment.)

Third Fleet's losses were scant. No ships took damage, and only 27 U.S. planes were destroyed by enemy fire, with another 27 put out of commission by: mechanical failure (7), empty fuel tanks (4), operational crashes (11), midair collisions (3), and 2 lost souls simply recorded as "unknown."

In triumph, Halsey ached to press his advantage. *Vae Victis.* Woe to the conquered. On December 16 he petitioned Nimitz to be allowed to refuel and chase what was left of the Japanese Combined Fleet into the South China Sea, where spies in Saigon reported it to have fled after the Battle for Leyte Gulf. The admiral's plan was typically succinct. He wanted to find it, engage it, and sink it. In his unwavering vision he saw a fleet-to-fleet showdown, a Midway redux. He knew he could not rest until he had caught the main Japanese armada right out in the open and smashed it for good. MacArthur's words to him in November 1942 may well have echoed through his mind: *"If you come with me I'll make you a greater man than Nelson ever dreamed of being."*

Like the acclaimed British lord admiral at Aboukir Bay and Copenhagen Harbor, Halsey had tasted triumph in the Coral Sea and Leyte Gulf. He realized, like Nelson, that the way to make your mark in combat was to seize any opportunity with sureness and boldness. Now he dreamed of his own Trafalgar, the missing golden thread in his nautical tapestry. "It is annihilation that the country wants, not merely a splendid victory," Nelson told his officers before the defining battle of the age of sail.

Halsey knew the speech; he yearned for the sensation. He surely also intuited that given the progress in modern military technology, the opportunity might be the last in history for two mighty armadas to slug it out at close quarters.

Admiral Nimitz denied Halsey his prize. CINCPAC determined that MacArthur's defenseless concentration of men and material on the Mindoro beachhead, as well as the flood of Kincaid's support ships just offshore, would be easy prey for land-based Japanese planes without Task Force 38's saturated air cover. He directed Halsey to refuel and return to his attack station in the Philippine Sea, a sentinel guarding the expeditionary force's soft underbelly. Halsey acquiesced, and trained his thoughts on the annihilation of the Japanese on Luzon.

By Saturday, December 16, Halsey's entire task force was low on fuel, his destroyers in particular riding as high in the water as Spanish galleons beneath the dove gray sky. Escorting a carrier task force takes its greatest toll on DDs, as they continuously steam at high speed screening for submarines and enemy sorties, run at flank speed for downed pilots, and sail against the wind at a maximum 30 knots to keep pace as flattops launch and recover aircraft.

In addition, subchasing destroyer commanders bore a unique obligation. They were, naturally, accountable for the security of their own ships. But they alone in the U.S. Navy's chain of command also bore responsibility for protecting the larger vessels they screened. This meant maintaining, uninterrupted, a submarine "sounding fence" of interconnected sonar arcs enveloping the American heavies around each of Halsey's three individual task groups. This need to accurately remain "on station" was paramount. As one DD commander said, "Even when unusually severe sea conditions developed, a destroyer skipper normally would not have felt he could say, 'To hell with the formation, I'm going to look out for my own ship.'"

This was an option, by contrast, open to the captains of battleships, cruisers, carriers, and even oilers. Because of this constant activity, many of Halsey's "small boys" reported their bunkers nearly bone dry, running on perhaps a day's worth of fuel. Among these was the former Little Beaver squadron stalwart *Spence*, which had been detached from the submarine screen on numerous occasions to run search-and-rescue missions for floating pilots.

That evening, his sailors and airmen exultant but exhausted, Halsey directed that Task Force 38 be withdrawn almost four hundred miles east into the Philippine Sea—to latitude 14° 50'N, longitude 129° 57'E—the prearranged rendezvous coordinates where Capt. Jasper Acuff's oiler Task Group 30.8 would be waiting. The plan was to begin refueling operations at 8:00 A.M. the following morning.

Zigzagging in antisubmarine group formations some twenty miles apart, the outer limit of TBS, or talk-between-ships, phone range, this was as close to Luzon as Halsey dared take the fleet while remaining beyond the reach of any stray kami boys. If the replenishment went according to schedule, it would take no more than a day. He radioed MacArthur that his carrier task force would return "as soon as possible," most likely within the next forty-eight hours, to commence another three-day series of strikes on Luzon.

MacArthur's engineers and Kinkaid's Seabees, slogging through unrelenting rain squalls on Mindoro, were already leveling large tracts of jungle and laying down heavy Marston matting runways over the ubiquitous mud. In a week or so, all-weather airfields for the Sixth Army's bomber corps would sprout like mushrooms.

Meanwhile, MacArthur needed Halsey's air cover. The Philippines campaign had reached a decisive moment. After securing Mindoro, looming just over the horizon was the invasion of Luzon, with its grand jewel of Manila. When MacArthur had vowed to "return" in 1942, no one doubted it was to the capital city that he'd directed his promise. He awaited Halsey's imminent rearrival.

In several ways the reckless admiral and the imperious general were the opposite faces of the same Janus coin. One senses that Halsey's overriding commitment to recapturing Luzon hinged as much on his desire to kill Japanese and avenge Pearl Harbor as to further America's greater war aims. (Much later, on the eve of VJ Day, after the Japanese sued for peace but before the actual treaty was signed, Halsey's "right arm," Slew McCain, advised any pilots encountering enemy planes "to shoot them down in a friendly sort of way.")

MacArthur, on the other hand, was a throwback, a Prussian in posture and thought, an atomic ego more at home in the eighteenth century than on the eighteenth green of Manila's Wack Wack Golf and Country Club, the oldest and most prestigious course in the city. His chief concern lay in reclaiming the "honor" forfeited during his humiliating retreat from Corregidor. MacArthur chafed to reoccupy his penthouse headquarters in the Majestic Manila Hotel, to parade his troops through downtown Manila's stately Rizal Park.

In the event, the crushing annexation of the largest and most strategic of the Philippine islands, a mere fifteen hundred miles from the southern tip of Japan, would be, foremost, the springboard for the coming invasions of Japanese soil—Iwo Jima, Okinawa, and beyond. Even the Imperial War Ministry understood this. "When you took the Philippines, that was the end of our resources," wrote Japan's naval minister Adm. Mitsumasa Yonai after the war. The Americans had indeed come far since December 7, 1941. This, Halsey knew, was something for its enemies to ponder.

Moreover, grinding just below the surface, as a sort of subconscious seismic fault, was Halsey's sanguine memory of his near-disastrous "wild goose chase" during the Battle for Leyte Gulf two months earlier. Halsey would not stray so far from MacArthur this time, no matter the circumstances or temptations.

Indeed, the fierce blowback from the Leyte Gulf incident weighed on Halsey's mind as Task Force 38 set its course after the successful opening salvos of the Mindoro invasion. Despite his personal belief that chasing the Japanese carrier fleet had been the sound military decision, and despite MacArthur's vote of confidence, the admiral knew that many of his peers were still sharpening long knives. In Washington, Admiral King was rumored to remain livid at the near disaster, and the perceived rebuke from Nimitz—"The World Wonders" —still stung. Halsey wanted nothing so awfully badly as to atone for the "Battle of Bull's Run."

The first three days of the Mindoro campaign had been a fine start, and for the first time since Ulithi, as he watched the fissures among the western cloudbanks fade from smoky crimson to violet on the evening of December 16, Halsey retired early as his task force steamed through the night to meet its oilers.

CHAPTER 10

That principle weight should have been given to the reports of the Chandeleur *search plane received at 14:24 Dec. 17th, since no definite reports of the storm location had been received since the 16th.*

That the aerological talent assisting Commander THIRD Fleet was inadequate in practical experience and service background in view of the importance of the services to be expected and required.

—General Opinions #4 and #6 of the court of inquiry's report investigating "Halsey's Typhoon."

At 5:00 A.M. on December 17, the crew of a seaplane flying out of Ulithi spotted what appeared to be the telltale "zero-zero visibility" of what its radio operator referred to as a "tropical disturbance" some 225 miles southeast of Third Fleet's rendezvous position. This was nearly 300 miles closer than fleet aerologist Comdr. George Kosco had forecast.

The scout plane returned to its tender, the USS *Chandeleur*, and its pilot encrypted the storm's last known coordinates by means of the deliberate, handwritten cipher required for weather reports—as opposed to the faster, electronic ciphering machine used to relay intelligence and orders. This message, the dog that didn't bark, failed to reach Halsey's flagship until nine hours later, where it was inadvertently buried under a stack of communiqués. Kosco was not to read it for another day and a half.

Meanwhile, farther north, Guam was being rocked by a series of torrential rainstorms, and Army Air Corps meteorologists stationed on Saipan launched their own weather reconnaissance flight. This aircraft's pilot filed an uncoded radio message saying that he had located what he believed to be the eye of a nascent typhoon. An army meteorologist on Saipan, Lt. Reid A. Bryson, teletyped an emergency transmission to Fleet Weather Central at Pearl conveying the storm's coordinates. He added that the disturbance was most definitely a typhoon, and it appeared to be curving north.

No one on Saipan, including Bryson, was privy to the exact movements of the Third Fleet. But across the Pacific, scuttlebutt was rampant regarding the Mindoro operation. It did not take much calculation for the meteorologist to determine that the cyclone appeared to be on a collision course with the island, and thus with Halsey's vessels. It wasn't often that the weathermen under Bryson's command got to feel they were a real part of the war. This was such a moment.

They were thus stunned at the four-word response Bryson received from an unknown navy aerologist at Pearl Harbor. "We don't believe you," it read.

Agitated, Bryson again sat down at the teletype machine. He assured Pearl that his report was not an educated guess. He had personally spoken to the recon flight's radio operator as his plane flew through the typhoon's eye!

"We still don't believe you, but we'll watch," came the reply. Bryson and his small team slumped in their chairs and waited for what they feared would be horrible news.

As Task Force 38 steamed east, away from Mindoro and Luzon, it remained well out of reach of Typhoon Cobra's most powerful gusts, although remote picket ships radioed reports to flag plot describing the sea making up fast. The eastern sky was swirling with fantastic, multicolored clouds, a Turner watercolor come to life, and the olive green ocean's surface was beginning to agitate and flow, like water coming to a boil.

Outlying destroyer and destroyer escort crews sensed that some unseen, if powerful, force was driving the mounting swells, and aboard the DD USS *Hunt*, Gunner's Mate 2nd Class Dominick Legato noticed that the incessant whitecaps were beginning to release sheets of atomized vapor. His chief warned him to batten down for "a big blow."

There was something vexing about the whirl of the sea's currents. They were, as one ship's officer noted, "not tentative, exactly, but encouraging of ambiguities and multiple meanings."

In fact, although Typhoon Cobra's core winds had reached 70 to 80 knots, with gusts topping 120 knots, the storm was still so compact that her "wind spread" extended no farther than one hundred miles from her eye—not yet close enough to be felt by the main body of the task force. Halsey certainly betrayed no apprehension, referring in his log on the morning of December 17 to the mariner's Beaufort wind scale: "Force 5—fresh breeze—25 to 31 mile wind."

There were, however, ominous auguries. Captain Kernodle of the "jeep carrier" *San Jacinto* instituted a two-man deck order: No seaman was allowed topside unless roped to a shipmate. Chief Petty Officer William Christensen on the carrier USS *Essex* raised Kernodle's ante. As the officer in charge of the flight deck, Christensen worried that his flight crews would be blown overboard by winds approaching gale force and ordered his sailors tied together into six-man teams as they shepherded home returning combat air patrols, or CAPs, charged with detecting enemy bogeys. And in the ready room of the jeep carrier USS *Savo Island*, Avenger tail gunner Bob Winn was warned by a veteran squadron commander that any man taking to the sky in this weather was a sure bet to end up in the drink.

Winn's squad leader proved prescient. By daybreak on December 17, commanders of Halsey's attack carriers had already begun receiving distress messages from the smaller and lighter escort carriers, which requested permission to land their CAPs on the larger, more stable decks of the CVs. And when it became too difficult to put down at all on any of the heaving, dancing flattops, Halsey directed the pilots of, first, one, and then a second returning scout plane to bail out and ditch their aircraft into the sea. At this Halsey ordered all planes temporarily grounded and instructed his carrier deck crews to let the air out of all aircraft tires and relash the planes with triple steel cables. The fleet had withstood big storms before, and it would damn well ride this one out, too.

Aerologist Kosco caught the essence of the admiral's martial mood. "Weather information at hand from the three reporting fleet weather stations did not disclose that a typhoon was on the rampage, or even existing," he wrote. "As a matter of fact, the possibility that [a typhoon] might be snaking toward the Fleet was not given serious thought. In time of war, when combat objectives rise above all other priorities, it is not the rule to bestow grave concern on incidental dangers. Planes do not stay grounded and fleets do not run scared because of ugly weather if in doing so they jeopardize military or naval missions."

It need be pointed out that Kosco was facing these "incidental dangers" aboard a 45,000-ton battlewagon and not a floundering destroyer. When a DD low on fuel rolls, the oil in its bunkers sloshes from its center of gravity to leeward, thereby increasing the roll. Third Fleet destroyer commanders had been issued a standing order to ballast their fuel tanks with "sufficient" seawater whenever their fuel capacity fell below 70 percent, particularly when encountering heavy weather. The DDs were indeed encountering mounting seas this morning, but the combined operation of spilling ballast and refueling could take upward of ten hours. His Tin Can skippers were loath to keep an anxious Halsey waiting that long, well aware of the admiral's desire to return to Luzon as soon as possible.

Anticipating his wrath should anything delay that goal, many of his destroyer commanders thus opted to remain running their ships perilously high above the waterline as the sea continued to roil. By

the time Acuff's oil tankers approached Halsey's task force, a bracing cross-swell and 30-knot winds would make refueling nearly
impossible.

At 1:00 A.M. on December 17, the deck log of Admiral Halsey's
flagship *New Jersey* recorded a barometer reading of 29.88, with
winds at 23 knots out of the northeast. This aroused no suspicion,
as normal barometric pressure at sea level is 29.92. Yet Third Fleet
was dispersed across such a wide swath of the Pacific that, at the
same time, more than two hundred miles east-southeast of the *New
Jersey*, the entry for the log of the destroyer USS *Dewey* noted a
barometer reading of 29.72.

While destroyer skippers depended upon the barometer and
thermometer as their primary weather forecasting instruments,
aboard the *New Jersey*, Kosco was monitoring multiple weather
transmissions coming into flag plot. These included reports compiled in Kwajalein from weather stations in the Western Pacific
and broadcast at six-hour intervals; transmissions every three hours
from Manus in the Admiralties; twice-daily search plane reports
from Saipan, Guam, Kossol Roads, Peleliu, and Ulithi; reports four
times a day from Oahu that covered the Central and North Pacific, and, of course, the overall weather map analyses sent every
six hours from Fleet Weather Central at Pearl. In addition, each
U.S. Navy vessel operating in the Western Pacific was issued a
monthly pilot chart from the navy's Hydrographic Office that
plotted the course of past typhoons in the area going back several
years.

Although their accuracy and timeliness was ever in doubt, Kosco
pored through these forecasts and charts as Halsey's task force approached Acuff's oiler group. In recognition of the worsening
weather, the scheduled refueling had been advanced one hour, to
7:00 A.M., but even by then the wind had intensified to just shy of
gale force, the cross-swell resembled rolling pewter hills, and the
sky was completely overcast.

Like William Dampier's terrified sailors two and a half centuries earlier, crewmen from Third Fleet watched as a dark, heavy cloud blackened the southeastern horizon, its upper reaches tinged with a dull, reddish cast. This mass approached slowly, its facade as thin as an ax blade, which then fanned out behind like the furrow of a plow. It was like nothing they had ever seen.

Atop the center mast of the carrier *Cape Esperance*, sixty feet above the deck, eighteen-year-old seaman Paul Schlener was pulling lookout duty as these "waves of dark clouds were coming down on us like I could reach up and touch them." As a child, Schlener had witnessed violent thunderstorms rolling down from the mountains near his parents' ranch in Idaho. Yet as the *Cape Esperance* began to sway in the heaving ocean, it seemed to the young seaman as if the lightning bolts emanating from the low-scudding rain clouds bearing down on him were arrows, all aimed at the metal pole to which he clung. He was, he told friends, "as scared as a kid could be."

Soon other vessels began pitching heavily, "slamming" up and over waves that tested their rivets, which buckled and emitted a sound like popping corn. As ships rose and fell, the clappers on their huge, three-foot-tall bells swung fore and aft constantly, and sailors spoke of becoming almost as sick of hearing those "damn bells" as they did of the bucking seas. Though it is doubtful that either Halsey or Kosco physically experienced the tossing ocean on the bridge of the hulking *New Jersey*, Capt. C. Raymond Calhoun of the oiler task group escort destroyer *Dewey* noted sardonically, "On the smaller ships, the weather took on a distinctly more personal dimension than it did on the carriers and battleships."

The main body of Acuff's replenishment task group consisted of five escort aircraft carriers, twelve oilers, and three oceangoing tugs. The jeep carriers were scheduled to deliver replacement planes and pilots to Halsey's attack flattops as well as—theoretically—launch combat air patrols. The oilers, their bunkers bursting, were transporting some 100,000 barrels of fuel oil and 800,000 gallons of aviation gas.

Oilers were the lumbering oxen of the sea. As such, they were easy prey for Japanese pilots and submarine commanders, and five destroyers and ten destroyer escorts screened this movable feast against enemy subs and aircraft. Standard procedure held that these escort vessels would form a wide circle around the oilers and fill the air with ack-ack at the approach of an enemy sortie.

It was rare that a Japanese pilot was hardy or lucky enough to fly through the barrier of air bursts. Moreover, the odds of a Japanese submarine rising even to periscope depth in these high seas were slim; the arrival of an enemy scout plane from far-off Luzon even slimmer. But even one lucky sighting could foul the entire refueling operation, and all vessels posted lookouts, most of whom tied neckerchiefs or kitchen rags around their mouths and noses to protect them from the stinging spume.

Along with the *Dewey*, sailing in the oiler group's screening detachment were four more of the old *Farragut*-class, double-stacked destroyers: the *Hull, Monaghan*, USS *Aylwin*, and USS *Farragut*. Although, as noted, by 1944 the *Farraguts* could not match the tonnage or firepower brought to bear by the newer *Fletcher* and *Sumner* classes of DD, the original eight *Farraguts* had once been considered pearls, and their crews took pride in their heritage. When one, the USS *Worden*, a veteran of Pearl Harbor, Midway, and Guadalcanal, split her seams open athwart a rock off Amchitka Island in the Aleutians and went down without a trace in January 1943, her loss was mourned throughout the fleet.

Among the remaining seven—as destroyer squadron commander Capt. Preston Mercer was to testify during the court of inquiry—the five *Farraguts* steaming with Third Fleet during the Mindoro invasion were led by some of the most junior destroyer skippers in the navy.

Calhoun aboard the *Dewey*, the *Hull*'s James Marks, William Rogers of the *Aylwin*, Conway "Connie" Hartigan on the *Farragut*, and the *Monaghan*'s Bruce Garrett had all been classmates at the Naval Academy in the late 1930s, and each was in his first combat command. Lieutenant Commander Garrett had been in the *Monaghan*'s captain's chair less than twenty-four hours before departing Ulithi, having replaced her former skipper, Comdr. Wally Wendt, the day before.

While replenishing on Ulithi, the *Dewey* had taken part in anti-aircraft gunnery exercises with, among other destroyers, the *Hull*. Although the *Dewey*'s thirty-one-year-old Captain Calhoun noted that he was "favorably impressed with the appearance of his sister vessel and the quality of her underway performance," he also remarked, portentously, that his classmate Lieutenant Commander Marks struck him as "very serious and very regulation."

In fact, since Marks's transfer to the *Hull* three months earlier, the ship's morale had plummeted. Veteran sailor Archie DeRyckere, the ship's chief quartermaster, described this feeling best when he told shipmates that, from the outset, he had sensed "something of the night" about the new skipper. The new captain was a short man, and slight, with dark eyes and an olive-toned complexion. He was a smart officer, to be sure, Academy class of 1938, who had given DeRyckere his shipboard examination when he'd fleeted up to chief. But even the Academy made stony ground for a certain kind of grain, and despite having spent twenty-nine months running convoys across the North Atlantic before taking command of the *Hull*, there lingered about Marks the scent of the pretender who had alienated the crew from the moment he'd toted his seabag up the gangway.

The *Hull* had been undergoing refitting at Bremerton when Marks came aboard. The new commander had the ill fortune of replacing the able and beloved Capt. Charles Consalvo, with whom the *Hull*'s marlinspike crew had forged a bond tempered by combat. But Marks's first official pronouncement—"I'm going to make history with this ship"—had not sat well with veteran Tin Can sailors who had already earned twenty battle stars in the Pacific campaign.

To make matters worse, Marks had forbidden fraternization, even social conversation, between officers and enlisted men. He canceled shore leave for negligible infractions. He dressed down a navigator for fancifully naming a star on the plot chart after his wife. And he enforced petty edicts with such gratuitous discipline that one of the ship's first class gunners' mates had to be physically restrained from attacking him with a submachine gun after a particularly roisterous Stateside evening.

In short, the *Hull*'s crew felt that Lieutenant Commander Marks was not a seaman, the worst insult that could be hurled at a captain in the Tin Can Navy. It was as if he knew the words, but not the music. A member of the *Hull*'s black gang was said to have named his daughter's new kitten "Captain M," as the creature did nothing all day but mewl, preen, and strut. And DeRyckere was not alone at reading it as an omen when, after a visit to a Seattle fortune-teller, more than a dozen crewmen jumped ship the night before the *Hull* departed Bremerton for Pearl.

"They just stood there on the docks with their seabags, refusing to come aboard," Pat Douhan, the *Hull*'s sonar man, told a crewmate. In Hawaii several more sailors, mostly old-timers with a weather nose for such things, managed to finagle themselves off the ship by picking bar fights and getting themselves tossed into the brig. These former shipmates, many of them old friends, crossed DeRyckere's mind as the *Hull* encountered heavier and heavier seas.

Just past sunrise on December 17, Acuff's oiler task group hove into view of Halsey's Task Force 38 through a dirty, yellowish haze. Its first order of business was to replenish the admiral's thirsty "small boys." The operation instantly proved problematic. The wind and waves tossed and rolled the vessels, and fuel transfer hoses and mooring lines lashed and snapped until they parted. Oiler crews risked life and limb as green water sloshed over decks and white lather over housings. Helmsmen grappled with corkscrewing vessels, and collisions were narrowly avoided.

Finally, parallel fueling became so dangerous that attempts were made to transfer fuel over the sterns of the few oilers so equipped. This, too, proved untenable for the majority of ships, as it required the dismantling and rerigging of hoses and other gear, impossible in these seas. The few trailing hoses successfully manhandled across a destroyer's pitching forecastle deck whipped and broke off well before they could be secured to the forward fuel oil trunk beneath the pilothouse.

Reports of refueling problems began streaming into flag plot from destroyer commanders, and given the speed with which the sea was running there existed the unnerving possibility that some of Halsey's small boys would run out of fuel before they could take on more. This was unprecedented in modern U.S. naval history. Yet as Halsey lifted binoculars to peer from the *New Jersey*'s bridge wing through thickening spouts and spiral rain bands, every DD within his field of vision was having difficulty maintaining station alongside the tankers. As the morning wore on, the admiral haunted flag bridge, smoking, pacing, apprehensive.

CHAPTER 11

*Having spent a great many years in destroyers and having been
in some very severe weather in ships ranging from 160 tons to
1,200 tons, I knew there had been grave doubts as to their stability from time to time, particularly when in a light condition.*

—TESTIMONY OF ADM. WILLIAM F. HALSEY JR.,
COMMANDING OFFICER, THIRD FLEET, TO THE COURT OF
INQUIRY INVESTIGATING "HALSEY'S TYPHOON."

The United States Navy had always been, and remains, the most
tight-knit of all the military services. Far-flung news—as well as mad
rumors—of triumphs and disasters flow fast and free through its
ranks. Thus sailors throughout Halsey's fleet in December 1944
were aware of the fate of the destroyer USS *Warrington*, which three
months earlier had sunk in a great Atlantic hurricane off Florida,
with 248 men drowned. One officer who took a particular interest
in the loss of the *Warrington* was Bob Surdam, the destroyer escort
Tabberer's XO, who had been detached from the *Warrington* in
order to take over as Capt. Henry Plage's number two.

The fate of the *Warrington* was also fresh in the mind of Seaman
Bob Ayers aboard the destroyer *Spence*. After the breakup of Arleigh
"31-Knot" Burke's DesRon 23 "Little Beavers" squadron, the *Spence*
had been dispatched to San Francisco for refitting and remanning,
and had returned to join Third Fleet at Ulithi two months earlier.
Upon arriving at her anchorage, one of her first orders had been to

dog down for weather, as at the time all ships berthed in Ulithi lagoon were on Typhoon Condition Standby. The alert lasted three days before the storm veered away and typhoon conditions were canceled. But though the blow had bypassed the atoll, the alert had left a daunting impression on the *Spence*'s raw crew, many of whom were teenage enlistees sailing into their first combat assignments. Among this gang was brand-new nineteen-year-old Gunner's Mate Striker Harley "Bob" Ayers.

Ayers had shipped out from Great Lakes Naval Station to his new berth as a "deck ape" on the *Spence* only eleven days earlier. Growing up on the fringes of Lake Michigan, Ayers was an avid swimmer and water skier who had never been afraid of the water. When he was fourteen years old, a family friend in Michigan City had invited him to crew on an old, gaff-rigged sixty-foot schooner, and the jangly, gawky teenager had taken to sailing like a seal to the sea. It was natural that when it came time to choose a service, he had enlisted in the navy.

On the first day Ayers reported to the *Spence* on Ulithi, the ship's bosun's mate had ordered him and another young crewman to wash down the skipper's gig, the captain's small launch, which was still swung outboard over the rail. A few moments later the bosun's mate found another task for Ayers and hollered for him to come back in. As he made his way from the gig to the destroyer's deck, instinct took over, and instead of edging across the launch and leaping down onto the deck, he grabbed a secure line and slid over. For an instant his momentum carried him out of sight of the bosun's mate, who thought he'd fallen into the lagoon. When Ayers popped back up into view, the shocked and angry bosun's mate cursed him long and loud.

Young Ayers's fearlessness, however, was to inadvertently help save his life. For, following this inauspicious debut, he had spent the next four days on punishment duty fashioning the *Spence*'s ratlines—thin, meshlike ropes running horizontally from the ship's shroud, the iron rod extending from the mast to the futtock plate, used to brace the base of the topmast. These ratlines were to prevent men from falling overboard. Ayers had but recently written to his parents about how proud he was to be a part of "Bull" Halsey's Big Blue Fleet, sailing with the Tin Can Navy to boot. Respect and affection for the "fighting admiral" were such that whenever a Third Fleet sailor ran into another seaman, the response to the immemorial navy greeting—"What ship you on now, sailor?"—was a proud, "I'm with Halsey." Yet less than a week into his service, Ayers now found himself muttering to any crewmate who would listen, "I'm so sick and tired of making them damn ratlines. Damn, dirty, creosote-coated hemp."

Yet, on the morning of December 17, as the gathering storm tossed the *Spence* like driftwood, Ayers decided that those damn ratlines might just come in handy after all. At a few moments past noon, Halsey himself signaled the *Spence*'s captain, Lt. Comdr. James Andrea, to steam along the starboard beam of his flagship and begin taking fuel from the *New Jersey*'s forward and aft bunkers. The *Spence*, down to between 10 and 15 percent of her fuel capacity, was sailing close enough to the *New Jersey* that the admiral could see that she was riding high and struggling mightily in the brutal wash.

Fueling a destroyer from a battleship, as opposed to from an oiler, is often less treacherous in confused seas, as the battlewagon's higher freeboard, greater mass, and maneuverability create, in theory, a natural lee to protect the smaller vessel from wind and horizontal rains. Like her *Farragut*-class counterparts, the *Fletcher*-class *Spence* was top-heavy. Additional radar scanners and antiaircraft guns had been installed on her deck in San Francisco, and this supplementary weight combined with her empty fuel bunkers to make her that much more "tender" as she approached the *New Jersey* in the escalating winds.

Nowhere was this more apparent than on the *Spence*'s pitching topside, where fueling gangs assigned to secure marker lines and hoses from the battleship were tossed about like straw men. One member of this gang was Gunner's Mate Striker Bob Ayers. Ayers's job was to tie in the destroyer's bow marker line. But as Halsey's

big battleship towered above him, he found that in the deteriorat-
ing weather he was having all he could do just to remain on his feet.
Once he managed to shoot the line up to the *New Jersey*'s deck crew
and secure the hawsers, he crouched near the prow of the ship,
paying the rope in and out as the two vessels rose and fell together
atop the heavy swells.

At one point, with green water crashing over him, Ayers sensed
that he was about to be washed over the side. Still gripping the bowline, he backed off and burrowed into what he thought was a sheltered cranny beneath the ship's number 1 gun mount. Just as he
wedged himself in, a huge comber rocked the *Spence*, sending her
rolling profoundly to port. Ayers lost his footing and began sliding
across the deck.

"Then I find out what the ratlines were for," he later told a
messmate. "One foot was through one hole and one through another, and my ass is hanging overboard. Without the ratlines, I
wouldn't be here."

Ayers untangled himself and was still hunkered down on the
deck, this time gripping the bowline much tighter, when an even
more colossal wave pitched the *Spence* again to port. So powerful
was this wave that it parted the thick hawsers' hemp fibers as if
they were threads and sent the 2,150-ton destroyer's mast and rigging swinging bow-on toward the *New Jersey*'s bridge. The *Spence*'s
mast came so close that Halsey, by now taking lunch near the open
door of the flag mess in the island superstructure, instinctively
ducked. Paint chips flew as the two ships sideswiped.

Near simultaneously, the destroyer USS *Collett* radioed flag plot
that both her hoses had been ripped asunder and carried away as
she attempted to take fuel from the battleship USS *Wisconsin*. The
destroyer USS *Maddox* reported narrowly avoiding a collision with
the oiler USS *Manatee* as she tried to refuel, and in rapid succession the destroyers *Hunt*, USS *Stephen Potter*, USS *Mansfield*, USS
Lyman K. Swenson, USS *Preston*, and USS *Thatcher* filed similar
messages. The skipper of the heavy cruiser USS *San Francisco* threatened to hack through the refueling lines of the bucking destroyer

USS *Brown* if she didn't break off. It was clear that something big was barreling down on the fleet.

Ten minutes later Halsey directed all refueling operations to be "suspended at the earliest time possible."

"So Halsey doesn't want to scratch his boat," Bob Ayers thought when he received the orders. Within moments the *Spence*, her foredeck and hull blackened by spilled fuel oil, broke off from the *New Jersey*. She had managed to pump some six thousand gallons into her bunkers. Ayers had no way of knowing that this would not be nearly enough.

In flag plot, Halsey and Kosco returned to their weather charts and forecasts. By 2:00 P.M. the barometer read 29.70. It had dropped .13 inches in three hours. In his chapter on tropical cyclones, Bowditch writes, "If the wind remains steady in direction and increases in force in heavy squalls while the barometer falls rapidly, say, at a greater rate than .03 of an inch per hour, the vessel is probably on or near the track of the storm and in advance of the center." Aboard the destroyer *Dewey*, Lt. Watson T. "Watso" Singer, a veteran China station hand in his mid-fifties, had reduced Bowditch's cyclonic counsel to its salty essence, which he dubbed "Singer's Law":

"When the barometer drops .10 of an inch or more in three hours or less, you're in the path of a typhoon, and you'd better haul ass."

But Kosco's calculations still placed the center of the "tropical disturbance" a good 400 miles southeast of the fleet. It was, in reality, a mere 120 miles distant. Nonetheless, on his aerographer's advice, Halsey plotted a new rendezvous with the oiler group some 160 miles to the northwest. The linkup was scheduled for daybreak the next morning, December 18, at latitude 17 degrees north, longitude 128 east.

With his options restricted by the necessity of remaining close enough to Luzon to fulfill his commitment to MacArthur, Halsey thought he was angling away from the storm. In fact, he was running parallel to and ahead of it. As the fleet fanned out in a great semicircle and steamed west-northwest, the faster carriers, cruisers, and battleships of Task Force 38 began outpacing by three to six knots the slower-moving typhoon. The sea thus moderated slightly, the *New Jersey*'s barometer inched higher, and Halsey was furnished with the illusion of security.

One hour later, at 3:00 P.M., Kosco received an updated weather report from Pearl indicating that the storm had also changed direction. A quick glance at his charts persuaded him that Halsey's current rendezvous coordinates could place the fleet directly in its new path. He informed the admiral, who, at 3:30 P.M., again changed the refueling site, ordering a course change to nearly 185 miles due south. This would take his vessels precariously close to the Japanese-held Legaspi Peninsula in the far southeastern corner of Luzon. But Halsey's staff argued that even the most desperate, Bushido-infused squadron commander would not put planes in the sky in this scud and wind.

They were correct about the Japanese dogging down, albeit for the wrong reasons. What was left of Japan's scattered navy, as well as its Philippine-based air squadrons, was very nearly spent. In fact, by the time of MacArthur's Mindoro invasion, the Imperial War Department had already written off the Philippines, save for last-gasp "prolonged holding operations" on Luzon. Japan's only effective remaining weapons were the kamikazes, who could no more aim their suicide flights at specific U.S. Navy ships in this weather than those same ships could refuel.

Thus, as the Third Fleet steamed south, it had only a nonhuman enemy to fear—a foe just 135 miles distant and roaring toward it on a collision course.

Far astern of the bulk of Task Force 38, Capt. Jasper Acuff's wallowing oilers struggled to keep pace with Halsey's faster "heavies." The tankers' low horsepower and high freeboard left them especially susceptible to the strong winds, and their task was further hindered by continued attempts to refuel the fleet's thirstiest ships—the destroyers *Spence*, USS *Hickox*, and USS *Maddox*. In spite of the dire conditions, the three vessels had been exempted from the fuel-cancellation orders, detached from Task Force 38, and left behind with Acuff's replenishment group with orders to seize the first opportunity to fill their bunkers. The effort proved disastrous.

After the *Spence*, now running on less than 10 percent fuel capacity, collided with an oiler—her second crash of the day, this one causing several injuries to her crew—all attempts at parallel refueling were abandoned. The *Spence*, *Maddox*, and *Hickox* would have to take oil stern-to-bow. The oilers dropped inflated canvas balls attached to ropes for the destroyer deck crews to gaff so they could attach fuel lines. But the swells had grown so large, blotting out the seascape, that the gaffing gangs could not even spot the balls. Next, an oiler tried floating an empty forty-two-gallon drum with a line attached to the *Spence*, but a tanker deckhand became fouled in the line and it had to be cut loose.

Finally, in desperation, one oiler ran a surfboard attached to a hawser off her stern, hoping that the *Spence*'s deck gang could scoop it up and reel it in. Though *Spence* sailors did manage to retrieve the board and run it through the ship's bull nose ring, when they attempted to bring fueling hoses on line, they snapped in the gale like rubber bands.

With his ship running on fumes, the *Spence*'s chief watertender, George Johnson, turned to a shipmate and ventured a prediction. "I believe we are doomed," he said.

By this time all of Acuff's narrow-hulled destroyers, even those with adequate fuel, were taking the brunt of the increasingly confused seas. A struggling DD would bury her nose in the base of an undulating cliff of water and begin the climb of fifty feet or more to the crest. Once atop the wave, her keel would be exposed nearly back to the bridge, and her screws and half her bottom would clear the surface as she plunged into the next trough.

In the pilothouse of the *Dewey*, sailing with 78 percent fuel capacity and thus fairly well ballasted, Captain Calhoun nonetheless noted that the heavy swell was causing his ship to yaw about 20 degrees with each wave. At one point the *Dewey*, locked in irons and out of control, hove to within five yards of an unknown cargo ship, nearly ramming her bow.

Among the most precious commodities that Acuff's replenishment group carried was mail. The navy realized the morale value of letters from home and tried to deliver them, even in combat zones, at least twice a month. Back on Ulithi a barge had split open on a reef and sank with twenty-five bags of mail, and the pall cast over enlisted men and officers alike was worse than if the atoll had run out of Iron City beer.

The destroyer *Hull*, screening the northernmost of the oiler group's three units, carried in its hold 120 sacks of letters to Third Fleet sailors from wives, sweethearts, and parents. The *Hull* had managed to refuel to 75 percent of her capacity, and late in the afternoon of December 17 she attempted the transfer of 40 bags of mail to the battleship USS *South Dakota*. Twenty-two-year-old Petty Officer 2nd Class Pat Douhan, nominally the *Hull*'s sonarman, had also signed up as the *Hull*'s mail clerk, primarily because it meant an extra $25 added to his monthly $75 paycheck. Back in California, Douhan's wife was three months pregnant, and he needed every dollar he could earn. (Thirteen *Hull* sailors had left pregnant wives behind following the ship's last Stateside overhaul; crewmen joked that theirs was the most prolific ship in the U.S. Navy.)

Douhan had wanted to be a sailor since he was a child. His father had been a navy man in World War I, and young Pat had watched his dad don his uniform and march in every Armistice Day parade thereafter. When war with Germany and Japan broke out, Douhan had enlisted at age nineteen, finished boot camp as a "twenty-one-day wonder," and was shipped off to sonar school. After completing his technical courses, he'd chosen destroyers over submarines, the "workhorse" Tin Can Navy seeming so much more romantic and glamorous. In March 1943 he picked up the *Hull* in San Francisco while she was refitting.

As the *Hull*'s "newbie" sonarman, Douhan had taken much ribbing over his several momentary failures to distinguish enemy tin fish from meandering whales. But he soon discovered he was drawn to the ethos of the old destroyer's rough-riding crew. He enjoyed the fact that their "work hard, play harder" attitude had gotten them banned from more than a few gin mills up and down the West Coast—it was rumored that San Diego posted a "Hull alert" whenever the ship entered the city's harbor. Moreover, to Douhan, veteran chiefs such as Archie DeRyckere and Chief Bosun's Mate Ray Schultz seemed as knowing of the sea as Ahab.

Now, however, Douhan wondered exactly what he'd gotten himself into. He'd sailed through some rough weather when the *Hull* had patrolled the Aleutians, but this storm was much more than he'd bargained for. During the heaviest rolls he imagined himself sitting safely ensconced on the seabed in a cozy sub, no swells or spindrift or combers to fret over.

When the high seas forced several sacks of precious mail to be dumped into the drink during transfer to the *South Dakota*, Douhan convinced the *Hull*'s Captain Marks to defer delivery of the remainder until the ship found better weather. But with the sea rising precipitously and the thick, black clouds above him swirling into grotesque shapes, Douhan discovered that mail transfer was the least of his problems.

The *Hull*'s sonar operators worked together with the ship's radarmen in a jury-rigged room adjacent to the captain's sleeping quarters behind the bridge. There was no radar or sonar when the *Hull* had been commissioned in 1934, and in order to accommodate the new equipment, the sleeping quarters had been subdivided by a canvas curtain. On one side was the captain's bunk; on the other, sound and radar gear, both surface and air, had been installed. As afternoon turned to evening on December 17, Douhan found Captain Marks unrelenting in his demands.

The thick salt spray of the waves crashing over the *Hull*'s superstructure combined with the wind-driven rain to "black out" the ship's radar gear, and in this weather there was no way to fix it.

This did not stop Marks from entering the compartment regularly to loudly berate the radarmen. "He's gone bonkers," Douhan told a radar operator after one of Marks's tirades. As the weather worsened, Douhan sensed that the havoc had spread to the bridge—as did the *Hull*'s chief bosun's mate, Ray Schultz.

Schultz grumbled often about the new commander's lack of seamanship—"All handle and no jug" was one of his phrases—particularly in contrast to Capt. Charles Consalvo, the *Hull*'s previous skipper. Consalvo, for instance, had been renowned for his docking ability. "He could bring that ship into a buoy and all the bosun's mate would have to do was drop down and hook that thing in," Schultz liked to recall. But after Marks took command, the running joke among the *Hull*'s crew was that no dock was now safe, and the destroyer's bow had the dents to prove it. The *Hull*'s chiefs had even come up with a private nickname for Marks, lengthening his initials "J. A." into "Jackass."

Douhan and Schultz were not the only *Hull* crewmen considering precisely this when their ship, now lacking radar, lost visual contact with the rest of its task group shortly after nightfall. Earlier, on the bridge, Archie DeRyckere had stifled a laugh when Marks had poked his head through the port window and nearly had it ripped off by the wind, scud, and rain. Marks had often boasted of the high seas he had steamed through in the North Atlantic, and his swagger seemed to be returning to haunt him.

But now DeRyckere saw nothing funny in the captain's comportment. Since the moment Marks had peered out the window, he had barely moved a muscle, wedging himself into a corner between the port wing of the bridge and the four-foot-high Polaris stand, the instrument used to mark the ship's bearing. The skipper, DeRyckere thought, appeared frozen with indecision.

Even had the oiler Task Group 30.8's commander Jasper Acuff been aware of the *Hull* crew's discontent, he had more pressing matters to worry about than one rogue destroyer commander. Acuff had chosen as his flagship the destroyer *Aylwin*, and after assessing the brutal conditions from her bridge, he closed down the refueling attempts to the *Spence, Hickox*, and *Maddox* shortly after 4:00 P.M.

The rain-washed sky modified from gunmetal to silver to tarnished brass as thick, high-altitude stratus clouds left an eerie red glow on the horizon. Except for the frothing white water capping the waves, the sea was the color of coal. In the gloaming, Acuff radioed Capt. H. P. Butterfield, commander of the escort carrier USS *Nehenta Bay* sailing with his task group.

"What do you think about running out of it?" he asked.

"My weatherman says that we may possibly run out of it by morning," Butterfield replied. "But we are going with it."

Acuff then broached the delicate subject that was by now edging into every seaman's mind: "Do you think the old man was mistaken on his course?"

"That is the best way for him," said Butterfield, alluding to the fact that Halsey's heavies had outdistanced both the weather and the oiler group. "But we've come quite a ways with it. Big swells from the east make us move with it."

Acuff pressed. "I think we will come close to making rendezvous in the center of the storm."

There was a slight pause on Butterfield's end. Then, "He probably thought the center was more to the north. But it is actually more to the east, I think. If he took report of the fleet broadcast from Pearl, he made an error."

No sailor in the Pacific dared question Halsey's acumen, intuition, or seamanship. He had led them through too much; he must have known what he was doing. Acuff and Butterfield assumed the admiral had better weather intelligence than either of them could hope for.

Still, as driving rain tattooed the pilothouses of Acuff's beleaguered oiler group, Captain Calhoun on the *Dewey* was not alone in fretting over Halsey's latest refueling plan. In fact, he called it "unrealistic," and even his young and inexperienced staff officers— "And none of us were geniuses," the captain noted—had reached the conclusion that the fleet was being threatened by a massive typhoon. Didn't anyone in flag plot understand how close they were running to this blow?

One officer sailing aboard the *Dewey* who did was Capt. Preston Mercer, Admiral Nimitz's former assistant chief of staff and commander of Destroyer Squadron 1. The destroyers of DS1 had spent the past eight weeks ferrying between Pearl Harbor and Ulithi in various, disparate stages of shipyard overhauls, tactical exercises, and shakedown cruises for new crewmen. Although this was the first time since October 18 that they had sailed together as a squadron, Mercer was familiar with their shortcomings, specifically with their inherent instability.

Three months earlier he had telephoned the navy's Bureau of Ships to express his concern over the "gross deficiency" in the weight distribution of the *Farragut*-class vessels, but he'd never received a reply. This did not surprise him. The Bureau of Ships had come into existence only four years earlier and was still a bureaucratic work in progress.

Prior to 1940, and reaching back to the Civil War, the responsibility for U.S. Navy ship design and construction had been shared by competing offices: the Bureau of Engineering and the Bureau of Construction and Repair. Such was the petty infighting between these two administrations that they were said to have inspired the age-old line about a camel being a horse designed by a committee. Now, as Typhoon Cobra descended upon Destroyer Squadron 1, no one was joking.

It was no secret among seamen of every stripe that certain classes of DDs, in particular the *Farraguts* and the even older *Mahans*, were prone to hazardous rolls. Yet no one in Washington seemed to want to address the matter. Although Mercer had never heard back from the Bureau of Ships, he had won a small bureaucratic skirmish when, during the *Dewey*'s last refitting, he'd vigorously lobbied to have her steel, 20mm gun mounts replaced with lighter aluminum. As a result, the *Dewey* had shed over three thousand topside pounds. But she was only one ship.

As night fell on December 17, Mercer radioed the struggling *Spence*, now sailing with DS1, to inquire if she had sufficiently ballasted. In a few moments it would be dark, and Mercer also wanted to relay Halsey's command to cancel the fleet's zigzagging course. The *Spence*'s skipper, Lieutenant Commander Andrea, replied, inexplicably, that no, he had not pumped ballast, "although it would have been helpful." Andrea reported that, given his fuel gauge readings, the *Spence* could probably steam for another 24 to 48 hours at 15 knots. Mercer "recommended" that Andrea immediately fill his empty tanks with seawater to 50 percent of total capacity.

Mercer's strategy for the *Spence*—as well as for the *Hickox* and *Maddox*—was to ballast down half their bunkers to provide at least some stability, while still leaving enough room to take fuel, if possible, first thing the next morning. Both the *Hickox* and *Maddox* complied. For reasons never explained, the *Spence* did not.

CHAPTER 12

Com3rdFlt's Aerological Officer [George F. Kosco] *completed a three-year course in aerology in 1940; since, he has had two years' experience in carriers and 2 years ashore on aerological duty, including three months in West Indies flying around in hurricanes to determine their location. He had had about six years' naval experience before taking aerology course. He had been on his present station about one month. He is the most experienced aerological officer in THIRD FLEET today.*

—FROM THE FINAL REPORT OF THE COURT OF INQUIRY
INVESTIGATING "HALSEY'S TYPHOON."

By 10:00 P.M. on December 17, the destroyer *Dewey*'s barometer reading had dropped to 29.54. Long, sinuous cross-swells, outriders of the storm, bruted against diagonal waves whipped up by a 36-knot backing wind. The sea about Capt. Jasper Acuff's oiler Task Group 30.8 rose and fell like a carousel, and in the dark of the *Dewey*'s pilothouse, the luminous glow of the ship's instrument dials limned the ashen faces of the DD's exhausted bridge crew, men gone gray from lack of sleep. Herman Melville noted that "meditation and water are forever wedded," and even Calhoun, a spit-and-polish officer not given to lyrical odes to nature, declared the night's conditions "eerie, and ominous."

Calhoun ordered that additional lifelines be rigged around the *Dewey*'s weather deck, all loose gear be lashed down or struck below, and that the ship's supply of fresh water be transferred from high to low tanks. At the last minute Calhoun realized he could have reduced topside weight and "sail" even farther by lowering the ship's twenty-six-foot motor whaleboat into the sea, but he had forgotten. Listening to the gale whistling through the ship's taut guy wires—the chorus of Ulysses' sirens, one erudite sailor called it— he recognized it was now too late. He wouldn't risk the lives of a deck gang for this. "If we lose it, we lose it," he thought.

Simultaneously, aboard the *New Jersey*, running at flank speed well to the south, Third Fleet chief aerologist Comdr. George Kosco logged a comfortable barometer reading of 29.76. Although the big leviathans of Task Force 38 were still outpacing the typhoon, Kosco's chart table was covered with piles of weather forecasts, including new reports from MacArthur's command on Mindoro, and even intercepted Japanese messages. Yet he still could not locate the center of the storm.

Kosco had also been reading dozens of Third Fleet ship-to-ship weather communiqués and was aware that many commanders did not believe they could reach Halsey's rendezvous site by dawn. Shortly before midnight he sought out the admiral in flag plot and advised him to again alter his refueling station, suggesting latitude 15° 30' north, longitude 127° 40' east, about midway on a north-south axis between the two previous rendezvous sites. Halsey reluctantly acquiesced and issued the fleetwide order, his third course alteration in the past twelve hours. On vessels spread about the heaving Philippine Sea, helmsmen and navigators began to smell panic—and some sailors began to experience it.

Clinging to the top of the *Cape Esperance*'s center mast with every muscle in his body, Paul Schlener was not sure what to do as the storm increased in intensity. His watch was technically over, but whether through oversight or intention, no crewmate had relieved him and no officer had signaled for him to climb down. In fact, the scud was so thick that he could barely make out the deck sixty feet below. He was petrified.

With no other recourse, Schlener began to pray. Only the Lord, he believed, could save him now. He promised God that if He spared him, he would dedicate the rest of his life to His work. He prayed for several hours atop the mast before an officer fought through the winds and flashed a light, relieving him of his duty. Gingerly, he inched down the long pole.

By midnight on December 17, the western edge of Typhoon Cobra's counterclockwise windstream was swirling into the cold front Kosco had tracked sweeping out of the arctic. But instead of bouncing off the mass of cold air to the northeast—away from the fleet—the storm accelerated and gained strength as it chewed through the suddenly weak front. Typhoon winds now exceeded 100 knots at its center.

Oddly, this meteorological donnybrook was witnessed by long-range radar operators on several vessels near the eastern fringe of the fleet, but they did not know how to interpret what they were viewing on their newfangled "picture machines." The science of radar was still in its infancy, and radarmen were typically trained to look for short-range "pips," indicating either Allied or enemy vessels. As the fleet's radar operators watched the atmospheric phenomenon of a cyclone swirling nearby, in some cases just sixty miles east of their position, they had no idea what to make of it.

At 2:00 A.M. on December 18, Kosco made his final report to a pajama-clad Halsey in the admiral's flag quarters. The aerologist confessed he still could not pin down either the tropical depression's center, or its direction. Despite Occam's famous razor—the simplest explanation is usually the right one—Kosco was still not ready to admit that the storm had already matured into a typhoon.

Exhausted sailors sacked out fully dressed in dungarees and blue cotton workshirts, but any man who relaxed too much was liable to be catapulted into a bulkhead. Some tried to nod off with their arms and legs wrapped around bunk chains and stanchions, while the savvier veterans lashed themselves in with belts. It did not help. It was, said one seaman, "like sleeping on a trampoline."

Cooks slapping together piles of cold bacon, Spam, or bologna sandwiches—there would be no hot chow for breakfast—secured themselves to cutting tables with lengths of rope, and so many were burned by boiling coffee sloshing out of sixty-gallon coppers that most simply shut down their stoves. Aboard one destroyer, a cook's assistant started a betting pool on the number of knives and forks that would fly across his galley and embed themselves in bulkheads.

And in the wee hours of December 18, Lt. Comdr. George Kosco continued to assure Adm. William F. Halsey that he had made the correct decision in shaping the fleet south. The admiral, pacing his flag quarters, preferred somewhere, anywhere, north of their current heading. The Japanese air squadrons on the Legaspi Peninsula still gnawed at him. He felt his ships were sailing too damn close. What if some samurai flight commander did in fact order the unthinkable, and sent his kamikazes aloft in this blow? The entire Third Fleet would be trapped between the enemy to the west and the onrushing storm from the east. Defenseless, refueling vessels presented a powerful lure to an adversary already knocked back hard on his heels.

It was just the sort of reckless counterattack Halsey himself would order.

But kamikazes did not concern Kosco, who struggled to keep his mind from drifting elsewhere. The Japanese were not the primary enemy at this moment, he knew, and he argued that the weather made any course other than their current, southerly heading too risky. Station discipline was already falling apart, he informed Halsey. There was a good chance that many of Acuff's vessels, including several of his oilers, would not even reach the existing rendezvous site by daybreak. He handed the admiral the stack of grim messages he'd received from the task group commanders. Acuff's destroyers and destroyer escorts were in particular distress. To turn back north now would invite disaster.

With a final glance at his charts, the admiral agreed, and sent directions for the fleet to maintain its present course. He would take his chances with both the Japanese and the storm. He bid Kosco good night.

At the same time, steaming forty miles northeast of the *New Jersey*, Lt. Comdr. Henry Lee Plage prowled the open bridge of the destroyer escort *Tabberer* in quiet alarm. The open bridge on a DE is just that, forty feet above the waterline and completely exposed to the weather, offering a 360-degree view of the surrounding sea. From this vantage point, young Plage, eight weeks shy of his thirtieth birthday and with a five-month-old baby boy at home, could hardly believe what he was witnessing.

Towering masses of dull gray water rose on his port quarter and overtook the *Tabberer* until its fantail was awash in swirling fingers of foam that probed as far as the depth charge racks. The confused heap would then pass under the entire length of the three-hundred-foot destroyer escort like some huge, humpbacked sea creature, and Plage held tight as the vessel yawed in a drunken motion as it was lifted along on the crest. The *Tabby*'s bow would rise sharply, and then the skipper could feel a heavy drag, as if that very sea creature had wrapped its tentacles around his ship and was pulling her backward. The vibration of her twin screws, at times spinning free of the sea, caused the vessel to shudder like a paint mixer as the bow finally fell, only to be smothered in another mantle of eddying foam. And then the process would begin again.

Plage, who had not slept in twenty-four hours, looked as if he'd been ridden hard and put away wet. He had two black eyes from the battering wind, which had bent to a 45-degree angle the thick coach-whip antennae mounted about the ship's wheelhouse. Spindrift, sliced as if by razor from the crest of the breakers, scudded through the troughs far below him like eerie, white tumbleweeds. When the wind slammed into the ship's superstructure, it hissed against her stack, an ungodly sound that forced the captain to shout at full lung to make himself heard to his officer of the deck and helmsman.

Plage knew his Bowditch and had skirted the edges of hurricanes chasing Nazi subs for ten months in the Caribbean. This weather was far more frightening. Throughout the night and early morning, between what he took to calling the DE's "surfing runs," he periodically crouched down on his hands and knees and pulled himself out to the open bridge along the lifeline strung from the wheelhouse. Measuring the moments between rolls reaching 62 degrees, he would stand facing the wind and extend his right arm just as Buys-Ballot's Law instructed. Most tropical rainstorms, he knew, progressed in a circular motion, and this did not necessarily signify an approaching typhoon.

The wind direction of this blow, however, never wavered as the hours passed. Watching his barometer drop, occasionally checking the radar screen mounted in the four-foot post in the center of the open bridge, he was fairly certain that the fleet lay smack in the path of a major cyclone.

He had already directed the *Tabberer*'s crew to batten down for weather and make the ship watertight. He set fore and aft lookouts, moved heavy equipment to starboard compartments to offset the deep lists to port, and had all hands don life jackets. He also instructed his chief electrician to construct tunnels out of canvas, three feet in diameter, to intercept and redirect any saltwater that infiltrated the companionways leading to the ship's electrical boards. Until Plage heard different from his task group commander, there was nothing more to be done.

Plage at least had the satisfaction of knowing that he and his XO, Lt. Bob Surdam, a twenty-seven-year-old former track and soccer star from upstate New York, had trained the *Tabby*'s crew of 124 for just such an emergency. He had confidence in his sailors, and despite their precarious position, he felt a frisson of pride in his officers' and crew's preparedness.

Down in the *Tabby*'s galley, Shipfitter Leonard Glaser, the sailor to whom Plage had delivered kosher food, was not certain what to make of his vessel's predicament as he drank a carton of milk with one hand while holding on to a roll bar with the other. He was hungry, and Cookie Phillips had someow managed to bake pies, but given the body blows the *Tabby* was taking, eating was out of the question.

Glaser, like the majority of the DE's green crew, had scant experience with Pacific storms. Snug in his kapok life jacket, he was not all that frightened until a chief bosun's mate with thirty years' experience, one of the few veterans on the ship, rushed past him in a daze. The man's face was drained of color. The bosun's mate had earned a reputation as a garrulous seaman who rarely stopped talking, yet now he pushed by Glaser without so much as a word.

"What's your hurry, Chief?" Glaser said. "What's goin' on up top?"

"Never seen as rough a sea like this," said the bosun's mate before stumbling off down the companionway.

Glaser immediately began reevaluating his circumstances. As he wobbled through the galley, a sudden bucking motion sent him airborne, nearly into the arms of a haggard-looking Cookie Phillips. Phillips must have read the fear in the skinny shipfitter's eyes.

"Nuthin' to worry for," said the cook. "Ol' Cap'n, he got it all under control. He's a seaman, dontcha know?"

Back in flag quarters, Halsey tossed fitfully in his bunk. He could not shake the idea of an enemy sneak attack. Shortly after 3:00 A.M. he draped a thin, cotton robe over his pajamas, stepped into his slippers, and padded to the office adjacent to his sleeping quarters. There were maps of Luzon and weather reports strewn about the bulkhead. Something, a gut feeling, left him off balance and jittery. With his finger he drew a line across one chart, in a northwesterly arc. Toward northern Luzon. Away from the enemy-held Legaspi Peninsula.

Nearly simultaneously Kosco sat upright in his bunk. He was overwhelmed "with a feeling of great, leaden weights pressing on [my] shoulders." He threw on his heavy weather gear and scrambled up the iron skipper's ladder to the navigation deck. Leaning into the wind and listening to the pounding surf, he surveyed the otherworldly tableau; giant, mottled whitecaps stretched endless in every direction under a black, starless dome. If the dark side of the moon were covered by sea, he thought, this is what it would look like.

And in that instant the word "typhoon" took shape in his mind. He realized he needed more than intuition before suggesting to Halsey, much less CINCPAC, that an official, fleetwide warning to break stations be issued. Still. He groped his way back to Halsey's quarters, found the admiral awake, and laid out his concerns.

Halsey sent for his chief of staff, Rear Adm. "Mick" Carney, and Capt. Ralph Wilson, his operations officer. The four spent the next forty-five minutes in flag mess gulping coffee and weighing various options. A fug of cigarette smoke obscured the charts they passed among themselves. Halsey had Kosco radio Task Force 38 commander Slew McCain on the *Hancock* and Task Group 38.2 commander Rear Adm. Gerald F. Bogan aboard the carrier USS *Lexington*. Both were sailing a-weather of his flagship; perhaps they could provide more firsthand information. Neither offered much of substance.

Given the cross-swell and backing winds, McCain and Bogan ventured that the storm was somewhere to the fleet's east, and probably bearing northwest. Where, specifically, to the east? Their answers varied. Bogan guessed 220 miles northeast; McCain 240 miles southeast. McCain appears not to have mentioned that his carrier's aft metal gun shields had already been buckled by a gale strong enough to rip the steel hatch off a magazine storeroom and flood the compartment.

Halsey was no closer to knowing that at this moment Typhoon Cobra was ninety miles east-southeast of the *New Jersey*. He lit another cigarette and paced. His subordinates wondered at his indecision. He felt, he told Carney, "like a matador going into the bull ring with a splint on his leg."

Moments before 5:00 A.M., with the robust gale running hard out of the north, Halsey made his decision. He canceled the previously arranged rendezvous site and ordered all task groups to begin refueling "as soon as practical" after sunrise. His fleet commanders were taken aback. Only in poetry do fighting men refrain from asking the reason why. How did the Bull expect ships sailing south to take fuel with this blow running at their backs? Hadn't the old man learned anything from yesterday's fiasco? There were already scattered reports of vessels locked in irons, 100-knot gusts nipping at their sterns.

In fact, Halsey was unaware that one of his ships was already fighting for its life. One hour earlier, the destroyer USS *Aylwin*, flagship of Acuff's oiler group, had gone dead in the water.

"Tough as a sandbag" is how one enlisted man described the *Aylwin*'s young skipper, Commander William K. Rogers. Rogers had come aboard the DD seven months earlier, and though only in his first command, in that time he'd acquired an instinctive feel for both his crew and his ship. He knew how she came about under fire, and how she reacted to unsteady seas.

The previous morning, during the aborted fueling attempts, he'd confessed to having a "bad feeling" about this storm to his XO, and ordered the deck crew to carry below every object that could be blown overboard and to double-lash all essential topside gear such as torpedoes and depth charges, including their ready tubes and racks. He had his oil gang pump seawater into the ship's empty holds as ballast, and damage control parties were formed up to fight any electrical fires that might break out. Belowdecks, Rogers also ordered stowed any loose clothing or rags that might conceivably clog suction-pump stations.

Rogers was not only tough, but smart. He was well aware that, in a crisis at sea, the danger to a ship's survival rapidly becomes exponential. The more trouble a ship is in, the likelier she is to run into more. Blown hatches lead to flooded bilges and flooded bilges lead to electrical shorts and electrical shorts lead to failed steering mechanisms. The list, Rogers knew, was endless. Like all the commanders of the *Farragut*-class destroyers, he was especially wary of the *Aylwin*'s ability to remain upright in high seas and heavy wind.

Every craft on water, from a ketch to an aircraft carrier, has a degree of roll from which she will no longer return upright. Depending upon the size of the ship, this usually falls within the 60-to-80-degree range. Upon the *Aylwin*'s commission in 1940, her stability rating showed a relatively adequate GM, or metacentric height, of 2.41 feet. A vessel's metacentric height determines the length of her righting arm, which is the lateral distance between the two opposing forces of buoyancy and gravity. On a trim ship, these two forces are equal and cancel each other out. This means a vessel will roll easily, but also snap back quickly. By contrast, the smaller the GM, the slower a ship's return to an even keel.

Calculating a ship's GM involves a complex mathematical formula that, in essence, subtracts a ship's center of uplifting buoyancy from her center of down-pushing gravity. Very simply put, a large GM gives a ship a large righting arm, which in turn gives a ship a large righting moment. The larger the righting moment, the more stable the ship.

But in the four years since the *Aylwin*'s keel was laid, the Navy Department's technology had outrun its vessels' utility. Rogers's ship, like the other *Farragut*-class destroyers, was now burdened with tons of supplementary topside weight, including a new combat information center and modern radar antennae, transmitters, and platforms at the tip of her mast. Her deck was also fully loaded with additional machine guns as well as cumbersome crates of ammunition. Given her already high center of gravity, when this added tonnage was taken into account, her GM had decreased accordingly, by .78 feet, to 1.63 feet. In other words, she was now much easier to push over.

On the night of December 17, Rogers retired to his quarters with nagging apprehensions. He had good reason. Roused from his bunk at 3:48 the next morning, he was dismayed, if far from surprised, when an aide handed him a copy of the distress call his officer of the deck had just broadcast to all her task group's escort carriers, oilers, tugs, destroyers, and destroyer escorts:

"Aylwin to TG-30.8. We are broken down. Have lost all power on generators. Am trying to come to base course."

Despite Rogers's precautions, the ocean had poured in through a sprung hatch on the *Aylwin*'s weather deck and shorted all her generators. Her lights were out, her electronic steering control gone. When Captain Butterfield on the *Nehenta Bay* received the *Aylwin*'s distress call, he directed his carrier to close on her in support. Rogers, meanwhile, donned his foul-weather gear, raced to the bridge, and ordered his chief quartermaster to make his way through the sea foam gushing from the scuppers to the ship's after steering compartment under the aft fantail, where the hand-steering mechanism was located.

Although oiler Task Group 30.8 commander Jasper Acuff was sailing aboard the *Aylwin*, Rogers was her captain, and it was his job to save his ship. He took the conn. With his main turbo-generator out of service, Rogers employed various engine-thrust combinations to try to regain course. But the roiling seas pummeled the DD out of control, and she swung wildly due north. When the hand-steering wheel was finally manned, her helmsman was able to wrestle her back on station. But she was now lagging well behind the rest of the oiler group. Sometime after 4:00 A.M. the ship's lights and electronic steering were brought back on line. Presently Rogers picked up Halsey's new fueling directive, via McCain on the *Hancock:*

"Cancel previous rendezvous. All groups come to course 180 degrees. Commence exercises when practical. Suggest leading destroyers take it over stern, if necessary."

By now Acuff had joined Rogers on the *Aylwin*'s bridge. Acuff was in a peculiar position, commanding a task group that was sailing well ahead of him. Before he fell out of TBS range, which carried only to the horizon, he radioed all vessels to comply with McCain's directive and designated Butterfield on the *Nehenta Bay* to take tactical command of the escort carriers. The oilers and their escorts swung to course 180, due south, running on a parallel track, and behind, Halsey's task force.

The new heading placed the entire fleet nearly at a right angle to the typhoon. Already buffeted by a backing gale force—a wind so savage it was lopping the tops off slate gray sixty-foot combers and driving the whitewater like horizontal rain—Task Group 30.8's bobbing vessels were now being broadsided by long, sweeping swells out of the east. Sailors were thrown from their bunks—the *Dewey's* Captain Calhoun was buried under a pile of books—and galley coppers crashed.

In the long tradition of frontline fighting troops, seamen eyed the heavy seas, joked with false bravado—"Weather great for buildin' character, huh?"—and bellyached about the brass. Outside the wheelhouse on the destroyer *Hull*, Chief Bosun's Mate Ray Schultz turned to Chief Quartermaster Archie DeRyckere and asked, in all seriousness, if he thought their "bullheaded *fighting admiral*" actually had a death wish. "Guy's supposed to be the smartest officer in the fleet, but every seaman second who just came aboard and don't know nothing abut the navy knows we're in a typhoon."

In fact, more than one DD commander was wondering about the ambiguity of the orders being transmitted, not the least of which was McCain's directive to "commence exercises when practical." Easy for an admiral riding a carrier as big as an apartment complex to say. But Comdr. William K. Rogers aboard the *Aylwin* did not have the luxury of contemplating the impending perils involved with refueling. He eyed the seven large, upright machine gun shields strewn across his vessel's deck. In his ship's precarious condition, if the swells and howling gale pushed her over into a deep roll, those "sails" would make sure she stayed pushed over.

North of the *Aylwin*, on the fleet's most vulnerable perimeter, Capt. Bruce Garrett of the *Monaghan* was entertaining similar thoughts. With each sledgehammer roll the destroyer took, the level of lubricating oil in her engines dropped below its suction point. If Garrett lost engine power, he knew, the ship was done for. The *Monaghan* was being bruted wildly off course like driftwood, albeit, as Garrett well knew, driftwood does not sink.

Although steaming with what should have been a sufficient bunker capacity of 76 percent, close to 130,000 gallons of viscous black fuel oil, the *Monaghan* was being buffeted unmercifully as she took the brunt of the storm's leading edge. Her anemometer registered 100-knot winds, the needle was still climbing, and no matter how much power Garrett rang up to keep her on a southern heading, the sea continued to push the little destroyer almost due west.

As the vessel heeled and pitched through the dizzying seas, sailors below clung to handholds and wrapped their arms and legs around any stationary object available, often lying in puddles of their own urine and vomit. As one officer noted, "It was bruising, painful, and exhausting. At any moment it could be fatal. It took a healthy measure of guts to stay below under those circumstances."

Finally, Garrett realized that no amount of rudder and screw combinations would turn the *Monaghan* back south and, in desperation, concluded that the only way to avert the ship's capsize was to ballast her aft bunkers with seawater. Given the weather conditions, this was close to suicidal, a thought not lost on twenty-year-old radar technician Keith Abbott as he listened to the skipper give the order from his station on the *Monaghan's* bridge.

Not for the first time that morning, "ghost sailor" Abbott marveled at the wicked fates that had carried him from his family's sugar beet farm in Idaho to this reckless place and time.

Now he watched in anguish as Captain Garrett, with a total of seven days in command of the destroyer, transmitted a general distress signal reporting that his generator and steering motor had failed, and that the *Monaghan* was out of control, bucking violently, and taking water.

Captain Calhoun on the *Dewey*, sailing parallel and perhaps three thousand yards west of the *Monaghan*, picked up one of Garrett's TBS messages. Calhoun grabbed his own TBS microphone and tried to reassure his Academy classmate that he, too, was taking major rolls. He received no reply. By now the *Monaghan's* onboard communications system had also failed, and Garrett could not even talk to his engine room from the bridge.

In a final bid to save his ship, Garrett ran a messenger to his "oil king," Watertender 2nd Class Joe McCrane, instructing him to open the valves to two of the *Monaghan*'s empty aft fuel tanks and connect them to the main waterline attached to the bilge pumps. McCrane dutifully notified the engine room to fire the pumps. But since he was using the failed steering motor telephone to communicate, he never found out if the black gang received the order.

McCrane had no way of knowing that, because of the pounding the ship was taking, the overhead in the engine room was starting to rip loose from her bulkheads. The *Monaghan*'s ferocious swings up fluted waves and down into troughs were beginning to tear her hull apart. In dark compartments below, men gathered in groups to pray in tender oblivion. And on the *Monaghan*'s bridge, Radar Maintenance Technician 2nd Class Keith Abbott thought once again of his former berth on the faraway and safe destroyer escort *Emery*.

CHAPTER 13

---

*Without meaning any particular criticism of our present-day aer-
ologists, I'm inclined to think that they have been brought up to
depend on a lot of readings they get from other stations. I think
they are much weaker than the older officers in judging the weather.
. . . I think they should be taught to judge the weather by what
they actually see.*

—TESTIMONY OF REAR ADM. FREDERICK C. SHERMAN,
COMMANDING OFFICER, TASK GROUP 38.3,
TO THE COURT OF INQUIRY INVESTIGATING
"HALSEY'S TYPHOON."

Back on the *New Jersey,* Halsey and Kosco continued to compare
forecasts from Pearl and outlying Allied weather stations. There was
by now a frantic undercurrent to their deliberations. Even the im-
mense battleship was taking disturbing rolls, and Halsey's apprehensive glances at the ship's barometer could not prevent its needle's
plummet, down now to 29.67.

Outside flag plot, the wind was howling, the ceiling was resting
practically on the deck, and saltwater was blowing in horizontal
sheets at bridge level. The admiral had a decision to make. He knew
that fueling would be difficult, but his destroyers were staggering.
The USS *Stockham* and USS *Welles* reported 22 percent fuel capacity; the USS *Moore* 21 percent; the USS *Yarnell* 20 percent; the
USS *Taussig* 18 percent. Some were even worse off. The USS

Colahan, USS *Brush*, USS *Franks*, and USS *Cushing* radioed that they were at 15 percent of capacity. The *Maddox*, *Hickox*, and *Spence* were at 10 percent or below.

One of the enduring questions surrounding the events of December 18 is why, at 6:16 A.M., Vice Admiral McCain ordered a fleetwide 120-degree course change, from due south to northeast. Halsey was aware of his task force commander's directive, yet he said nothing as Third Fleet steamed directly toward the eye of Typhoon Cobra.

McCain later testified that "he did not appreciate the speed with which the storm was overtaking" the fleet. Uppermost in his mind, he added, was the commitment to strike Luzon, and for that his small boys needed fuel. Halsey, for his part, was never asked by the court of inquiry to explain why he permitted the course change, and never spoke nor wrote of this decision thereafter.

One theory posits that Halsey was merely acting in character, the personification of the heedless servant in the Robert Frost poem who understood that "the best way out is always through." As a sailor once remarked, "Bull Halsey. My God, even the name swaggers." More skeptical minds speculated that in some recess of the admiral's psyche, he was still being guided by the powerful memory of leaving MacArthur's flank unguarded during the Battle for Leyte Gulf.

Thus, despite the fact that by 8:00 A.M. on December 18 virtually every ship's commander in the Third Fleet, one by one, on a direct axis running southeast to northwest, had concluded that they were steaming into a massive typhoon, Halsey insisted on attempting to refuel his destroyers. He had vowed to provide MacArthur's beachhead on Mindoro with every gun and plane he could muster. That this was wishful thinking, if not a hallucination, seemed lost on the admiral.

Soon more vessels joined the *Aylwin* in distress. The attack carrier USS *Wasp* reported a life raft to her port that appeared to carry three men. The fleet tug USS *Jicarilla* requested assistance due to engine trouble. The carrier *Independence* reported two men overboard, swept into the sea by a geyser of green water. And the destroyer *Hickox* lost steering control after her aft steering compartment was flooded, nearly drowning the sailors stationed inside; only a makeshift bucket brigade had saved their lives.

Across the Philippine Sea, Halsey's "small boys" were careering blindly, their lookouts pulled in and their surface radar too cluttered with heaving black contours to differentiate between looming waves and out-of-control vessels on collision headings. And aboard one ship, panic was prompting thoughts of mutiny.

Moments before dawn on December 18, Archie DeRyckere bolted from his bunk in the chief's quarters in the bow of the destroyer *Hull* to the sound of a refrigerator bouncing from bulkhead to bulkhead. After helping to lash it down, he was making his way through the wardroom in officers' country when he felt the ship lie over on her side.

Men tumbled from their beds, and DeRyckere was staggered. He regained his balance only by standing on the starboard bulkhead. As the vessel slowly righted herself, he ran through the chart house and onto the second deck. The ceiling was below him and the spume stung his face like a sandblaster. The starboard side of the *Hull* was submerged.

Making his way from the chart house to the captain's bridge, DeRyckere could not differentiate ocean from air, and visibility was so low that he could not make out the ship's bow, no more than 120 feet away. He began climbing the starboard skipper's ladder when, midway to the bridge, another wall of water slammed into the *Hull*'s port beam. He hung on as she lay so far over that the back of his head grazed the ocean's surface.

Thus began a synchronized rolling that would last for six hours. The vessel's towering masts and stacks served like the bantam tail of a weathervane, and the relentless winds would seize them and spin the ship into the tossing broadsides of enormous waves. DeRyckere knew that none of Halsey's ships would be refueled that day. It was a constant fight for crewmen just to remain on their feet.

The *Hull* was a tough old tin can that had survived rough seas before. Three years earlier, in 1941, she had been escorting the carrier *Lexington* from Pearl Harbor to San Diego when an unexpected low front had fallen on her like a lid. She'd plowed through waves so steep, the vessel's metal housing had shrieked and the crew felt the shuddering vibrations in their kidneys. The beating she'd taken had warped her main frame, but she'd docked safely, all hands accounted for.

That experience now seemed like a shakedown cruise, and DeRyckere was frustrated. His responsibilities as chief quartermaster also included winding, reading, and comparing the *Hull*'s three chronometers and reporting his findings to the ship's captain. But besides qualifying the instruments in this blow, DeRyckere felt like a "big zero." Taking his station on the bridge, he yearned for Captain Marks to give him something, anything, to do. He offered to take reports from the engine room, where the scowling throttleman "Buddha" Wiemers, the water rising almost to his great, heaving belly, had only moments before cursed the captain to DeRyckere with strings of oaths novel even to the veteran chief—"damn pogey-bait sailor." But Marks appeared petrified.

Wiemers was an old China hand, a veteran of the USS *Panay*, the small, shoal-drift river gunboat that Japanese dive bombers had sent to the bottom of the Yangtze River in 1937 during the Rape of Nanking. Wiemers manned the whaleboat that ferried the *Panay*'s survivors to the river's reedy banks until rescuers arrived. With his barrel-shaped physique, Buddha Wiemers may have appeared as if he needed a tugboat escort, but the man had a lot of hard bark on him. If his tone of voice was tinged with a tremolo of fear, DeRyckere was a sailor to take notice. Now DeRyckere paced behind Marks, not ten feet away, practically willing the man to give him something to do. Marks never said a word.

Irritated, DeRyckere stepped out onto the starboard bridge wing. Surging seas the color of pewter crashed about him. Driving rain stung his face. "This is not good," he thought. He was an understated man. "We're going down and there's nobody around to help us." He couldn't believe that Admiral Halsey had gotten them into this pickle.

Halsey was an icon to every sailor in the Pacific Command. The word was out among even the most humble jack tar that Halsey was a sailor's sailor and a leader's leader, a commander who was motivated by only two ambitions: to kill Japs, and to watch over the safety of his sailors. The tough old admiral was known to weep while greeting returning vessels that had lost men in combat.

But now Ray Schultz, the *Hull*'s chief bosun's mate, approached DeRyckere on the bridge wing with incredible news. Schultz had just come up from the communications shack, where Chief Radioman Burt "Sparks" Martin had copied a TBS message between Halsey's *New Jersey* and the light carrier USS *Monterey*. The *Monterey* was in trouble, dead in the water after having lost steering control. She was also fighting an aviation fuel fire in her hangar deck. The *Hull*'s radioman had overheard her reporting her damage to flag plot.

During the exchange, someone on the *Monterey*—Sparks Martin assumed it to be her captain—asked Halsey for permission to break station and plot coordinates to sail around "this typhoon." It was the first use of this loaded word anyone on the *Hull* had picked up; all other descriptions of the violent weather had referred only to a tropical storm or a tropical depression. Sparks also overheard the *Monterey*'s commander express concern for his "small boys," meaning the task group's destroyers and destroyer escorts. Halsey's reply, rather too nonchalant for Ray Schultz's taste, was that the rough seas would give the destroyer crews an opportunity to practice their seamanship.

"Jesus, you believe that?" Schultz said to Martin. He was angry enough to explode. "Practice our seamanship?"

Unlike most draftees and enlistees in the dark days after Pearl Harbor, John Ray Schultz had not come lately to the colors, having been billeted aboard the *Hull* since June of '38. A slender twenty-four-year-old with wavy, pomaded blond hair set atop a boyish oval face, he was fair-skinned and freckled, handsome in a sidekick sort of way. He reminded DeRyckere of the Hollywood actor Ralph Bellamy, the good-looking guy who, in the movies, never got the girl.

He was also a wildcat. Once, back at Pearl before the war, Schultz had missed curfew and subsequently commandeered a fast crash boat to return to the *Hull*. But he was spotted and chased by the Shore Patrol. He outran them and, nearing the *Hull*, dived off the boat, climbed aboard the destroyer over the screw guards, and hared to his bunk in his soaking dress whites. He pulled a blanket up to his chin, and when the officer of the deck "woke" him, he professed outrage at any dirty rat who would dare to steal one of the U.S. Navy's crash boats.

Weeks later, when the Japanese attacked on the morning of December 7, Schultz was still in the sack at Pearl. He refused to believe the sailor who came running through the bunkroom shouting a warning and beaned him in the back of the head with a shoe for waking him. Then Schultz heard the explosions. He rushed topside, manned a .50-caliber machine gun, and shot down the Japanese plane that crash-landed into the seaplane tender USS *Curtiss*.

DeRyckere knew Schultz's moods, and now, in the middle of this blow, he could see that the chief bosun's mate was seething with anger. A few hours earlier, he told DeRyckere, he had petitioned Captain Marks for permission to order all hands to don life jackets.

"What do you want to do?" Marks replied. "Frighten the crew?"

Incensed, Schultz left the bridge and headed belowdecks. He rousted unnerved men and ordered each to break out his kapok. It was Schultz who had crusaded back in Bremerton to have all the *Hull*'s worm-eaten, inflatable "Mae West" rubber life tubes replaced with the newer kapok designs constructed from the waxy, fibrous seedpods of tropical silk-cotton trees and sealed in vinyl. This inspiration now looked prescient. Down in the hold, men were praying in corners, dredging the bottom of their faith. Others were puking, or writing letters to their mothers. Desperate men, Schultz knew, never wrote to their fathers. Somewhere aft, Schultz could hear voices singing the navy hymn: *Eternal father strong to save, whose arm does rule the restless wave. . . . Oh hear us when we cry to Thee, for those in peril on the sea.*

Since the argument with Captain Marks over the life jackets, Schultz had made periodic trips to the bridge to urge Lt. Griel Gherstly, the *Hull*'s executive officer and second-in-command, to convince Marks to rig the *Hull* for heavy seas. Schultz wanted to strike all superfluous topside weight, the ammunition lockers in particular, and move it belowdecks. He argued that the ship's high port side desperately needed ballast. When Marks dismissed Gherstly's request to stow the ammo by reminding his subordinate that the *Hull* was "in a war zone," Ray Schultz stomped away in frustration.

Sometime around 11:00 A.M. another vertical sheet of ocean slammed into the *Hull*, accompanied by a sucking, hissing noise that sounded to the crew like a giant vacuum cleaner. The wave rolled the ship 75 degrees to port and sheared off the forward davit securing her motor whaleboat. The dory swung in the wind on its remaining davit like a scythe, banging against the deck housing. Schultz burst into the bridge, demanding that it be jettisoned. Marks would not cut it loose. Instead, he ordered Schultz to form up a deck crew to resecure the boat.

In the midst of the operation the whaleboat broke completely free, crashed into a torpedo tube mounting, slid across the deck, and took several crewmen over the side with it. There was no way the *Hull*, locked in irons, could reverse course to retrieve them.

Upon news of this tragedy, the men on the *Hull*'s bridge went silent. DeRyckere was in shock. The chief quartermaster had always felt that the crew makes the ship; it did not matter who was in charge. Now he wasn't sure. After a moment, Gherstly, stationed behind the helmsman, quietly asked Schultz to find him a life jacket. His was below, Gherstly said, and because he was the officer of the deck, Captain Marks would not allow him to leave the bridge.

Schultz pivoted toward Marks wearing a lion-tamer's look. When he saw that the captain's own kapok was buckled across his chest, his emotions slipped their brakes. Without taking his eyes off Marks, he addressed Gherstly, loud enough for Marks to hear.

"Why don't you ask him for his? He's supposed to go down with the ship, anyway."

Marks glared back at Schultz, but said nothing. It was an exchange Chief Quartermaster Archie DeRyckere never expected to witness on a fighting ship of the United States Navy.

A few minutes later, his watch finally over, Gherstly left the bridge to find a life jacket. Schultz trailed after him.

"Mr. Gherstly," he said, "you know the captain is sinking this ship. You've got to relieve him."

Gherstly paused, the rain streaming from his peaked cap. At first he said nothing. Then he told Schultz he was talking mutiny. If they didn't drown they'd all be shot. Then he walked away, and the opportunity to save the USS *Hull* passed.

CHAPTER 14

DDs lost were maneuvering to maintain stations prior to sinking; were unable to extricate themselves from trough of the sea. COs failed to discontinue, sufficiently in advance, attempts to maintain position and emphasize all attention on saving their ships. Knowledge that fueling would be resumed as soon as possible may have caused COs to delay ballasting.

—ONE OF THE FINDINGS IN THE REPORT
OF THE COURT OF INQUIRY INVESTIGATING
"HALSEY'S TYPHOON."

More than a hundred miles away from Halsey and Kosco on the *New Jersey*, the destroyer escort *Tabberer* and her picket group had drifted to the far fringes of the fleet. The little ship's thin metal hull plates groaned as tons of gray-green water washed over her deck, and she rolled ever more violently. Captain Plage had attempted to keep lookouts posted, but with visibility no more than a few hundred yards, the act was not only life-threatening, but futile.

Unknown to Plage, just before dawn the last lookout he'd pulled in, nineteen-year-old Signalman 3rd Class John Cross, had spotted another vessel atop a swell mere yards from the *Tabberer* as she struggled to escape a deep trough. Cross, who had wrapped his body around a crossbar attached to the door of the wheelhouse in an effort to keep from being blown overboard, had not recognized the make of the ship. All he saw was the bottom of her hull as she crested the wave almost directly above the *Tabby*.

Cross, in his first combat posting, had not known what to do. In a panic, he'd slithered across the deck to the DE's signal shack, found a powerful flashlight, and crawled back to his post. But by the time he returned, the ghost ship had disappeared, and Cross never told anyone about the incident for the remainder of the war.

Now, having ordered Cross belowdecks, Plage was acting as his own lookout. He balanced himself in the *Tabby*'s wheelhouse, scanning in every direction for what he guessed, what he hoped, was the horizon. Suddenly he glimpsed a dark shadow through the rack of scud off his port side. A moment later the shape took sharper image, and Plage recognized it as the bridge of one of the *Tabby*'s sister destroyer escorts, the USS *Robert F. Keller*. She was slicing through the waves less than one hundred yards away, pitching wildly and closing fast on a collision course.

The *Keller* was skippered by Plage's friend Lt. Comdr. Raymond J. Toner, a seaman with a poetic bent who, after the war, would go on to become a military writer of some note. Like Plage, Toner had sailed through hurricanes in the Caribbean and helmed his "sea dwarf" through heavy gales in both the Atlantic and Pacific, including two previous combat commands. Without ever forming his thoughts into words, Toner had sensed that this morning's blow would turn into nothing less than a struggle for his ship's, and his crew's, survival. Thus, as the bottom dropped out of his barometer, he decided to point his craft in whichever direction the air pressure appeared to be rising and plowed forward with no more reason than to keep his vessel afloat.

Throughout the gray morning Toner had noticed that "a strange, shrill sound had been impinging upon my consciousness." As the noise grew louder, he realized it was the shriek of the constant wind whistling through the *Keller*'s halyards and antennae. He felt as if he were inside a bass fiddle, and because of the difficulty in relaying orders, he had relieved his officer of the deck and taken the conn himself, personally issuing directives to his helmsman and engine room operator.

At nearly the same moment Plage spotted the *Keller* heading for him bow-on, Toner felt someone pulling ferociously on his arm, "pointing violently toward the murk, the color of burnt umber, on our starboard bow." It was Toner's OD, who, the commander learned later, was screaming as loud as he could. Toner could not hear him above the ocean's roar. With eyes stinging from saltwater, Toner swiveled his body to starboard and spotted the *Tabberer* bearing down on him.

"All engines ahead flank!" he screamed to his engine gang.

Simultaneously, Plage ordered the *Tabby*'s black gang to back down full reverse. He had no choice but to plow into the tremendous seas stern-first and accept the risk that the *Tabby* might break in two. He relayed his movements to Toner via TBS. (Or, as Toner heard it in Plage's slow, Georgian drawl, "Rogah, aha'm backina full.")

Both ships lurched madly, and Toner could feel his insides quiver as the two DEs avoided ramming each other by feet.

"In periods of such intense concentration," Toner would note after the typhoon with a typical lyricism, "the body and its demands recede and fuse into a mental-spiritual sensing. It extends one's reactions to the utmost limits of the ship so that her next movement becomes as responsive and anticipated as the movements of one's own limbs."

In the *Tabberer*'s wheelhouse, Lt. Bob Surdam's thoughts were somewhat more prosaic. After witnessing the *Robert F. Keller* lurch out of the *Tabby*'s path, Surdam felt as if his thumping heart were near to breaking through his chest wall. He turned to the *Tabby*'s captain.

"How the hell did we get into this mess, Skipper?"

"I don't know," Plage said to his XO. "What bothers me is how the hell we're going to get out of it. I believe we're right in the middle of a typhoon, and no one has yet acknowledged it."

The *Tabberer*'s full reverse had forced her into another trough, from which she could not now escape. On the bridge, Plage and his officers prayed silently as waves formed a canyon on either side of them. Plage glanced at the inclinometer as the *Tabby* heeled into another 50-degree roll. Murmuring more to himself than to his officers, his voice barely audible, he added, "No warning at all." His men were not sure if he was talking about the near miss with the *Keller*, or the storm.

There was now no question that what the *Robert F. Keller's* Captain Toner described as "this inhuman force" was engulfing Halsey's fleet. After one destroyer skipper estimated he heard the chilling distress call "Man Overboard!" over his TBS radio at least twenty times in an hour, oiler task group commander Capt. Jasper Acuff radioed McCain that fueling under these conditions was impossible. His tankers were lolling like water buffalo, their deck crews fighting for their lives. Moreover, the aircraft in his escort carriers' hangar decks were breaking loose and being pounded to scrap.

At this, McCain finally directed Acuff's carriers to run to the lee of the storm, wherever they could find it—"to select a course and speed at their own discretion." He ordered Butterfield on the *Nehenta Bay* to try and keep them together as a unit. Straightaway the small flattops turned back due south, their speed barely topping 10 knots.

Halsey's entire fleet was dysfunctional and scattered, as if a ball of quicksilver had been smashed with a hammer. At 8:18 A.M. he radioed MacArthur to inform the general that his planned return the next morning, December 19, was out of the question. The storm had reduced the business of war to an insignificant consideration. He set a new, tentative date with MacArthur for December 21 and ordered the entire fleet to follow Butterfield's carrier flotilla south.

The admiral was clearly confused—or, to some fleet officers, mule-headed. In his zeal to remain within striking distance of Luzon, he had waited too long to batten down his task force for heavy weather. Even his friend Kosco, keeping a journal, seemed to have changed his opinion about "the incidental dangers of ugly weather."

He now noted that Halsey's "primary mission should have been to get his fleet away from there fast. The enemy could wait. The storm did not."

Telling evidence of Halsey's obduracy was the communiqué he sent to CINCPAC Nimitz at 9:15 A.M. December 18. In it he relayed the *New Jersey*'s position and blithely referred to the storm as a "tropical disturbance." A mild description, considering. He had either still failed to diagnose that his fleet had met a powerful typhoon—or he simply refused to admit it. In any event, the result was as inevitable as a simple axiom of Euclidean geometry: Two forces cannot occupy the same space at the same time.

U.S. Navy rules and regulations can often be chloroform in print, but Adm. William F. Halsey Jr. was nothing if not versed in maritime canon. As Typhoon Cobra encircled his Third Fleet, he was surely familiar with Bowditch's entry on tropical cyclones as well as the relevant passages of his navy-issue *Heavy Weather Guide*. It is doubtful, however, that more than a handful of the thirty-six thousand sailors he commanded had any concept of the raw power of the typhoon that was about to embrace them.

"A perfectly ordinary afternoon thunderstorm has the energy equivalent of about thirteen 20-kiloton atomic bombs," Capt. William J. Kotsch writes in the U.S. Navy's *Heavy Weather Guide*. Further, he continues, "in a 24-hour period, even a small-scale typhoon will release about 20 billion tons of water. This is an energy equivalent of close to 500,000 atomic bombs, or almost six bombs per second."

Halsey had once leafed through an aerologist's copy of the *Heavy Weather Guide* and noticed the single word "Odysseus" scribbled in the margins next to that particular passage. Poetic, perhaps, but his Third Fleet was a state-of-the-art deepwater navy, not some misbegotten bark on a wine-dark sea. Nevertheless, as the morning wore on, disturbing reports continued to flow into flag plot from foundering ships, the smaller, more southeasterly vessels at first. Men swept overboard. Loss of steering control. The bow of the destroyer USS *Grayson* was buckled by one wave, and her aft gun mount was stove in by another.

Then, more ominously, Halsey began hearing from his larger vessels, particularly his escort carriers. Fighter planes were being swept off decks and into the sea. Aircraft stowed in hangar decks were breaking loose from their moorings, bouncing off bulkheads, and exploding. Aboard the USS *Monterey*, the admiral learned, one such conflagration was close to sinking the venerable aircraft carrier.

To Lt. (j.g.) Jerry Ford, officer of the deck on the USS *Monterey*, each descent down the face of a wave was like the downbeat of an ax. From his station on the bridge, Ford contemplated the implausible scene unfolding before him. Lashing rains and 60-knot winds had whipped the sea into a liquid palisade, and few, if any, of Third Fleet's vessels were visible through Ford's binoculars. As the presiding officer on the midnight-to-4:00 A.M. midwatch, it was Ford's responsibility to ensure that the little jeep carrier maintained station. In particular, he was tasked with securing her heading and avoiding collisions at all cost. Yet now, as he scanned the shifting, undulating horizon, not a single ship hove into view.

It suddenly struck the lieutenant that in his eighteen months at sea he had never seen waves so large. They reeled in from starboard in constant sets, an unbroken chaos of gray-black water that appeared to defy gravity. They battered the *Monterey*'s hull and washed over her flight deck, fifty-seven feet above the waterline. To Ford, their vibrations resonated like a basso organ chord in some vast European cathedral.

Since he'd drawn a billet on the *Monterey* in the spring of 1943, the thirty-one-year-old Ford—blond and broad-shouldered, with the square-jawed countenance of a young Johnny Weissmuller—wrote that he'd seen "as much action as I'd ever hoped to see." As a gunnery division officer, Ford had directed fire during the great

Marianas Turkey Shoot only six months earlier, where Japanese Zeros had fallen like autumn leaves. Four months after that, during the Leyte campaign, waves of enemy aircraft out of Formosa had hit the *Monterey*'s task group with everything they'd had for two solid days. It had rained iron, and Ford, commanding a 40mm antiaircraft gun crew from the fantail deck, had watched as a torpedo narrowly missed his carrier and tore out the bow of the nearby Australian cruiser HMS *Canberra*.

Ford thought he'd seen the worst of it . . . until this morning, watching the Philippine Sea churn. Now, as another breaker crashed over the carrier's housing, Jerry Ford wondered if nature was about to accomplish what the Japanese could not. Sometimes, in those rare, eerie hollows when the wind abated for an instant, he could just make out the distress whistles sounding about him, the deep beeps of the battlewagons, the shrill whoops of the destroyers. By the end of his watch there was already scuttlebutt on the bridge about 2,000-ton destroyers rolling abeam and taking water down their stacks.

When his midwatch ended, Ford crawled into his bunk belowdecks, his nerves on edge, functioning in that liminal state between sleep and wakefulness. It seemed to him that his head had barely hit the pillow before the *Monterey*'s skipper, Capt. Stuart H. "Slim" Ingersoll, sounded general quarters. Ford bolted upright in his dark sea cabin. He thought he smelled smoke from somewhere amidships.

Racing through a rolling companionway dimly lit by red battle lights, he reached the catwalk encircling the flight deck. His foot hit the first rung of the iron skipper's ladder leading to the bridge at the precise moment a gigantic white comber broke over the wheelhouse like an avalanche lit by glints of moonlight. The sound reminded Ford of branches being ripped from giant trees.

The carrier pitched 25 degrees to port, and Ford lost his footing and was knocked flat on his back. He began skimming across the flight deck "as if I were on a toboggan." By this time the waves were up over the ship's island superstructure, and Ford was taking a twenty-second slide down the flight deck. "It scared the hell out of me," he later admitted. "I was going overboard."

Before the war, Ford had been an all-American football player at the University of Michigan and had passed up a professional contract in order to attend Yale Law School. But he remained in good shape, and aside from his duties as a gunnery officer he was also the *Monterey*'s athletic director. Crewmates groused that Ford was "an exercise nut," who, if he caught them goldbricking or loafing, even off duty, would order them to break into sets of jumping jacks. To his credit, Ford would jump right alongside them. It was likely that this dexterity is what saved his life as the white-veined water washed him across the flight deck of the carrier.

Around the deck of every aircraft carrier is a tiny steel lip, about two inches high, called the deck combing, designed to keep the flight crews' tools from slipping overboard. When Ford's feet collided with the combing, he managed to slow his slide enough to twist like an acrobat, grab the ridge with his fingertips, and fling himself down onto the ship's catwalk.

He landed flat on his back. As the *Monterey* reeled through another trough, he got to his knees, made his way back belowdecks, and started back up again. "Well, let me tell you," he said, "my second trip back from that catwalk to the bridge, I was much more careful. I was scared as hell."

When Ford reached the bridge, he found Captain Ingersoll struggling to keep the *Monterey* on her heading. Moments past 9:00 A.M., Ingersoll sent a distress message to Rear Adm. Alfred E. Montgomery, commander of the *Monterey*'s task group.

"Cannot hold present 180-degree course. Am coming to 140 degrees at 15 knots."

But it was futile to attempt to sail into the cross-swell. A moment later Montgomery received a more alarming message from Ingersoll: "Present course 220 degrees. All planes on my hangar deck on fire."

The *Monterey* carried thirty-four aircraft—fighters and torpedo bombers—divided and stowed between the flight and hangar decks.

Before retiring the previous night, Ingersoll had ordered all topside planes as well as any movable gear lashed down with half-inch cable. He'd also had the aviation fuel drained from the aircraft stored below.

Oddly, the exposed aircraft on the *Monterey*'s flight deck remained knotted tight for the moment. Down in the hangar deck, however, one plane had burst its cables and begun bouncing about "like a pinball." When it crashed into other aircraft, they too broke loose, and showers of sparks flew like the Fourth of July as warbirds collided with each other and slammed into the ship's bulkheads. The sparks from the collisions ignited the planes' gas tanks and turned them into skidding torches. Although the tanks had been drained, it was impossible to deplete them of every last drop of fuel, much less the explosive gasoline vapors.

The hangar deck of the *Monterey* became a burning cauldron of aircraft fuel, and one flaming plane plunged down into the carrier's elevator shaft, threatening the magazines stored in the ship's bowels.

As all hands worked frantically to jettison the ammunition before the heat touched it off, flames from the burning aircraft were sucked down into the air intakes of the lower decks, and fires began breaking out below. Jerry Ford remembered the smoke he smelled when he bolted from his rack. Because of a quirk in her construction, the vents designed to channel fresh air into the *Monterey*'s engine and boiler rooms were now funneling thick, oily, black smoke. One black gang sailor was already dead, and another thirty-three were down with asphyxiation.

With no one to tend them, three of the ship's four boilers were out. If she lost her last boiler, the carrier would also lose pressure in the fire hoses now fighting the conflagration in the hangar deck.

The *Monterey* was ablaze from bow to stern as Ford stood near the helm awaiting orders from Ingersoll. From a distance she must have looked like she'd taken Greek Fire, for over the TBS the officers in her pilothouse overheard a transmission from an unknown vessel. "Well, check off the *Monterey*," came the disembodied words.

But Ingersoll would not let go so easily. He directed Ford to lead a team down to the hangar deck, evacuate the wounded, and try to douse the flames. Before Ford could comply, Ingersoll received an order from Halsey relayed via Admiral Montgomery. Halsey, informed of the *Monterey*'s plight, had decided to abandon her. Ingersoll was told that two cruisers and several destroyers had been directed to steam abreast of his carrier to rescue survivors, more of a pipe dream than a practical reality in these seas.

Ingersoll mulled Halsey's directive for a moment, then scanned the raging ocean. He turned to look into the faces of the men huddled about him in the pilothouse. Each, including Ford, was a pale silhouette in the dark. "No," he said. "We can fix this."

He radioed Montgomery to advise Admiral Halsey of his decision. There was precedent to Ingersoll's resolution. War planners in Washington had long suspected, if not exactly articulated, that in the early stages of World War II too many American vessels had been lost due to hasty orders from panicky captains to abandon ship. The Navy Department was clearly displeased. As a pointed reminder, the cover line on the department's 1944 *Damage Control Manual* was a none-too-subtle "Don't Give Up the Ship."

Now, with a nod from Ingersoll, Ford donned a gas mask and led a fire brigade below. Aircraft gas tanks exploded as hose handlers slid across the burning hangar deck. Into this furnace Ford took his men, his first order of business to carry out the unconscious survivors. As one firefighter was overcome by smoke, or burned by the shooting flames, another sailor took his place.

At 9:41 A.M. the *Monterey*'s Captain Ingersoll radioed Admiral Montgomery, "Have fire under control. Prefer to lie to until we can make formation speed."

In near-miraculous fashion, one by one the carrier's boilers were brought back on line. Of her 34 aircraft, she'd lost 18 burned in the hangar deck or blown off the flight deck, with the remaining 16 seriously damaged.

Thirty years later, after Lt. (j.g.) Jerry Ford became president of the United States, he wrote of that morning, "I remembered that fire at the height of the typhoon, and I considered it a marvelous metaphor for the ship of state."

Aboard too many of Halsey's ships on that December day in 1944, however, reality was outpacing metaphor. About the same time that Halsey received word of Ingersoll's refusal to abandon the *Monterey*, the carrier USS *Cowpens* reported fire raging across her hangar deck and was saved only when the wind and water tore off the deck's heavy steel roller door as if it were Styrofoam and the sea flooded in knee-deep, dousing the flames. On the USS *Altamaha*, a bomb truck snapped its fastening cable and collided with a fighter plane. The aircraft's fuel tank detonated, igniting planes on either side of it. The ship's fire extinguisher system drowned the fire, but the torrents of water gushing down her fractured ventilator shaft flooded her lower compartments. Thirty-two of her planes would eventually be swept overboard.

And the 11,000-ton USS *San Jacinto* reported rolling so precipitously that her skipper glimpsed the carrier's screws in the air above him as she tottered on the edge of a giant comber. She then keeled over to port at a 45-degree angle and planed into a trough. The strain of the water crashing over her palisades was too much for the steel cables lashing down aircraft in her hangar deck. The planes broke free and ran amok, lacerating the ship's ventilator ducts, steam pipes, and oil lines. The oil ignited, and the deck proved too slippery for firefighting teams.

As the fire spread, the pilots aboard the *San Jacinto* were instructed to abandon their ready room, and her captain considered the situation hopeless—until one enterprising junior officer ordered that hand lines be strung from overhead beams bracing the hangar deck. "One hand for the ship and one for yourselves, boys!" he shouted, and the fires were brought under control.

Halsey's drawbridge eyebrows rose when he was told of the young man's heroism, and he made a mental note to find the officer and personally commend him. In fact, across the entire fleet spontaneous acts of individual valor by boys and men barely out of their teens, and some still in them, became routine. *Quick's the word and sharp's the action.*

When the destroyer USS *Taussig* lost all its power, the ship's physician, Dr. John Blankenship, tied himself to a makeshift operating table and performed an emergency appendectomy, his scalpel sparkling in the vessel's guttering oil lamps. And when a forward fireroom airlock hatch blew on the destroyer *Dewey*, Chief Watertender Andrew Tolmie struggled toward the flooded airlock over scorching steam lines and up a swaying ladder. The seas in the lock bruted him violently, yet, stunned and battered, Tolmie reached the flapping outer hatch and managed to reseal it.

Aboard the destroyer *Thatcher*, two seamen, Jack Maurey and Stan Lubinsky, volunteered as ropechockers to keep taut the hawsers strung fore and aft that men used as handholds while crossing the deck. When they saw a depth charge break from its rack, roll loose, and bounce into the sea, Maurey held fast to Lubinsky's legs as he crawled to the cage and wrestled the gate's locking pin back into place.

And on the *Monterey* a flight deckhand, fresh from fighting fires with Lt. Jerry Ford below, attempted to secure a runaway fighter plane that had broken its mooring. He was lifted like a kite by a 100-knot gust and blown into the sea. A fellow crewman risked his life by shimmying to the edge of the deck to hurl a fire hose in his general direction and, miraculously, the sailor came to the surface right beside it. He grabbed the hose and pulled himself, hand over hand, back aboard. On the flight deck, he joked to his rescuer that he'd needed "a good cold bath after fighting those damn fires."

At the same time, as black smoke and fire edged toward the pilots' ready room on the *Monterey*, the airmen stationed on the carrier made their way topside to escape. Strapped into their yellow Mae West life vests, they lay flat on their stomachs clutching the heaving deck's pad eyes, watching aircraft crash about them like rogue elephants. Among them was twenty-five-year-old Lt. Ronald P. Gift, commanding officer of the carrier's torpedo plane squadron.

Presently the *Monterey* crested a wave, and Gift squinted through the spindrift and spotted a destroyer in the distance. The ship was nearly vertical, bow up, as if rearing and about to fly like an arrow from a bowstring into the gunmetal sky. Gift lost sight of the vessel as the *Monterey* slid into a trough. But a moment later, climbing another giant comber, Gift again saw the DD, still vertical, but this time bow down, its screws spinning freely in the air.

Suddenly there was a commotion among the pilots, laid out like sardines in a tin. A flier, Ray Thorpe, XO of the fighter squadron, had lost his grip and tumbled over the side. Squadron mates squirmed on their bellies to the edge of the flight deck. Forming a human chain, they slid down to the catwalk as the *Monterey* crested another wave. From this vantage point they watched as Thorpe, more than one hundred feet below, floundered in the wash, the carrier's hull threatening to crush him. When the *Monterey* descended into the next trough, its catwalk nearly dipped into the sea. And there, not two feet in front of his fellow airmen, was the flailing Ray Thorpe. They reached out and pulled him back aboard just as the ship began to roll and climb the next swell.

Such valiant narratives, however, proved the exception to the rule. By midmorning, Third Fleet communications shops were in chaos. Radar stations were unable to plot the locations of individual ships in task groups, and though flag plot was still capable of receiving TBS messages, few were encouraging.

Aboard the jeep escort carrier *Cape Esperance*, lookout Paul Schlener may have been recovered from the center mast, but so many planes had broken loose from their lashings on the flight deck that her commander, Capt. R. W. Bockius, feared that his bridge would topple, as it was being slammed by rogue aircraft. Ignoring protocol that forbade smoking in the wheelhouse, Bockius turned to his officers and offered each a condemned man's final cigarette. Having smoked them, however, and finding themselves still afloat, they left the bridge and joined their crews, including men released from the brig, in fighting fires burning on both decks.

Two war correspondents aboard the *Cape Esperance* noticed that the ship's enlisted men had already begun referring to the vessel, constructed by Kaiser Steelworks, as a "Kaiser coffin." The ship listed so perilously that the starboard gun wells were taking water, and the wind blew so hard that it sandblasted paint from the bridge. One seaman standing watch atop a gun mount high over the flight deck drew his hands back in horror after wiping what he thought was saltwater from his cheeks. The capillaries in his eyes had burst, and the liquid trickling down his face was blood.

Even before her fires were contained, Captain Bockius radioed Halsey that his deck guns and sights had been so severely damaged by aircraft ramming into their mounts before flying overboard that they were useless for combat. The *Cape Esperance*, he added, was dropping out of formation because of steering malfunction. Every one of her planes except a single, unmarked Hellcat fighter was wrecked or had been lost over the side.

In rapid succession the escort carrier USS *Kwajalein* transmitted that she, too, had been forced to heave to, and the light carrier USS *Langley* reported that she was rolling consistently to 70 degrees from side to side in a snapping, pendulum motion. The destroyer USS *Buchanan*'s gyro compass had broken down, and the disabled *Cowpens* was being assisted by the cruiser USS *Baltimore* and three destroyers.

On top of this, salt to the wound, Halsey also learned from Slew McCain that the oiler group's flagship, the DD *Aylwin*, was again broadcasting distress signals.

CHAPTER 15

Storm losses and damage incurred by Fleet were basically due to (a) Maneuvering the Fleet unknowingly into or near path of a typhoon under false sense of security [based on] unsound aerological advice, based on insufficient data. (b) Certain amount of delay and maneuvering in face of storm in effort to fuel destroyers. In some cases a lack of appreciation by subordinate commanders and COs that dangerous weather conditions existed, until storm had taken charge of the situation.

—ONE OF THE CONCLUSIONS DRAWN BY THE COURT OF INQUIRY INVESTIGATING *"HALSEY'S TYPHOON."*

Though she'd managed to regain power in her generators after her midwatch calamity, the *Aylwin*'s Capt. William Rogers now sent word to McCain that his destroyer was pitching violently and steering blind. At 9:35 A.M. he reported narrowly avoiding a collision with another of the task group's screening vessels—which one he had no way of determining—and by 11:00 A.M. the ship was sluicing through waves so huge that her inclinometer was registering 70-degree rolls.

At one point she lay over on her beam-ends for twenty minutes, completely out of control. "Hanging on the brink of nothingness," one seaman described the sensation. Her radar and communications gear hung in ruins, and the pounding ocean had torn her port lifeboat from its davits. In a moment the davits were gone, too.

From his station on the bridge, Rogers warily eyed the tons of green water crashing into the *Aylwin*'s depth-charge racks. He briefly considered jettisoning the ash cans before their "safe" settings were jarred loose. But the ship was now nearly prone, her engines having failed again. Rogers worried that he would be signing his crew's death warrant should one of the sub killers explode directly beneath her.

He coped as best he could, directing all hands to don life jackets and packing as many men as he could spare into the starboard living compartments in an attempt to offset the giant rolls to port. Fire-control parties dashed from stem to stern as electrical fires broke out about the ship, one even blazing across the bridge. Each was eventually brought under control.

In the end, however, Rogers had no choice but to cede the battle to the sea. He stopped all engines and allowed the *Aylwin* to settle in irons, heading downwind, wallowing in the trough of the huge waves like a bathtub toy. Lying to like this, however, allowed tons of seawater to course through her engine-blower intakes. One generator was washed out, and five feet of water stood in the engine room bilges. Without its ventilation blowers the engine room seethed, and across the ship the thin steel of the bulkheads grew superheated as steam filled the engineering spaces below. Fireroom personnel attempting to restore power could work no more than ten-minute shifts in the 180-degree heat.

The *Aylwin*'s chief engineer and his machinist's mate had doffed their life jackets in the sweltering conditions. They kept them off in order to slip through the narrow overhead hatchway leading topside. Before they could don them again they were both blown overboard. Crewmates tossed them lifelines, but could do nothing more.

Neither man was recovered. Rogers wondered if he and the rest of his crew would shortly join them.

Just after 10:00 A.M., Commander Kosco stepped outside flag chart on the *New Jersey* to again observe, firsthand, the hellacious winds and spume. The salt spray was vicious, cutting into the skin on his face like tiny knives. And the gale-force wind was backing counterclockwise, meaning only one thing: Third Fleet was indeed sailing through a typhoon.

Kosco's gut feeling became official when the carrier *Wasp*, steaming well east of the *New Jersey*, reported picking up the eye of the storm on her short-range radar. Someone looking at the radar screen knew what that vortex meant. At 11:49, Halsey finally issued the order releasing all vessels from fleetwide formation. Among his ship's captains, this was likened to Mrs. O'Leary reporting her cow missing. It would still be another two hours before he sent an official typhoon warning to Fleet Weather Central at Pearl Harbor.

As the hours passed, the fleet's more easterly vessels began to fill in the bleak picture. Kosco was informed that winds near the typhoon's center were blowing steady at 125 knots. Seas had grown from "high" to "very high" to "mountainous," although the rain and swirling scud made accurate height recordings difficult. Ships caught in irons reported waves, streaked with white, foamy veins, as tall as one hundred feet. On some vessels crewmen were already gathering in afterdeck houses awaiting orders to abandon ship.

Aboard the *Dewey*, steaming southeast near the typhoon's eye, not a few sailors were making peace with their maker. The blown forward fireroom airlock hatch that Chief Watertender Andrew Tolmie had managed to close had nonetheless allowed nearly a thousand gallons of saltwater to flood the main distribution board. Her power had been shorted, she had no generators, and she was rolling heavily to starboard, dragging her shattered, flapping antenna wires behind her like broken wings. She was in fact listing so precariously that waves were cresting her gunwales, and her starboard weather deck was submerged for sixty seconds at a time.

On the deepest rolls the *Dewey*'s crewmen watched from the wardroom as her XO, Lt. Comdr. Frank Bampton, stepped off the bridge and crawled onto the side of the now-horizontal conning tower in "absolute certainty" he would presently drop into the sea. Bampton wore a look of bemusement when, on each occasion, the

Dewey ever so slowly righted herself and he crawled back down to the pilothouse.

In one sense, if it can be construed so, the *Dewey* was fortunate that destroyer squadron commander Capt. Preston Mercer had chosen her as his flagship. Mercer was the screening commander for all the destroyers in the *Dewey*'s unit, and when Captain Calhoun realized it was idiocy to attempt to maintain fleet formation, he simply turned to Mercer and said, "Commodore, I'm concerned about my ship. I have to save my ship."

Mercer nodded. "I agree with you," he said. With that Calhoun broke station and, in all likelihood, saved the lives of his crew.

At noon the *Dewey*'s barometer read 28.10, a drop of .74 inches in the last hour. Venturing topside was suicide, and her terrified crew huddled belowdecks, where her bulkheads were stove in, leaking badly, and the groans from her creaking frame reverberated through the thin metal plates like the cries of ghosts. Men kneeled in common prayer, and though the *Dewey* sailed with no chaplain, a Protestant lay leader, Quartermaster Lawrence "Preacher" Johnson, gathered as many sailors as possible and led them in a continuous recital of the navy hymn.

In the wardroom on the main deck, the thoughts of Chief Warrant Officer Steven F. Yorden turned to "the poor guys down below; I felt so sorry for them. You know, you're holding on for dear life, with no lights. Those guys dogged down in them compartments—they didn't have a Chinaman's chance to get out of there."

Chief Yorden, dark, squat, with a huge walrus mustache, was in charge of the construction and repair division of the *Dewey*'s shipfitter's shop, and as the destroyer rolled helplessly, he decided to dare an ascent to the bridge to offer assistance. This was treacherous, as Yorden had to await the ship's roll to starboard before opening the compartment's port hatch and making the mad dash across the ship's hull to the skipper's ladder that led up to the wheelhouse.

Timing his movements perfectly, he emerged face-to-face with Captain Calhoun, who shouted above the gale, "What can you do?"

The chief could think of only one option: sever the destroyer's seven-ton gun director, which along with her mast and main stack were acting as sails to keep the ship heeled over. If that didn't work, Yorden added, then cut off her mast, too.

"Cut 'em off," Calhoun ordered.

Yorden returned to the wardroom and asked for volunteers to help him retrieve acetylene torches and oxygen tanks from the shipfitter's shop in the bow of the vessel. An electrician and a gunner's mate stepped forward. The three made their way to the stem and managed to drag the heavy acetylene and oxygen bottles back to the wardroom through the pitch-black interior of the *Dewey*. It was only after Yorden ran the oxygen hose out onto the deck that he realized that the acetylene torch would not cut through the aluminum at the base of the gun director. He crawled back to the pilothouse.

"Can't do it," he told Calhoun. "She's made out of aluminum. I'll start working on the mast."

After crewmates tied a lifeline around Yorden's waist, he began belly-crawling across the deck. Twice he was washed overboard. Twice he was "fished back out." Reaching the base of the mast, Yorden now realized he could not keep his acetylene torch lit in the gale. He tried several times; in each instance the wind and spume immediately doused the flame. He returned to the bridge, his eyes met Calhoun's, and he motioned wordlessly in the direction of the destroyer's portside lifeboat. It seemed their last, best hope.

An instant later a stupendous wave, slashed with blue shadows, slammed into the *Dewey*, rolling her over more than 70 degrees to port. Seawater cascaded through the bridge's smashed windows. The helmsman swung with the wheel, water up to his armpits. Calhoun was slammed against the bulkhead, where he landed in a tangle of arms and legs with his officer of the deck. The two scrambled to their feet and watched incredulously as the inclinometer climbed past 70 degrees, past 80 degrees, before finally coming to rest at 84 degrees.

Lieutenant Commander Henry Plage (sunglasses) and Lieutenant Howard Korth of the USS *Tabberer* enjoying R&R on one of the American-held Pacific islands in 1944. *(Courtesy of Russ Plage)*

An official portrait of Admiral William Frederick Halsey Jr. *(National Archives photo)*

A still-unfinished USS *Tabberer*, a destroyer escort, being launched on February 18, 1944, at Brown's Shipyard in Houston, Texas. *(National Archives photo)*

The USS *Tabberer* (DE 418), nicknamed by its crew the "Tabby," steams off to join the Pacific Fleet. *(Courtesy of Russ Plage)*

General Douglas MacArthur on the USS *Nashville* overseeing the invasion of Luzon in the Philippines. By his side is General Richard K. Sutherland, the supreme commander's chief of staff. *(National Archives photo)*

"Nothing more than my right arm" is how Halsey characterized Vice Admiral John S. McCain (left), conferring with Halsey en route to the Philippines in December 1944. *(National Archives photo)*

The USS *Hull*, a *Farragut*-class destroyer, returning from maneuvers in the Pacific Ocean. *(National Archives photo)*

The USS *Monaghan*, the destroyer that drew "first blood" at Pearl Harbor. *(National Archives photo)*

The USS *Spence*, a proud member of the "Little Beavers." *(National Archives photo)*

"Bull" Halsey conducts a staff conference aboard his flagship, the USS *New Jersey*, in December 1944. To his left is Rear Admiral "Mick" Carney, his chief of staff. *(National Archives photo)*

Navy pilots challenge USS *Monterey* personnel to a game of basketball in the ship's forward elevator well. Lieutenant (j.g.) Gerald Ford (left, center), the ship's recreation officer, leaps for the ball. *(National Archives photo)*

Pat Douhan, in a photograph taken before he joined the crew of the USS Hull. (*Courtesy of Pat Douhan*)

Evan Fenn, who turned out to be one of seven survivors of the USS *Monaghan*. (*Courtesy of Evan Fenn*)

Keith Abbott, who would become the "ghost sailor" aboard the USS *Monaghan*, pictured during basic training at Camp Farragut in Idaho in May 1943. (*Courtesy of Keith Abbott*)

As Typhoon Cobra intensifies, the USS *Astoria* tries to refuel and resupply. *(Herman Schnipper photo)*

An oil tanker trying without success to move into fueling position on December 17, 1944. *(National Archives photo)*

An unidentified destroyer in trouble as the typhoon overtakes the Third Fleet. The smaller the ship, the more vulnerable it was to capsizing. *(National Archives photo)*

The USS *Langley* is attacked by wind and waves on the morning of December 18, 1944. Even aircraft carriers felt Cobra's fury. *(National Archives photo)*

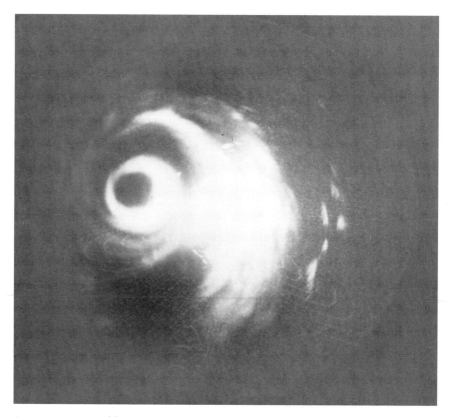

An image captured by U.S. Navy radar on December 18 showing the expanse of Typhoon Cobra. It was the first Pacific typhoon officially assigned a name. *(National Archives photo)*

The *Wisconsin* was one of the battleships that was not immune to the typhoon's onslaught. *(National Archives photo)*

An unidentified ship being swamped by the sea on December 18. Many of the smaller ships were at greater risk because they had become more top-heavy during the war. *(National Archives photo)*

One of the planes destroyed by the storm on the USS *Anzio*, which the *Tabberer* was assigned to protect from submarines. *(National Archives photo)*

Members of the USS *Altamaha*'s crew examine the damage on the carrier's deck. *(National Archives photo)*

The demasted *Tabberer* heading for shelter and repairs after Typhoon Cobra. *(Courtesy of Russ Plage)*

The survivors of the storm saved by Captain Plage and his crew, on the *Tabberer* as the destroyer escort heads to Ulithi. (*Courtesy of Pat Douhan*)

On Ulithi, Lieutenant Commander Plage is congratulated by Admiral Halsey for a job well done. The "Tabby's" captain had expected a court-martial instead. (*Courtesy of Russ Plage*)

Archie DeRyckere and his wife, Jackie, on their wedding day in 1946. It was a day he didn't think he would live to see while floating in the ocean in December 1944. *(Courtesy of Archie DeRyckere)*

A reunion of the men of the USS *Tabberer* in 1984, forty years after Typhoon Cobra. Henry Lee Plage is in his usual spot at such reunions—in the center, surrounded by his loyal crew. The captain was also an honored guest at *Hull* and *Spence* reunions over the years. (*Courtesy of Russ Plage*)

"She's going!" the helmsman shouted, unnecessarily, as every man in the wheelhouse knew well that only divine intervention would save a ship from a roll so precipitous.

And at that moment a sound like the firing of cannons drowned out the gale. Calhoun whipped around as the half-inch guy wire that ran from the deck to support the main forward stack snapped past his ear like a rifle shot. He watched in astonishment as the stack snapped at her base and slowly crumpled.

According to Bowditch, any wind's force increases proportionately as the square of its velocity. Thus, the 110-knot gales the *Dewey* was encountering would have produced about 78 pounds of pressure per square foot on the destroyer's 600-square-foot stack. This amounted to at least 23 tons of sustained pressure on the funnel, taking into account the increases in force due to the breathtaking gusts as well as the seawater now pouring down her spout. Against a weight of this magnitude, it is a wonder that the *Dewey*'s stack had not broken off earlier.

As the funnel collapsed and crashed across the destroyer's deck, it knocked into the sea a gun turret, two ammunition lockers, and the vessel's whaleboat, davits and all. The flattened heap of shredded metal, its tip now dragging through the waves like an abandoned oar, reminded Calhoun "of an old sock that had been thrown across the ship by some playful giant." Black smoke billowed out of the gaping hole on the deck, and white-hot steam shot skyward from a broken line. Yet, with the smokestack no longer holding her over, with this reduction of "sail," the crew of the *Dewey* felt her quiver and begin to stabilize.

Massive waves continued to pitch the vessel to starboard, but she never again rolled as deep. It was as well. For at 1:00 P.M., as she bobbed in a trough, the *Dewey*'s barometer needle went completely off the scale, down to the "U." of "U.S. Navy." One officer estimated that it dipped under 27 inches, perhaps to 26.30—which would have made it the lowest barometer reading ever recorded by the United States Navy. The *Dewey* was sailing through the eye of Typhoon Cobra.

* * *

As noon approached, oiler task group commander Capt. Jasper Acuff found himself out of TBS range on the floundering destroyer *Aylwin*. He dictated a clipped message to be sent via battery-operated VHF to the nearby carrier *Wasp* and forwarded to Vice Admiral McCain on the *Hancock*. Acuff, whose call sign was "Dracula," had moved his command post to the *Aylwin*'s chart house from the bridge, where the shriek of the wind through the smashed wheelhouse windows made it impossible to communicate orders. Acuff's radio operator, sloshing in knee-deep water in the flooded communications shack, dutifully sent off the terse communication.

"Dracula has lost control. Commander Task Group 30.8 unable to control his group."

McCain took the report and ordered the individual commanders of the oiler task group to fall in behind his Task Force 38 as best they could. Despite her tribulations, the *Aylwin* was also lucky. She was still afloat.

As bleak morning turned to bleaker afternoon, Halsey logged increasingly anxious entries into his war diary for December 18:

0942: *The [escort carrier] Kwajalein reported she had lost steering control.*
1007: *Wind 62 knots. Barometer 29.52.*
1012: *The Wisconsin reported one Kingfisher [scout plane] overboard.*
1016: *The [heavy cruiser] Boston reported one Kingfisher overboard.*
1017: *The [escort carrier] Rudyerd Bay reported she was dead in the water.*
1051: *The [light carrier] Cowpens reported fire on her hangar deck.*
1100: *Wind 55 knots. Barometer 29.47.*
1128: *The [escort carrier] Cape Esperance reported fire on her flight deck.*
1300: *Winds 66 knots. Barometer 29.30.*
1310: *Wind velocity increased sharply from 75 to 83 knots, with gusts reaching 93 knots. Barometer 29.23.*

By this time, the peak period of the fleet's encounter with Typhoon Cobra, the sky and sea seemed fused in one aqueous element. The oiler USS *Nantahala* recorded a record wind velocity of 124 knots (or 142.6 miles per hour), and visibility was reported at three feet. Sailors who dared crossed decks by snaking on their stomachs, and turning one's back to the wind created a vacuum in which it was difficult to breathe. Sopping, injured men belowdecks were manhandled as wind and waves pitched and battered their vessels like buoys. Bailing gangs—water penetration repair parties—felt as if they were pushing Sisyphus's rock, and one seaman wondered if he might actually drown *inside* his ship while it was still afloat.

Rising above all this was the cacophony of racked and groaning ships, the creaking of bulkheads, the working of stanchions, the slide and tear and roar of wreckage bouncing from bulkhead to bulkhead.

"No one who [has not] been through a typhoon can conceive its fury," Halsey wrote. "The 70-foot seas smashing you from all sides. The rain and the scud are blinding; they drive at you flat out, until you can't tell the ocean from the air. At broad noon I couldn't see the bow of my ship, 350 feet from the bridge. The *New Jersey* was once hit by a five-inch shell without my feeling the impact; the *Missouri*, her sister, had a kamikaze crash on her main deck and repaired the only damage with a paint brush; yet this typhoon tossed our enormous ship as if she were a canoe. Our chairs, tables, and all loose gear had to be double-lashed; we ourselves were buffeted from one bulkhead to another; we could not hear our own voices above the uproar."

He concluded his entry on a forlorn note: "What it was like on a destroyer one-twentieth the *New Jersey*'s size," he wrote, "I can only imagine."

CHAPTER 16

It was very difficult to see the men with searchlights as the sea was so rough the lights would pass over their heads unless the men were on crests of the sea.

—TESTIMONY OF LT. COMDR. HENRY LEE PLAGE, U.S. NAVY, CAPTAIN, USS TABBERER, TO THE COURT OF INQUIRY INVESTIGATING "HALSEY'S TYPHOON."

By midmorning the *Monaghan* had been drifting for hours without power. Despite Capt. Bruce Garrett's lack of command experience, he had done a magnificent job of helming her through the storm. Like a nineteenth-century sail master, he'd fought to keep her running before the wind, countering the ship's natural tendency to broach-to each time she yawed with only the use of his rudder. Yet for all Garrett's labors, the *Monaghan* had never been able to ballast her empty aft bunkers with seawater. She was down to thirty thousand gallons of fuel and sloughing like a rubber raft. Her crew sensed the inevitable.

Below, in the ship's forward fireroom, twenty-one-year-old Fireman 1st Class Evan Fenn had finished standing his 4:00-to-8:00 A.M. watch. Living belowdecks, Fenn, a rough-and-tumble former railroad worker, was accustomed to being bounced about the bowels of the ship by "a little rough water." Still, he had to admit his surprise when he came topside and, timing his sprints between pounders, it took him almost an hour to cross the heaving deck to his quarters in the stern. When he arrived, the berths about his were dark, nearly empty.

He spotted a shipmate running through the companionway and hollered to him. The sailor yelled back over his shoulder that men had already begun gathering topside, in the destroyer's after deckhouse. Fenn climbed up to the deckhouse and discovered 40 or 50 sailors wedged into the small compartment. They were standing shoulder to shoulder, adjusting an assortment of kapok and older Mae West life jackets. Among them was the ship's "oil king," Senior Watertender Joe McCrane.

At 11:30 the *Monaghan*'s last generator failed and all her lights blinked off. McCrane, Fenn, and a few others groped their way back to lockers below to retrieve flashlights. They returned to find every sailor reciting, aloud, the Lord's Prayer. *For thine is the Kingdom, the Power, and the Glory.*

The waves were coming in constant sets from starboard. With each stupendous roll, the man beside McCrane shouted, "Don't let us down now, Dear Lord. Bring it back, Oh God, bring it back." With every return from a list, more voices joined in, chanting in unison, "Thanks, Dear Lord."

McCrane counted seven giant rolls before he and his shipmates were lifted as one off the deck's steel plating. His stomach rose to his throat as the *Monaghan* slide-slipped down the face of a sheer wall of water. She landed on her starboard quarter. An avalanche of ocean entombed her, and another, and another. She lolled on her side as if gasping for breath, pummeled by whitewater. Her 1,400 tons of steel frame quivered, and began tearing apart.

On the bridge of the destroyer *Spence*, Lt. Comdr. James Andrea turned to his executive officer: "What's the Beaufort?"

"Force sixteen," said the XO. It was a grim joke. Force 12—or "that which no canvas could withstand," as Adm. Sir Francis

Beaufort calculated—is the maximum rating on the mariner's scale of wind intensity.

Andrea glanced at his barometer. It read 27.40. The anemometer was spinning at 125 knots. Great jagged bolts of lightning illuminated the starboard sky.

"It's impossible," the *Spence*'s navigator said. His voice was dull, resigned.

"I know," Andrea said.

The *Spence*'s power panels and circuits had already shorted out, one by one. Her lights, radio, and radar were gone, followed presently by her steering motors. Her masts were bent like saplings, her whaleboat swung in the wind like a ragged pennant, and she was running on one boiler. Her rudder was jammed hard right, which left her wallowing broadside to the waves, and a foot of saltwater stood in all compartments below. Men worked furiously to shore her crumpling bulkheads.

A runner appeared on the bridge. "After deckhouse buckled," he said.

Andrea nodded. He was staring at the destroyer's stern, where a fifty-foot gash in the hull, as ugly as an exit wound, stood in place of the two depth-charge racks that were ripped out and carried away by the wind and waves. The Pacific Ocean was cascading like a waterfall into the hold of the *Spence*.

"Sir, we must be taking fifteen hundred gallons of water a minute."

"Form bucket brigades," Andrea said. *For all the good they would do.* The *Spence* was dying, and her captain knew it.

By 11:00 A.M. the storm had stripped clean the *Hull*'s deck. Lost were her long-range communications equipment and whaleboat, and most of her depth charges had been swept from their racks. Chief Quartermaster Archie DeRyckere, bolted to the wheelhouse floor, watched from on high as the metal covers of her ammunition lockers blew away, their screw-down hasps snapped in the gale.

He wondered if the bridge itself would shortly disintegrate. Viking blood DeRyckere may have possessed, but so did Canute, and neither could stem this tide.

Since daybreak Captain Marks had inexplicably attempted to conform to Halsey's orders to remain in fleet formation, straining the engines at 22 knots, at one point even volunteering to aid the burning carrier *Monterey*. That was a joke. The *Hull*'s main propulsion systems were capable of developing close to 50,000 horsepower, but given the raucous state of the seas, DeRyckere thought it doubtful that she was making half that force as she tried to break free of the trough.

When the scud and spume had knocked out the *Hull*'s electrical grid and surface radar, Marks sent a general distress call via VHS radio, asking to be kept abreast of the whereabouts of any ships in the vicinity. He feared a collision. DeRyckere smiled, grim, at this. As if it would make a difference.

The wheelhouse's windows were shattered, and as the wind and waves whipped about him, Archie DeRyckere had already begun to consider his beloved destroyer in the past tense. The *Hull* had been a tough little fish. She'd fought nobly in the Aleutians and distinguished herself during Spruance's Turkey Shoot by rescuing several downed pilots. DeRyckere remembered the thrill of blasting enemy planes in the Marshalls and Gilberts, and "sinking" a Japanese schooner during the seesawing battle for Guadalcanal—until the crew discovered that the schooner had already been sunk and was sitting on the shallow bottom. They all had a good laugh about that.

He also recalled the *Hull*'s last refitting, when the vibrations of her turbines, striking a note as clear as a tuning fork, had told him that her engineering plant was in excellent condition. At flank speed, light brown wisps of smoke had coiled up from her stacks, trailing behind for 50 or 60 feet before dissipating into haze. White smoke would have meant the forced draft was giving her too much air, and too little air would have produced billowing black clouds. Now her funnel belched black, gaseous fumes.

The main difficulty had been her instability, and DeRyckere now wished he'd raised more of a protest about it. It was obvious that Nimitz and Halsey urgently needed firepower in the Pacific; the navy hadn't spent all that time and money repairing ships and training sailors to have them sit out the war. Still, the *Hull* had been pushed back in harm's way too soon, well before her top-heaviness could be addressed. Someone should have known. Someone should have said something. DeRyckere knew who that someone should have been.

Unlike the *Spence*, the *Hull* had been able to take ample fuel the previous day; she was sailing with at least 125,000 gallons, well above the minimum requirement for ballasting seawater. As one navy investigator was to note, "The ship's company of the *Hull* probably felt that no ship of the United States Navy could capsize as long as she remained in compliance with ballasting instructions applicable to her class."

DeRyckere recalled the edginess of the *Hull*'s crew when they'd arrived in Ulithi in early November. They were spoiling for a fight, and every man jack knew that the Philippines campaign was on deck, with the big invasions of Japan to ensue. More's the pity, he thought now, as he was fairly sure that the *Hull* would never get the opportunity to follow Halsey into Tokyo Bay.

Chief Bosun's Mate Ray Schultz now edged next to DeRyckere and shouted into his ear, "I joined the damn navy to fight, not to drown!" But the words barely registered, as DeRyckere was distracted by a strange noise emanating from the corner of the bridge. He turned to find the twenty-year-old enlisted man "Punchy" Parker weeping. Parker was the ship's intramural boxing champion, and DeRyckere considered him one of the toughest sailors he'd ever met.

"I can't swim," Punchy Parker sobbed. The man was shivering. "I can't swim."

DeRyckere grabbed Parker by the shoulders and shook him hard. "Listen, none of us are going to make it any better than you are," he said. "You don't have to swim. You got a life jacket, don't you?"

Then DeRyckere pointed to another huge breaker crashing over the *Hull*'s bow.

"Who the hell you think is gonna swim in that mess anyway?"

* * *

From his post high up in the *Monaghan*'s combat information center, radar maintenance technician Keith Abbott had a direct sight line to the ship's inclinometer. He'd watched it inch past 78 degrees on several steep rolls and marveled at the sensation of sliding down the crest of an eighty-foot-high wall of water. When the ship slapped into the troughs, she made an earsplitting noise, like a clap of thunder, and on each occasion Abbott silently thanked God that Lieutenant Commander Garrett had been able to pull her out. Abbott was in awe of the skipper, "a real destroyer navy man," who had not set foot off the flying bridge since dawn.

There had been little conversation in the *Monaghan*'s pilothouse since early morning, when she'd lost not only her power, but her forward stack. There was nothing left to say. At some point before the communications shop went silent, her radio operators had picked up anonymous TBS chatter, most of it desperate, much of it cursing Admiral Halsey's refusal to release Third Fleet from formation stations. Abbott also overheard a distress call from the *Hull*, her sister ship, which was apparently floundering. But the *Monaghan*'s crew had its own problems to contend with. There was a palpable feeling among the officers on the bridge that only a miracle could save their fabled little destroyer.

A few minutes before noon, Abbott stepped out onto the open wing surrounding the wheelhouse. On earlier occasions he had been able to snatch occasional glimpses of the tall masts of carriers and cruisers, and the proximity of friendly ships had somehow reassured him. Now what he saw on the horizon was the largest wave yet bearing down on the *Monaghan*. Beneath its foaming white crown, the comber was as black as a rolling sandstorm, and when it collided with the ship, she shuddered and lifted, as if blasted from the ocean by a depth charge.

Abbott leaped for a handhold and was knocked into the bridge railing as the *Monaghan* twisted, reeled, and began the long descent, as if in slow motion, down the face of the wave. She landed on her side, and seawater surged through her superstructure. The rush of ocean knocked Abbott back into the pilothouse, where he caught a final glimpse of the inclinometer. It had passed 78 degrees. He nearly laughed. It was the only instrument on the ship still working.

Abbott thought of his bride, and the baby daughter he had never seen, and for an instant wondered over the "simple twist of fate" that had conveyed him from his cozy berth on the destroyer escort *Emery* to this doomed vessel. As a sailor on temporary detail he had been something of a loner, and he hadn't gotten to know many of his *Monaghan* shipmates. There were the seamen in the communications shack, of course, and a few officers and enlisted men stationed regularly on the bridge. But he'd never acquired that sensation of camaraderie common to fighting ships' crews, and, now, in some bizarre sense, he regretted not knowing the names of the men with whom he was about to die.

He felt a thrum in his gut, and a slightly metallic sensation developed in the back of his throat. It took Keith Abbott a moment to recognize the taste of fear.

Bob Ayers asked himself if this could really be life in the United States Navy. Eight days into his first billet aboard the *Spence*, and he'd spent the first four making ratlines and the last four thanking God they were in place to catch him before he was pitched over the side. Bad luck had not yet abandoned him. At 8:00 A.M. he'd finished his watch in the pilothouse and headed below to eat yet another cold bacon sandwich. Two straight days of cold bacon sandwiches. Ayers was sick of cold bacon sandwiches.

In the mess he'd met his friend Floyd Balliett, with whom he had shipped out on the train from Great Lakes Naval Station, through Pearl, and on to Ulithi. Floyd was a Florida kid, just turned eighteen, and he and Ayers—two newbies among an established destroyer crew—had formed a greenhorns' bond. They finished their sandwiches together, and Ayers suggested they make their way topside. Balliett said he wanted nothing to do with that, and

Ayers, left alone, climbed as far as the companionway leading to the base of the bridge.

As he stumbled yet again from the ship's heavy heels, a blast of warm air whistled across the deck, and Ayers realized they were close to the eye of the typhoon. He was hanging on tight to a cross-bar near the starboard hatch of the radio shack, deliberating his next move, when the *Spence* took a huge roll to port. He ducked into the shack—fell in, really—and banged against four or five sailors clustered against the port bulkhead.

He said, "Hey, look at this." He was standing on the bulkhead, the vertical deck rising before his eyes. No one answered him.

The ship came back from the roll, but she never did swing to starboard like the manual said. Another wave sent her listing even deeper to port, and from this one she did not recover. The *Spence* was on her side now, at the bottom of a trough, and Ayers scrambled with his shipmates from the radio shack. His knees buckled as he stood on the side of the wheelhouse. Waves washed over him, but he was not sure where to go. The ship had two lifeboats as well as a dozen life rings; Ayers could see none of them.

He finally guessed that his only slim chance was to reach the bridge's starboard rail, the solid-panel rail, and from there shin out to the rigging. And then? He had no idea, but he'd worry about that when the time came.

In any event, Ayers never made it. He'd edged across the side of the starboard bulkhead and barely managed to swing himself up onto the bridge railing when the *Spence* began to turn turtle. He stood on the rail as the sea swirled and hissed about him, rising to his ankles, to his knees, to his waist.

It was only then that Ayers remembered he'd left his life vest at his battle station, number 27 gun mount, far back in the stern. He studied the rising sea and fretted for his new friend Floyd Balliett, trapped somewhere belowdecks. He wondered if Balliett had remembered to wear his.

* * *

Petty Officer 2nd Class Pat Douhan cursed himself. How could he have been so stupid, leaving his kapok up on the *Hull*'s bridge like that? He had meant to retrieve it at daylight—if you could call this spitty mess daylight—but when he'd been relieved from his sonar watch, he was bone-weary. He promised himself he'd go back for it after just a few moments of sack time. Now that Douhan thought about it, that had been pretty foolish, too, imagining that he could sleep through this blow.

Tossed from his bunk repeatedly, he'd risen, dressed, and just made his way across the vessel's treacherous deck from bow to stern—don't ask him how; don't ask him why; he was certain he'd seen men being blown over the side—when the *Hull* took the big roll to starboard. Douhan flung himself through the hatch of the house mounting the 5-inch guns. He was startled to find five or six terrified shipmates jammed into the compartment. He noticed straightaway that they all were wearing life jackets.

With a loud *bang!* the hatch on the gun mount's starboard side blew. The steel door soared into the gray sky as if shot from a howitzer, and the compartment began taking water. Each time the ship took a starboard roll, the deckhouse would fill with more sea, and in the confused recesses of his mind Douhan realized his fellow sailors were yelling, screaming, "Reverse those rudders! Reverse the goddamn rudders!"

Douhan knew Captain Marks better than that. The man would never break station, even if he could hear the hollered pleas, which he could not. No, Marks would sail the ship to hell first, and when that notion sank in, Pat Douhan, gripping an overhead roll bar for dear life, began to wonder how he would escape this death trap.

CHAPTER 17

Court: *"How did you get out of the passageway just forward of the galley when the ship capsized?"*
"I climbed on the side of the bulkhead of the issue room just alongside of the port hatch. I sat there until all the rush had gone by. I couldn't get out because of the number of men going up. They were just knocking you every way."

—TESTIMONY OF ROY G. MORGAN, FIREMAN 2ND CLASS, USS HULL, TO THE COURT OF INQUIRY INVESTIGATING *"HALSEY'S TYPHOON."*

When she broached to starboard for the final time, the *Monaghan's* oil king, Joe McCrane, was knocked over with violence and became snarled in a sweaty ball of men's bodies. The destroyer bobbed on her side, and the after deckhouse's portside hatch was nearly directly above him, perhaps ten feet away. McCrane watched three or four crewmates put their shoulders into it, balancing precariously on the prone bulkhead.

The wind and waves were beating hard against the door, and it took several moments before it swung open, and in good order sailors began filing out. McCrane felt an incongruous flush of pride. There was no panic. Each seaman waited his turn patiently. Given the circumstances, there was little, if any, confusion.

Third Class Gunner's Mate Joe Guio, with no concern for his own safety, squatted outside the hatch in the lee of the gun mount, pulling men out one by one in a chain, like tent caterpillars ascending a tree. But the waves were too strong, and when sailors reached the open deck, most were lashed overboard unless they quickly found something to cling to.

For the fireman Evan Fenn this was a single depth charge, the last still attached to its rack. Soon enough, however, Fenn's grip gave out, and he was carried over the destroyer's fantail and into the sea. About him the ocean foamed and bubbled under a cloud of black smoke issuing like a death rattle from the *Monaghan*'s coughing boilers.

Fenn became tangled in the wires trailing from the ship's wrecked antenna, and as they whipped him about like a gaffed marlin, he saw several crewmates being pounded to pulp against the side of the heaving vessel. He managed to disengage himself and began swimming away from the gurgling *Monaghan* as fast as he could.

Since early morning, gun mechanic Floyd Balliett had been certain the *Spence* was going to sink. He didn't know quite how to explain the premonition, and he certainly had not articulated his thoughts to anyone, not even his new friend Bob Ayers as they shared cold bacon sandwiches down in the galley. It was just a gut feeling, and though he was only several months in the navy, Floyd Balliett had learned to trust his gut. It was why he was wearing his kapok.

Most of his shipmates had not followed suit. The kapok life jackets were bulky, and the access hatches leading topside were so small that it was difficult to wriggle through them while wearing one. Many of his crewmates had stashed theirs on the deck outside the hatches, within easy reach should they need them in a pinch. Of course, many of Balliett's crewmates had not figured that the *Spence* would go "Tango Uniform"—Tits Up—in the blink of an eye.

Balliett was in his compartment below the bow when a huge comber rolled the *Spence* hard to port. Tons of seawater lashed her exposed hull, and he heard men screaming, crying—the noise reminded him of newborns in a hospital maternity room—as they raced from their berths into the narrow, clogged companionways. They were bashed against bulkheads as they hauled themselves up hand over hand, clawing and fighting each other as well as the deluge streaming into the passages.

Balliett was lithe and quick, and even while strapped into his kapok he was able to pick his way among the berserkers until he was standing almost directly beneath a starboard hatch in the bow of the ship. The knot of sailors flailing and rolling and crawling beneath the hatch were either too confused or too frozen with fear to move. They wouldn't mount the ladder, and they wouldn't get out of his way.

Balliett lifted himself to the top of the scrum and began climbing over men until he reached the open air. A jet stream of water gushed in through the opening, and he fought it hard, forcing first his head, then his shoulders, and then his entire torso through the hatch until he was standing on the starboard hull. He looked back, reached down, and extended a hand through the foaming cataract. No one grabbed it.

Any damn fool could see that the *Hull* was sinking. Archie DeRyckere reckoned that someone forgot to tell the ship. She was trying to sit up, God bless her, fighting like hell to come out of her roll. DeRyckere could feel the vibrations of the engines straining beneath his feet. She was gutsy, all right, but as the old tars often said, there was the devil to pay and no pitch hot. She was at too much of a disadvantage in this wind and big sea, at nature's mercy, and at the moment nature did not appear very forgiving.

DeRyckere was on the bridge, bucking up the panicky kid Punchy Parker, when he looked aft and noticed the eight-foot screws ticking over in the air from whatever pressure was left in the boilers. Across the stern, any sailors who could scrambled from belowdecks—crawling from hatches, wriggling through portholes and blower vents. Men streamed out of the after deckhouse like ants poked with a burning stick. Some were washed overboard and cut to pieces by the turning propellers. Others made the mistake of attempting to climb back aboard. But as the syncopated break-ers drove the ship deeper into the sea, the nearest floaters were crushed.

DeRyckere watched as one crewmate, a fire controlman from Cincinnati, tried to claw his way back just as one of the 5-inch guns swung down and caved his head in like a melon. Even in this mael-strom the chief could make out the blood in the water. He won-dered about sharks. Did they attack in high seas?

Groups of sailors huddled together on the side of the heaving vessel, clinging to gun screens, radar mounts, anything to keep from plunging into the roiling water. But as the ocean scoured the floun-dering *Hull*, each successive wave thinned their ranks. He caught a movement out of the corner of his eye and turned to see a seaman, he couldn't tell whom, calmly stroll to the end of the horizontal main stack and step off into the water.

DeRyckere glanced one last time at his navigation charts. Another hundred miles south, less than two degrees of latitude, and they'd all be laughing about the close call with the typhoon. Now the *Hull* was almost horizontal, and DeRyckere stepped out onto the side of the wheelhouse to watch the stack dip into the sea. The funnel came back up slightly, but he knew what it meant. How many tons of water the *Hull* "swallowed" was anyone's guess. More sailors arrived on the bridge from below, huddled together, no one saying a word.

The *Monaghan* bobbed on her side, and "oil king" Joe McCrane clung to the ship's gun shelter. His eyes scanned the waterline as shipmates and friends were crushed to death beneath the rocking destroyer. He frantically adjusted his rubber-tube life vest and re-minded himself to stroke for all he was worth when his turn finally came. The ship's metal plates were keening when a spout of foam-ing green water snatched him and swept him over the side.

McCrane was pushed deep under the wave and lost all sense of direction. He felt as if he were caught in a whirlpool. He clawed like a madman for the surface, banging off flailing bodies as he forced himself upward. Unseen hands clutched at his arms, his feet, his head; he shook them all loose. When he emerged at the waterline, another large swell lifted him and rammed him shoulder-first into the side of the *Monaghan*'s port torpedo tubes. This, he thought, was a chance.

He hefted himself back onto the ship and picked out the highest point he could make out through the spume, the side of the 20mm gun shield. He started climbing, crawling really, his hands and feet seeking any purchase, his fingernails nearly digging into the steel hull, like a child inching up a jungle gym. He had nearly reached the gun shield when another wave enveloped him, tossing him sideways and wrapping him around the ship's prone antenna. The current spun him about the metal pole three or four times, propelled him into the air, threw him loose, and deposited him back in the sea.

The pain was like electricity shooting through his torso, and McCrane thought his ribs were surely broken. He again found himself almost beneath the ship, her wheelhouse churning like a piston. It was all he could do to keep from being pummeled. Water and fuel oil choked him, gagged him. He began beating the water, "like a puppy," trying to will himself away from the pounding steel. He was on the brink of panic.

"No," he told himself, "conserve your strength. Close your mouth and breathe through your nose. Stop swallowing saltwater and oil, now. Swim."

Midway through his first stroke he was washed under again, this time not as deep. When he surfaced, the *Monaghan* was gone. Vanished. Where? He turned in a 360-degree radius, searching for his ship, his crewmates. It was impossible. The rain and spume stung his face like shrapnel. Visibility was zero. The ocean was empty. Joe McCrane was alone.

It was close to noon, and nineteen-year-old Radioman James Elder was monitoring the TBS from his combat station in the rocking combat information center of the jeep carrier *Cape Esperance*. The frantic chatter he'd listened to all morning had been broken only by static. Now, inexplicably, came a long silence, followed by an all-points distress call. The speaker identified himself as Capt. James Andrea, skipper of the destroyer *Spence*.

"We are taking water down our stacks," Andrea said. His voice was calm, almost matter-of-fact. "We can't make it."

Elder listened for more. No words followed. Moments later the *Cape Esperance*'s executive officer dashed into the CIC.

"Did you get that, did you get that recorded?" said the XO.

Elder read the message back to the officer. He would remember the exact words for the rest of his life.

The *Hull* was rolling unmercifully, locked tight in the trough. She wasn't getting out, and the sonarman Pat Douhan knew it.

The opening to the after gun mount's blown-away starboard hatch lay flush with the sea, and the handle to the portside hatch was now above him. He scrambled over several bodies—men yelped as he stepped on their hands—turned the latch, and flung open the door. He crawled out on deck and was blown flat on his back. The hatch, swinging on its hinges, came down on top of him and knocked the wind from his lungs. He was trapped beneath the heavy steel door for several minutes.

Two seamen who followed him out managed to free him, and when Douhan got to his knees, he spied a life jacket tied to one of the aft guns. It was one of the old, rubber-tubed Mae Wests, just hanging there, forlorn. He grabbed it and threw it over his shoulders.

No sooner had he donned the Mae West than another wave snatched him and swept him amidships, depositing him just below the 40mm gun director. A few yards away he spotted a shipmate—he couldn't see a face—pinned against the bulkhead by a rogue life raft. The balsa-floored donut had broken its mooring and been caught in the rigging, and when the rigging collapsed it had wedged the seaman in tight. Douhan and several others tried to wrench it loose. It wouldn't budge. The trapped sailor had freed one of his arms, and with it he waved them away. "Fight on!" he cried.

Douhan was at a loss. He could not just leave the man. The decision was made for him. The next comber, the size of a building falling on him, washed him into the sea.

At the exact moment the *Monaghan* broached—her overhead buckled, her rivets popped, water pouring in through the seams—Nathan Abbott was eight thousand miles away working a field of his sugar beet farm in Nampa, Idaho. Bent over a hoe, he was abruptly overcome with a tremendous feeling of despair. It was if a dark cloud was encompassing him, and the distress was unbearable.

Nathan Abbott, father of the *Monaghan*'s "ping jockey," Keith Abbott, fell to his knees and began to weep. His tears fell into the fresh-turned, loamy soil. Nathan Abbott had two other sons as well as a son-in-law fighting the war. But he instinctively knew what the premonition portended.

Clearing his head, he rose on shaky legs and ran as fast as he could toward his farmhouse, some three hundred yards away. He burst through the door and shouted for his wife, Mary.

"Keith is in great danger," he hollered. He was nearly wailing. "He needs our prayers."

For the next two hours Nathan and Mary Abbott knelt in their living room in landlocked Nampa, Idaho, beseeching the Lord to save their son from the sea. The contours of battle had not changed in over two thousand years, since Cicero noted that, in peace, sons bury fathers; in war, fathers bury sons.

CHAPTER 18

*It is the opinion of the court that the commanding officers of the
Hull, Monaghan, and Spence failed to realize sufficiently in advance of the fact, the necessity for them to give up the attempt to
maintain position in their disposition and to give all their attention to saving their ships. It can be said that the good judgment
for such decisions will, in many cases, require more experience than
had the commanding officers of those ships.*

—OPINION #59 OF THE REPORT OF THE COURT OF INQUIRY
INVESTIGATING "HALSEY'S TYPHOON."

Lt. (j.g.) Alphonso S. Krauchunas was making his way from the
Spence's galley to the disbursing office amidships when the destroyer's whaleboat was wrenched from its davits, sailed into the
air, and nearly took off his head. Sopping and shaken, Krauchunas
reeled into the passageway leading to the wardroom. A mess steward was inside, "as white as a ghost," attempting, with no success,
to tie down the compartment's recoiling tables, chairs, and couches.
Presently the ship's lights blinked, dimmed, and went dark.

Struggling to remain upright, guided by guttering emergency
lights, Krauchunas stumbled down the dim passageway toward a
hatch that led to the main deck. He paused at the captain's compartment, where in the shadows he recognized the ship's doctor,
Lt. George C. Gaffney. Gaffney had just transferred on to the
Spence, and he looked terrified. There was little Krauchunas could

do about that, but he stopped anyway to reassure the new sawbones that the destroyer was as sturdy and watertight as any ship in the navy. He was seated on the captain's lower bunk, still heartening Doc Gaffney, when the *Spence* rolled.

Krauchunas was flipped backward off the bunk into the passageway, a drop of five or six feet, and buried in a shower of books, ashtrays, papers, and charts. His heart in his mouth, he scrambled on all fours toward an open hatch leading to the deck, Doc Gaffney, he thought, in close pursuit. He had nearly reached it when another wave rolled the destroyer, this time much farther, and gushing water poured in through the hatch and flooded the companionway.

The tide swept Krauchunas along with it, and as the long roll continued, the lieutenant found himself trapped underwater. He grabbed a bulkhead railing and held tight as the sea sped past him toward the wardroom. He lost sight of Doc Gaffney.

Krauchunas sensed that the *Spence* had flipped almost completely upside down. Holding his breath, he swam toward the outline of the open hatch, now twenty feet away. But the onrushing water was sucking him back like a river's current, his lungs were bursting, and Alphonso Krauchunas began to contemplate his death. How would it come? Painful or peaceful? Fire or water? He relived a moment from his youth, when he was six years old, and he'd stolen a box of animal crackers from the grocery store. Stabbed by a sudden pang of regret, he fantasized that he was standing in that grocery store right now. He wished he could do something, anything, to atone for the theft.

Now the ship was rotated by another swell and bucked briefly back onto her side. This halted the flow of ocean inundating belowdecks, and Krauchunas saw the passageway leading from the radio shack deck rise momentarily from the water. He lunged, broke the surface, and gasped for air. He took four or five huge gulps, and as the *Spence* began to settle back into her overturned position he pulled with all his might for the open hatch.

*   *   *

Fireman Tom Stealey's mouth engaged before his brain had time to stop it. He'd done it again, volunteered for an assignment that was likely to kill him. He wondered if he'd ever learn. The forward boiler on the *Hull* was shot, done, the sea surging down her stack having just knocked it completely out of commission. Now the chief was asking for men to crawl down the stern shaft to try and get the aft boiler back on line. Stealey said he'd go. He was joined by an engineer he did not recognize and a watertender named Cal Miller from Forsyth, Montana. "Dumb," Stealey thought.

Back on December 7, 1941, Stealey had been a civilian contractor stationed at Pearl when the Japanese planes tore up the harbor. It was sometime during the second wave when he'd jumped in a truck and volunteered to fight fires on the two destroyers berthed next to the capsizing battleship USS *Oklahoma*. After several hours of this, there'd been a huge explosion, no more than a quarter mile away.

Someone raced over and said they needed a volunteer to swim out to the drifting and blazing destroyer USS *Shaw* to attach a fire hose. Stealey, being young and stupid and a good swimmer, well, somehow his hand had flown into the air. "Give me a rope," he'd said.

And he'd swum out to the *Shaw* and attached the hawser to her stern and pulled the fire hose aboard and fought those damn fires. He'd even ventured below to make sure all the bodies scattered about were really dead, which they sure were. Stealey figured they'd never known what hit them. And then, after twenty-four solid hours of fighting fires, his reward had been to be thrown in the brig because some nervous young sentry with a tommy gun didn't trust a civilian who had lost his papers.

Stealey had enlisted after that and thought he'd learned his lesson—"Never volunteer." But upon reflection, he guessed now that he really hadn't, because here he was crawling belowdecks through the bowels of the sinking *Hull* on an assignment sure to end badly. He and his two shipmates had just reached the aft boiler room when the destroyer capsized. Stealey lurched for the escape hatch that opened to the tunnel-like shaft that led to the deck. When he hit the handle that pressurized the shaft, all three of them shot to the surface like skyrockets.

Stealey landed hard and found himself trapped beneath a cargo net entangled on the waterlogged deck. Half the ship was underwater, and waves were roaring in from every direction. Even though it was close to noon, it seemed dark as midnight. Stealey watched in horror as a group of sailors, more than a dozen, were sucked under the keel and battered to death.

There were just two of them now, Stealey and Miller the watertender—Stealey had no idea what had happened to the engineer. When they crawled out from under the cargo net, they hoisted each other up to the davit used to raise the ship into dry dock. Stealey decided that their only fighting chance was to time a wave overrunning the ship, jump into it, and allow it to wash them away.

"We're gonna run down the stack and jump on that water as soon as you see it coming," he told his crewmate. "Holler when you're ready."

The watertender yelled, and they both ran down the stack, jumped, and the comber carried them well free of the submerging hulk of metal that had once been their ship. And that was the last Tom Stealey ever saw of the *Hull*. Or of his crewmate the watertender.

Al Krauchunas didn't know how he made it, where he swam from, when he'd arrived. All he knew was he was floating in the sea, no more than a dozen feet from the capsized *Spence*. He vomited up oil and saltwater. He stuck his finger down his throat and retched some more. He was dazed, treading water with no life jacket, yet out of habit and officer's pride, he paused to admire the fresh coat of red paint on the upturned keel of the ship.

Out of the blue, as if he'd materialized from a magician's hat, Chief Watertender George Johnson appeared next to Krauchunas, handed him a kapok, and just as rapidly vanished. Another life jacket floated by—countless were strewn about the surface—and Krauchunas snagged it and strapped it around his legs.

Now he was driven against the hull of the *Spence*, and through the thin, one-inch steel plating he could hear the cries of shipmates trapped inside. The screams were curdling, as if coming from a mental institution. Again a man suddenly appeared, popped up to the surface right before Krauchunas, coughing for air. The lieutenant recognized the young sailor Charlie Wohlebb. He was snarled in wires and braces, and Krauchunas helped free him. Wohlebb said he'd escaped from the fireroom by wriggling through a small air hatch.

The *Spence* was now nearly broken in half, and it occurred to both men that when she sank, the suction would pull them to the bottom. Over the gale, Krauchunas heard shouts and screaming coming from beyond the mountainous swells. He and Wohlebb struck out "as if chased by crocodiles." While close to the metal mass of the ship, they had been protected from the ravenous wind, but after only a few strokes the needlelike spray blinded Krauchunas, putting him in mind of an arctic snowstorm. They pushed on—they had no choice—and somehow came into contact with a floater net that had rolled from its cradle adjacent to the ship's smokestack. Close to twenty sailors were already clutching at its mesh lines and buoys.

Krauchunas grabbed the net just as another comber broke over him. The floater net turned, rolled, and twisted, tossing everyone high into the air. Krauchunas hit the water and was pile-driven under for what seemed like eternity. Finally his two life jackets bobbed him back to the surface. When he found the floater net for the second time, he turned to look for the *Spence*. It was gone.

Now another young sailor, Signalman 2nd Class John Connolly, took hold of the net next to Krauchunas. Connolly looked to be in shock and moaned repeatedly, "I can't go on anymore. I can't. I can't." Krauchunas shook him by the shoulders and began shouting encouragement. He didn't see any wounds, and he was angry with Connolly for giving up so easily.

Another wave again tore the men from the net. When Krauchunas resurfaced, Connolly was gone. No one ever saw him again.

The last wall of water had submerged the *Hull*'s forward stack. Strain as she might, she could not right herself fast enough, and the ocean poured down her main funnel and into her boilers. It doused her fires, and Chief Bosun's Mate Ray Schultz raced below.

He was too late. The firerooms were pressurized, and in order to keep the firebox stoked, the compartment had to maintain its compression. With the ocean rushing in, this proved untenable, and the flames, thirsting for oxygen, shot into the after fireroom. Schultz saw several sailors fried to blackened crisps.

There was nothing Schultz could do except fight his way back to the bridge. For some reason he remembered the storm he'd encountered back in '38, when the *Hull* had been berthed off Long Beach, California. The winds had reached 80, maybe 90 miles per hour, nothing like this to be sure, but brutal nonetheless. The old destroyer had dragged anchor and shot along the bottom as her captain fled the harbor, taking the waves head-on, leaving at least half the crew back on the wharf. There'd been a halfhearted attempt to put out whaleboats, but the skiffs had ended up in some parking lot, resting atop civilian cars. The *Hull* had ridden that one out just like the book said, all buttoned up and steaming straight into it at 3 knots.

Schultz compared this quick thinking with his current commander's frozen uncertainty. He was beginning to despise Captain Marks, hate him more than the devil hated holy water. Schultz thought, *"This Marks, dumber than a turd. And a greenhorn to boot. No idea what to do in a blow. He said he'd seen storms in the Atlantic? I'll bet he never did."*

He was still stewing about Marks—if the captain had ducks, DeRyckere figured, they'd drown—when the final wave hit. The *Hull* went over, and stayed over. Schultz was almost to the bridge when he spotted Archie DeRyckere crawling out on the port face of the wheelhouse and pulling himself atop a twelve-inch signal searchlight fastened to the bridge railing. DeRyckere straddled the light with his legs and lifted Schultz up behind him to an adjoining searchlight. Then they both hefted Lt. Griel Gherstly, the *Hull's* executive officer, and cradled his limp body between them.

Gherstly's hand had been badly mangled when a piece of heavy equipment had torn loose from the bridge as the *Hull* heeled, and the XO was bleeding badly and in obvious pain. Gherstly was pale, and frightened, as he looked from DeRyckere to Schultz. "When we go down, will you help me?" he said.

"Yes, sir," said DeRyckere.

"Yes, sir," said Schultz.

The *Hull* was lolling on her side at a 90-degree angle, still locked deep in the trough between waves. Their height, incongruously, reminded Schultz of a visit to New York City, when he'd strolled down Fifth Avenue gaping up at the skyscrapers. *"Who knew the crazy things you think of when you're going to die?"* DeRyckere, meanwhile, suddenly recalled that he had forgotten to make his noon report to the captain informing him that the ship's chronometers had been wound.

And then the *Hull* dropped out from beneath them. It happened very fast. DeRyckere and Schultz each put an arm around Gherstly. They nodded their good-byes as the Pacific Ocean surged around them. DeRyckere had read the charts; he knew they were sailing close to the deepest part of the great Philippine Trench, an area named the Galathea Depth where the seabed was nearly seven miles below the surface. The pressure at that depth would be equal to over one thousand of the earth's atmospheres. But DeRyckere also knew that he'd be long dead before his corpse reached the bottom. Fish food.

Before he was sucked down into the vacuum with the USS *Hull*, before he was driven so deep he thought his eardrums would explode, the last thing Chief Quartermaster Archie DeRyckere from Laurel, Montana, heard was the rough, bitter plaint of his friend Chief Bosun's Mate Ray Schultz.

"Goddamn Halsey," Schultz said. "Sailed us right into the middle of this goddamn typhoon."

Aboard the mine lighter USS *Tracy* seaman Elwood Link had just been relieved from the forenoon watch. He was crouching low in the ship's wheelhouse when he imagined he heard an explosion over the roar of the gale. Link stood up, turned, and glimpsed something dark in the water several hundred yards to port. Bracing himself with his knees, covering his eyes with cupped hands, he squinted through the scud and rain.

His first impression was that the object was like no vessel he had ever before seen. Perhaps, he thought, it was a surfaced submarine. It disappeared into a trough and was raised again on the next wave. And only then did the thought dawn. Link was staring at the hull of a capsized destroyer. All about the floundering hulk the tiny figures of men flailing in the sea took shape.

The *Tracy*'s officer of the deck took in the gruesome scene at the same moment, and shouted for hard left rudder. The little lighter pitched over a wave and heeled precariously. Link watched the inclinometer register 61 degrees. The vessel, an ancient, converted four-stack destroyer remaindered from World War I, had been built for durability and speed, not for power. She was designed to roll a maximum of 64 degrees before her stacks took water. Link held on tight as the captain screamed for his helmsman to balance her. The *Tracy* rolled again, 59 degrees to starboard this time, and Link found himself standing on a bulkhead, the *Tracy*'s deck now a vertical wall.

By the time the *Tracy* climbed from the trough and breached the crest of the next wave, the capsized vessel had disappeared. Elwood Link and the bridge crew scanned the water with binoculars in every direction. They saw not a piece of flotsam nor jetsam. They never knew which vessel they had witnessed go under.

* * *

At 1:45 P.M. on December 18, Adm. William F. Halsey Jr. received a transmission from Vice Adm. John Sidney "Slew" McCain, and entered a notation in his war diary:

"Commander Task Force 38 reported the center of the typhoon showed on his radar at 000 (due north), distance 35 miles."

Halsey was finally driven to admit, officially in a message to CINCPAC Nimitz at Pearl Harbor, that his Big Blue Fleet had been swamped by a massive typhoon.

Almost simultaneously, Comdr. William Rogers, captain of the limping *Aylwin*, conveyed another report to McCain via VHS radio. His destroyer was on the fleet's far-eastern flank, and her barometer readings were rising.

She had been battered, beaten, inundated for twelve solid hours. Her secondary conn wheel and her annunciators had been torn from their foundations, and the cracked metal deck around her forward stack was a spider's snarl of lifelines and floater nets. The two main generators in engine room number 1 were inoperable, as were her engine room blowers. Her radar and TBS radio were out, and she'd finally managed to jettison her depth charges in order to lose topside weight. Rogers had tried to fire her torpedoes, but no crewmen could get close enough to the tubes without risking death. But now Typhoon Cobra had washed over her, its residue a rush of clouds trailing lightning bolts that dissected the western skyline.

Captain Calhoun on the *Dewey*, not far away, noted that exiting the vortex and seeing a brilliant white sun overhead was comparable "to coming out of a cloud formation in an aircraft. One minute we were in a thick soup of violent wind and spray, and the next we were out in the clear."

On the *Aylwin*, wind readings were down to 50 knots, but the seas were still so mountainous and confused that, seven hours later, Rogers would direct his crew to prepare to abandon ship. "That she did not capsize was miraculous," he would later tell the *Dewey*'s Calhoun. In the end, however, she survived. She was lucky.

As the afternoon wore on, most of Halsey's vessels continued to fight for their lives. The admiral ordered all ships to steam southeast, to within the left, or more navigable, semicircle of the storm's cyclonic winds. He set a rendezvous site for seven the next morning at latitude 12 degrees north, longitude 129 east, about seventy miles away. It was a belated command easier issued than carried out.

It would be several hours before Halsey learned he had already lost at least three of his ships, and possibly one more: The *Tabberer* had disappeared.

BOOK THREE

THE RESCUE

They attack the one man with their hate and their shower of weapons. But he is like some rock which stretches into the vast sea and which, exposed to the fury of the winds and beaten against by the waves, endures all the violence.

—VIRGIL, *THE AENEID*

CHAPTER 19

"It's all in the laps of the gods."

—Lt. Comdr. Henry Lee Plage,
USS Tabberer

By Lt. Comdr. Henry Lee Plage's reckonings—the plunge in barometric pressure, the strength of the gale, the movement of the
combers—the destroyer escort *Tabberer* steamed through the teeth
of Typhoon Cobra somewhere between 10:00 A.M. and noon on
December 18.

At 7:00 A.M., after a haggard night, the barometer in the DE's
pilothouse read 29.58. Four and one half hours later the needle
had fallen by almost two inches, bottoming out at 27.95. Around
10:30 Plage clocked the wind, blowing out of the north, at the
maximum Beaufort reading of Force 12, and—after the ship's
anemometer was ripped from its stanchion and blown into the
sea—estimated that gusts held steady at over 100 knots for several hours thereafter.

Titanic waves heeled the ship so hard to starboard that Plage
transferred as much oil as safety allowed to the portside bunkers
to compensate for the list. He also set special watches below to
protect the generators and switchboard, which he had ordered
draped with canvas tarps. And while the boiler water levels were
kept at full to prevent sloshing that would add to the ship's tilt,
he'd drained some of the lubricating oil in the turbogenerator in

order to prevent the windings from soaking. He had done, he thought, everything he could.

Throughout the storm, the remaining ships of the *Tabberer*'s hunter-killer submarine Task Group 30.7, at least the vessels Plage knew to be still afloat, had attempted to keep station about their flagship, the jeep carrier USS *Anzio*, steaming on a base course of 160 degrees, south-southeast. But because the *Tabby*'s helmsman was having such difficulty steering her through the mountainous swells, Plage radioed the *Anzio* that he was breaking station and ordered a course change to 90 degrees, nearly due east. Visibility was no more than thirty feet and—the near collision with his friend Capt. Raymond Toner's *Robert F. Keller* fresh in his mind—he was afraid of being run down by the larger ships of Halsey's scattered task force. The change of heading locked the *Tabby* in irons, but at least, settled deep in the trough, the rolls had decreased, to no more than 40 degrees.

When he felt he was well clear of any nearby vessels, Plage attempted to bring the *Tabby* back around to her south-southeast base course. This proved impossible. The ship pitched into the waves at full rudder with her engines dangerously stoked to 18 knots, and when this didn't work, he attempted full ahead with one engine while backing the other down full. It was like trying to ride a motorcycle up the walls of the Grand Canyon. By midday he'd given up trying to break out of the massifs of water engulfing his little "sea dwarf," and settled back into an easterly direction, the wind and sea pummeling his port beam.

The *Tabby* was sailing with 75 percent of her fuel capacity, which helped with stability, but the seas were just too high, an ocean conjured by Caliban. Her chief radioman, Ralph Tucker, became so anxious standing watch in the DE's communications shack that he tried to push the dread from his mind by reading, from cover to cover, the comedian Bob Hope's autobiography, *I Never Left Home*. He told crewmates he didn't realize the book was funny until two days later.

The confused seas combined to create "a delicate situation" for the *Tabby*, as the understated Plage noted in his log. The ship had suffered damage to one of her screws, her driveshaft, and her motor, which had been temporarily knocked off its bed. A flying ammunition locker had punched a twelve-inch-by-twelve-inch hole through the hull of her motor whaleboat. And there had been a few minor electrical shorts when saltwater entered the air vents during big rolls and doused the switchboards. But the canvas sleeves the ship's engineers had rigged to reroute seawater pouring belowdecks had done their job, and the tarps with which Plage had sheltered the generators kept them relatively dry. In fact, despite the rolls and spleen-rattling pitches, at no time during the height of the typhoon had the *Tabberer* lost all its power.

Those same rolls, however, had loosed several heavy 5-inch shells from their racks in the forward handling room as well as a number of aluminum gunpowder cases. The shells, their fuse caps knocked off (rendering them live), were ricocheting from bulkhead to bulkhead. Given the circumstances, Plage could not leave the bridge, and he refused to order any crewmen below to relash them—"It was almost a certainty that someone would get crushed trying to secure 5-inch shells under those conditions," he said.

But nineteen-year-old Gunner's Mate Tom Bellino needed no orders. He grabbed the first man he could find, a black steward's mate, and the two dashed into the room. The projectiles weighed 54 pounds apiece, and the gunpowder cases 27 pounds each, but the two *Tabby* sailors strained to heft them off the grating and tie them back into their racks. They most likely saved the ship. Plage only later learned of their heroics.

By early afternoon, Plage calculated the *Tabby*'s position to be somewhat northeast of the bulk of Halsey's flotilla. She was rolling heavier now, up to 55 degrees, as the wind backed around, first to the west and then to the south. But she was steaming fairly steadily at 10 knots.

Just past 1:00 P.M. the captain noticed his glass beginning to rise, and he picked up the destroyers *Hickox* and USS *Benham* as well as the destroyer escort USS *Waterman* on his radar screen. The three vessels, all from his task group, were bunched together some 2,000 to 5,000 yards ahead of him. Via TBS radio each skipper informed Plage that he had lost steering control. All three were steaming in troughs at no more than 3 knots. Plage backed his own vessel down to 3 knots in order to avoid running up their sterns, and with the loss of speed, the *Tabby* took a stupendous roll, the inclinometer registering 72 degrees.

Because she was "beamier" than a destroyer, with a lower center of gravity, the *Tabby* recovered from these heels much more quickly. But not long after another such roll, one of the mainmast's porcelain insulators gave way, and the long metal pole began to whip and sway. As it worked itself loose, Plage knew it was only a matter of time before the mast crashed. The only question was how large a hole it would gouge from the foredeck when it ripped from its base. He gazed at the seventy-foot waves pounding his ship and turned to his XO Bob Surdam. "It's all in the laps of the gods," he said.

Chief Quartermaster Archie DeRyckere was drawn so deep by the suction of the sinking *Hull* that he thought his eardrums would explode. They didn't, but his head ached for days afterward. Prior to helping the *Hull's* wounded executive officer, Griel Gherstly, up onto the doomed destroyer's searchlight and nodding good-bye to his friend Chief Bosun's Mate Ray Schultz, DeRyckere had managed to lash a kapok tight around his beefy chest.

Now, before he followed the *Hull* all the way to the cold ocean floor, the life preserver shot him back to the waterline, not that he could know it from the solid sheets of wind-driven rain. In fact, the spume was as thick as the sea, and the only sign that he had surfaced was the deafening sound of the gale. His ears hurt even more, and it felt as if someone were throwing sand in his face. DeRyckere had to turn away from the gusts and cup his hands around his nose just to breathe. Before long, the driving rain would chip all the skin from his nose, neck, and ears.

As the chief gulped for air, he silently thanked Schultz for procuring the new life jackets to replace the *Hull*'s old Mae West inflatable life belts. Third Fleet sailors liked the rectangular kapoks. They could be used as pillows while, say, standing long watches at general quarters, and in a pinch even served as a modest flak vest against shrapnel. But now, as he treaded water, Archie DeRyckere recognized their true worth. They would keep a man afloat much longer than a flimsy Mae West, perhaps up to three or four days. DeRyckere prayed it would not come to that.

Neither Gherstly nor Schultz was anywhere to be seen when, out of the corner of his eye, DeRyckere spotted a raft with several shipmates already on board. He made for it. The raft was donut-shaped, gray canvas stretched taut over balsa wood, and he was barely inside when a huge comber drove the craft down deep, held it underwater for what seemed like an eternity, and then blasted it back 15 to 20 feet into the air like a hollow stick. Every sailor was knocked from the float, and in the scramble to reboard, DeRyckere felt men grabbing at his hair, his ears, gouging his eye sockets. This happened three, four times in the next few moments before he thought, *"To hell with this, I'm getting the hell out of here."*

He started to swim, to where he did not know or care. Soon enough he realized he could "sense" by the surface current and wave action the impending crash of one of the huge crushers. As it closed on him he would hear the roar, and seconds before the wave broke, out of some primal instinct, he kicked his feet, folded his arms across his chest . . . and taught himself to bodysurf, as if learning to fly while falling. He began gliding down the face of ninety-foot combers.

He saw shipmates doing the same. He rode one wave with Fire Controlman 1st Class Al Taylor, who curved in midair with the resilience of a dolphin and hollered, "Woo-ee, Chief! What a ride!"

Next he found himself bodysurfing parallel to Chief Radioman Burt Martin, who screamed, "Any port in a storm, right, Arch?"

"You got that right," DeRyckere yelled back. And then Martin, like Taylor before him, was gone.

DeRyckere rode the waves like this for a good five hours. The water was warm, well over 75 degrees Fahrenheit he guessed, and he was not uncomfortable. But he knew the night air would be cold, and he was tiring. In the gloaming, as he skimmed down the face of another wall of water, he nearly collided with the *Hull's* skipper, Lt. Comdr. James A. Marks.

"Hey, DeRyckere," Marks said. "Like to know what time it is?"

What the hell was this man talking about? "Yes, sir, Captain. I would."

Marks glanced at his waterproof watch, still working perfectly, and said that it was a little past 6:00 P.M. Then the skipper disappeared. Not a word about attaching lines and staying together. Not a thought for his crew. Just gone. Archie thought this par for the course.

As night fell on December 18, an ashen-faced Halsey conferred unremittingly with his flag staff aboard the *New Jersey*. He had accounted for all his "heavies," from battlewagons to attack carriers to cruisers. Of the DDs and DEs, from which there was no word and no trace, he hoped that this was merely the result of their masts, or antennae, or both, having been blown away in the typhoon. Although the smaller jeep flattops such as the *Monterey*, *Cowpens*, *Cape Esperance*, and *San Jacinto* radioed flag plot that most, if not all, of their aircraft were either resting on the seabed or hopelessly demolished, Halsey was heartened by his escort carriers' sustained seaworthiness. Planes, he thought, he could replace. He would later learn that he had lost 146 of them.

Via his Task Force 38 commander, Adm. "Slew" McCain, Halsey directed the *Monterey's* Capt. Stuart Ingersoll to form up the battered vessels most in need of repair and, after refueling, shape course for Ulithi ahead of the rest of the fleet. Among these ships was the broken and limping destroyer *Aylwin*.

At 6:45 P.M., with the *Hull, Spence, Monaghan,* and *Tabberer* still unaccounted for, the admiral sent a TBS order to McCain alerting all ships to post lookouts for floating survivors. There was nothing else to do but smoke cigarettes, drink coffee, watch, and wait. As damage assessments dribbled into flag plot, Halsey paced between the port side of flag mess and his seat at the conference table. Occasionally he would peer over the shoulder of his chief of staff, Adm. "Mick" Carney, who kept a running tally sheet of the fleet's vessels on the table before him. Carney's damage assessment continued to grow.

CHAPTER 20

"It's a question of who wants it badly enough."

—*Fireman 1st Class Evan Fenn,*
USS Monaghan

Joe McCrane, the *Monaghan's* "oil king," was exhausted and for-lorn when he heard a familiar twang.

"Hey, Joe, grab that raft back of you."

The voice belonged to Joe Guio, the gunner's mate from West Virginia who had helped pull so many men from the *Monaghan's* afterdeck gun house just before she went under. Moments earlier Guio had cut the raft loose from the deck lines, and now McCrane lunged for the balsa-and-canvas float and seized it with the last of his strength.

As he looked around, he was, incongruously, reminded of Noel Coward's classic lifeboat movie *In Which We Serve*, which had de-buted two years earlier. He counted nearly twenty fellow crewmates hanging on for dear life. Several were injured, including the ship's cook, Ben Holland, who was bleeding badly from ugly, serrated gashes on his foot and the back of his head, and the fireman Evan Fenn, who had stripped much of the skin off both his legs nearly down to the tendons attempting to reboard again and again.

When McCrane wiped the spume from his eyes, he also saw that half of Joe Guio's foot was missing. He could tell easily, for Guio was naked.

As wave after wave battered the raft, spinning it topsy-turvy with each collision, McCrane and the healthiest seamen spent the afternoon helping the wounded back aboard. "It's a question of who wants it badly enough," Fenn told McCrane as yet another shipmate gave up and disappeared. These flips occurred four or five times before thirteen survivors finally managed to secure the craft in a bottom-down position.

The next several hours were a blur of onrushing wind and water as the sailors fought to remain afloat. It was only after dusk turned to total darkness that McCrane thought to fish through the emergency rations, and, as the ranking seaman, more or less take command of the tiny craft. He found watertight tins of hard biscuits, malted milk tablets (to slake thirst), and Spam as well as several five-gallon kegs of potable water and a medical kit containing sulfa powder and burn ointment.

Mentally dividing the stores by the number of survivors, he decided he would limit his "crew" to a biscuit and one cup of water two to three times a day. He guessed that would last them a week. There was no sense in stocking up for a desert island. He noticed that as soon as he knifed open a tin of Spam, huge, dark fins began circling the raft. He wondered how the sharks could smell it.

The *Tabberer*'s main mast snapped at 6:18 P.M. It crushed a flag bag and took the number 3 floater net basket with it over the starboard beam. The only wonder was that it hadn't collapsed earlier. For over five hours Henry Plage had watched pensively from the *Tabby*'s wheelhouse as the fist-sized, porcelain insulators that maintained the mast's guy wires crumbled and disintegrated with each stupendous roll. One by one the insulators washed away, and after each failure the gyrations of the sixty-four-foot-long pole increased exponentially.

Long before it began whipping in eight-foot arcs, Plage had ordered a deck crew tied into makeshift harnesses and sent topside, directing them to run a five-inch line through a lower eye on the main port guy in an effort to take up the slack. But though the sailors managed to get the hawser tied on, there was no way they could keep the mast taut in the throttling seas, and Plage dared not send any man aloft into the rigging.

The mast had shimmied in ever-widening arcs before ripping almost completely out of the step-weld on the main foredeck. Its base now rested on the signal bridge level, still attached to the ship by its wire stanchions and guys, and the large bullhorn was fouled in the main deck's starboard bulwark. The tip, trailing in the ocean, was banging hard, dangerously hard, against the thin metal plating of the DE's starboard hull. The *Tabberer* looked like a bomb had hit it.

Since the mast carried not only the ship's radar but all her antennae, the little destroyer escort's communications were now gone. Lost was any hope of sending out a distress call. The *Tabberer* was sailing blind, literally and figuratively, through the wild remnants of Typhoon Cobra.

The skipper turned to Bob Surdam and calmly ordered all engines stopped. They had to lose that mast completely before it punched a hole in the side of the ship. As tons of whitewater crashed over the *Tabby*'s stern, Plage broke out acetylene torches and axes, and called for volunteers.

Bob Ayers never saw the *Spence* slide beneath the sea. He had gone down with his destroyer while standing atop the bridge's starboard, solid-panel rail, and somehow, even without a life jacket, he was spit back to the surface by the currents. A moment later a crate of potatoes washed by, and Ayers hopped atop it and hung on for all he was worth. He snagged a kapok skirting the spindrift and tied himself to the wooden crate as best he could. The water about him was littered with the ship's flotsam, but he could make out no other survivors. The mangled *Spence*, hull up, refused to sink. She danced about the waves, threatening to crush him. He paddled his potato-crate raft away from the shattered ship as fast as he could.

Samuel Eliot Morison wrote, "For some reason that goes deep into the soul of a sailor, he mourns over shipmates lost to the dangers of the sea even more than for those killed by the violence of the enemy." So it was that as Bob Ayers raced to escape the dying *Spence*, he thought at that moment of his friend Floyd Balliett, trapped belowdecks in the bowels of the doomed destroyer. Then a mountainous breaker crashed over him and drove him deep below. When he came to the surface, his makeshift raft was gone, as was his life jacket. He could not see more than fifteen feet in any direction. The noise was earth-shattering, the waves towered above him, and the wind-driven rain stung him like needles.

A month earlier the eighteen-year-old Bob Ayers had been riding a train across America's heartland, seemingly bound for glory with the Tin Can Navy. Now the onetime Great Lakes schooner sailor, nine days out of port on his first seagoing assignment, was bobbing alone in the vast Pacific Ocean.

When Chief Bosun's Mate Ray Schultz broke the surface, he counted at least two dozen of his *Hull* shipmates bobbing in "a big glob" where the destroyer had once been. After one, and then another, and then a third giant comber washed over them, Schultz could locate no more than two or three men. The rest had gone under and not come back up. He spied a life raft, stroked for it, and looped a line from his life preserver through one of its small pad eyes. On board he recognized a hemp-haired giant, a young ship's steward named Chambers, and warned the big man to lash himself on.

"I'm gonna do better than that," Chambers said, and before Schultz could stop him, the steward had wedged his foot between the slats of balsa wood grating that constituted the raft's deck. The next wave lifted the raft high into the air, snapping Schultz's lifeline and most likely Chambers's leg. From a distance Schultz watched it land facedown. He saw the steward's foot sticking up through the grating as he drowned.

Swearing off rafts, Schultz rolled himself into a ball, smacking from wave to wave. Their convection created powerful, mini-whirlpools that alternately flung him into the air or drove him deep beneath the surface. He had gone into the water fully clothed, but by nightfall the sea had torn away every stitch except for his kapok life jacket and the belt and pockets of his dungarees. He soon learned to stop fighting the down-driving current—the honeycombed air pockets in his kapok would always propel him to the surface just as he felt he could not hold his breath a moment more. He rolled through the Philippine Sea like this well into the night.

Several planks washed by near him, but from the experience with the life raft, he had learned his lesson about latching on to anything rigid. He never thought to bodysurf, and though a good swimmer, he was certain he would soon join the steward Chambers at the bottom of the sea. Before the *Hull* had shipped from Pearl to Ulithi, she had picked up twenty-five new men, predominantly seventeen- and eighteen-year-old kids, and Schultz rued the fact that he'd never gotten to know them, to teach them what he knew, to pass on to the greenhorns the U.S. Navy's vaunted "chief's lore."

He was fairly certain the radioman on the *Hull* had failed to get off a distress signal before she capsized. This meant that no one knew he was out here. Sometime in the middle of the night, Ray Schultz began to think of his family, about how they would never get the straight story of his death. These thoughts left him angry, and sad.

Capt. Henry Plage handed Leonard Glaser a torch and an acetylene tank as several shipmates laced looplines in and around his life preserver. "It'll either bang a hole in the hull, or get caught in the screws, so it's got to go," Plage said.

Glaser glanced at the flopping mast dragging along the side of the *Tabberer* and nodded. When ax blades had proven futile against the thick steel, Glaser had volunteered to be lowered over the side to burn it off. It was the least he could do for the skipper who had gone out of his way to bring him kosher food.

Plage stopped all engines and ordered live power cut from all the mast's leads so as not to electrocute Glaser or the damage control party, and the twenty-six-year-old shipfitter was dropped down to the raging water level. A few times giant swells engulfed him, blinding him momentarily, knocking out his acetylene torch, but on each occasion he relit it quickly enough. Within five minutes he had severed the long pole and its cables and sent it all to the bottom without even scraping any paint, much less denting the ship. Glaser gave the "All clear," and as they hauled him back up, he felt the rumble of the *Tabby*'s engines being restarted.

Once the cumbersome mast had been jettisoned, the *Tabberer*'s roll was reduced immeasurably, and the ship was able to break free from the troughs that held her in irons. Yet with the mast went all the ship's communications equipment, and Plage now had no way of informing flag plot that his vessel was still afloat. He realized that the swirling vortex of Typhoon Cobra may have washed over him and his crew, but the tremendous seas worked up by the typhoon were still running. In fact, the wind and waves actually seemed to be increasing. He pointed his bow south and steamed on thin fumes of hope.

Meanwhile, attempts to rerig an emergency transmitter antenna across what was left of the DE's superstructure proceeded desperately. Ralph Tucker, the *Tabby*'s chief radioman who had spent the worst of the storm immersed in Bob Hope, was now on top of the pilothouse, lashed in, skipping over the cavity left when a solid wall of water had sheared off a section of its roof a few moments before the mast snapped.

Tucker worked for hours fusing cables to a spare, forty-four-inch-long TBS antenna rod, and by midnight he would establish a weak radio signal, albeit one that could not transmit farther than a few thousand yards. But for now the *Tabberer* was still sailing incommunicado.

Minutes before 10:00 P.M., Tucker was straddling the after bridge, jury-rigging the antenna wire between a gun mount and the remaining flag bag, when he glimpsed a pinpoint flicker of a light perhaps one hundred yards away.

"Man overboard!" he shouted. "Light off the starboard beam!"

Plage, pacing the bridge below Tucker, wheeled about. By then, what Tucker was certain he saw was the glint of a small, one-cell, battery-charged flashlight attached to all U.S. Navy–issue kapok life preservers as it had disappeared into a trough as black as a deep cave. It took a minute or two before Plage saw it cresting another wave. Had one of his crewmen been washed overboard? No, that was impossible. He assumed it was just an empty kapok blown off some vessel or another.

Nevertheless, he ordered the *Tabby* swung about. In spite of standing, antisubmarine blackout orders, he directed that his 12-inch and 24-inch searchlights be trained on the tiny, flickering beam bobbing atop the whitecaps. The sea lit up like a stadium at night.

Although he never lost consciousness, the twenty-one-year-old radarman Keith Abbott had no idea how he had been knocked from the *Monaghan*'s combat information center into the sea. All he knew was that the rain flaying his face stung like sharpened hailstones, and something was whipping into the back of his head. He turned to find the straggling rope of a four-by-eight-foot balsa-bottomed raft. His arms flailed and he grabbed the line. Without even trying to heft himself aboard, he held on as tight as he could.

The raft rode the combers with Abbott trailing behind it like the tail of a kite. Each wave presented its own private battle—up, over the crest, a dizzying descent—and his mind became so preoccupied with winning every one of these battles that it was some time before he realized there were no other sailors from the *Monaghan* in sight.

Hours later, when the bruised, battered, and drained Abbott finally eased himself into the raft as if there might be snakes inside, he began scavenging for provisions. There were none. He was alone with no water, and no food. He told himself there *had* to be people throughout the fleet who were aware of the *Monaghan*'s plight. He was not naïve. It would certainly be difficult to locate one man in a small raft in the middle of the Pacific Ocean. But if anyone could do it, Admiral Halsey could. Of this he was certain. He could not believe, he did not *want* to believe, that he had been the only survivor from the fabled destroyer.

Henry Lee Plage trained his binoculars on the bobbing light, and a living, waving form took shape. It was indeed a sailor, and as the *Tabby* closed on him, Plage heard the shrill keening of the whistle also affixed to every kapok life preserver. The captain assumed the floater had been lost from the destroyer *Dewey*, which had passed his ship several hours earlier.

Plage attempted several by-the-book rescue approaches into the wind, as if shaping toward a mooring buoy at anchorage. As an aircraft carrier screener the *Tabby* had plucked at least twenty-five downed American pilots from the drink since her commission (and always offered the puzzled flyboys a brimming bowl of ice cream from Cookie Phillips's pilfered machine), but no rescue rules applied in these high seas. The waves were still so precipitous that on each occasion, as the ship drew near to the desperate floater and slowed, the ground swell and the cross-seas would cause her to lose steering control and her bow would drift away from the man. "Normal procedures," Plage decided, "just won't work."

He could think of only one other maneuver, a highly dangerous course of action he'd once read about a squadron of Merchant Marines experimenting with off the wild coasts of New England. The naval reservist, with less than eighteen months at sea, drew the *Tabby* about fifty yards to the windward side of the floater, and turned his ship broadside into the heaving seas. It was a stroke of genius from such a novice seaman. Now the gale and waves plowed the *Tabby* sideways toward the drifting man, "rolling toward him like a hunk of tumbleweed." But it also exposed her thin-skinned starboard hull to a jackhammer pounding from the combers.

As the *Tabby* closed the gap, she listed so sharply that the portside edge of her main deck plunged underwater with every heel. On her final approach, even as it appeared she would roll atop and crush the man, a deck gang managed to heave a life preserver and a looped line. The floating seaman caught it and fastened the bight beneath his arms. On the *Tabby*'s next return roll, when the green swells and frothing white foam retreated from her deck, it left behind an unconscious heap swathed in a kapok life jacket, its rescue beacon still blinking.

When the sailor regained consciousness in sick bay, he identified himself to his rescuers as Quartermaster 3rd Class Vernon Lindquist, from the capsized destroyer USS *Hull*. When word of this was passed topside to Plage, the captain was staggered. He had no idea a destroyer had gone down. An old battlefield bromide cautions: Never believe a straggler and rarely believe a casualty. But here was living, breathing proof.

Plage rushed belowdecks to interrogate the seaman, who insisted "there are more of us out there." The skipper ordered cargo nets draped over both sides of the *Tabby* to provide handholds and footholds. All crewmen who could be spared were directed topside to search for lights and listen for whistles. Sailors crowded the weather decks and lined the rails, eyes straining.

Despite the high seas, despite the blinding rainsqualls, despite his lost radar and radio, Plage began a systematic, dead-reckoning boxed search of the area: fifteen hundred yards a side at a speed of 10 knots. Up, over, and down waves the *Tabby* flew. At ten-minute intervals, as regular as the Angelus, the skipper doused all running lights, turned off the bridge's ventilation blowers, and cut his engines in order to better see the blinking kapoks and hear the desperate whistles and hollers above the gale.

Presently, whistles were indeed heard in the distance. At first it was difficult to distinguish floating men from whitecaps, however, lights flickering unsteadily from the tor-like peaks gradually came into view before disappearing into the troughs.

When Sonarman Pat Douhan had splashed into the water, he lunged after the first object his hands brushed against. It was one of the

Hull's large life rafts, already carrying several sailors, and it bounced on the high seas attached by slack lines to a second raft.

Douhan pulled himself up so that his shoulders were nearly inside, his legs trailing in the sea. At that moment a thunderous wave broke over both rafts, and Douhan watched as the heads of the men trapped in the water between the two crafts were "crushed like popcorn." He let go, slid back into the sea, and allowed the current to take him.

The "ping jockey" was not wearing a kapok, merely the old Mae West life belt he'd grabbed off the aft gun—named, naturally, after the curvaceous vaudeville and movie star. He wondered how long the worm-eaten yellow rubber tube fastened about his waist would last in this ocean. Not long, he bet. He thought he was well clear of the sinking *Hull* when he was violently sucked downward in a giant whirlpool. His ears popped at first, and then his eyes, so hard he thought they would blow out of their sockets. He was certain he was being siphoned into the big screws of a passing carrier or battlewagon. He couldn't see a ship, he couldn't see anything in this muck, but he was sure it was there.

Then he shot back to the surface, as if fired from a gun. A huge swell carried him up its face, and from this vantage point, as if peering over a cliff, he watched the *Hull* gurgle and disappear beneath the slate gray sea. One moment she was lying on her side, a floating abattoir, and in the next she was gone. Douhan was too high in the air to make out how many sailors she pulled below with her.

Not long after this he sensed her boilers exploding, maybe her depth charges, too, a wave of pressure spiraling up from the deep. He felt it in legs, in his torso, in his bowels, in his kidneys, and he thought of all the good men who had not made it out. More surf broke over him and he curled up into a tuck position and let the current carry him.

Douhan was a "water bug" who had starred on school swimming teams since he was a little boy, but he knew there was no swimming through this maelstrom. Waves tossed him like a toy. Sometime around dusk, as he was lofted up another huge swell, he peered across a liquid valley and recognized a shipmate. It was the *Hull's* Storekeeper 3rd Class Ken Drummond, dropping through the gaps on the opposite face, as if falling from the heights of a ragged line of hills. He waved, but Drummond did not wave back.

And then it was dark, an inky, suffocating murk, blacker than Pat Douhan thought it could ever become.

The *Monaghan's* gunner's mate 3rd class Joseph Guio Jr., from Hollidays Cove, West Virginia, died naked in Joe McCrane's arms sometime after 10:00 P.M. He abruptly ceased shivering and passed away as the "oil king" cradled him in an attempt to keep him warm.

Moments earlier McCrane and his fellow survivors had spotted the running lights of a ship quite a far distance from their raft. They'd begun hollering and waving, but the vessel steamed on without noticing them. Guio had looked up and said to McCrane, "Joe, can you see anything?"

McCrane thought Guio was talking about the passing ship. It was obvious to all his raftmates that Guio was bleeding out from his severed foot, and McCrane had tried to buoy his spirits. Sure, he said, he could see something. A ship. Coming for them.

"I can't see a thing," Guio said, and closed his eyes.

McCrane and Seaman 1st Class Doyle Carpenter prepared the burial at sea. Carpenter said the Lord's Prayer, and McCrane gazed one last time at the pallid face of the man who had saved his life. Then he and Carpenter gently rolled Guio's body over the side.

They were now twelve.

CHAPTER 21

"Those bastards are gonna abandon us."

—Chief Quartermaster Archie DeRyckere,
USS Hull

Employing the same perilous maneuver they had on their first rescue, Henry Plage and his deck crew plucked nine more *Hull* seamen from the ocean over the next ninety minutes. The *Tabby*'s engineering officer, Arthur Carpentier, listened appalled as two of the survivors described how they'd twice nearly been run over by the DE before being spotted. When this news was relayed to the skipper, he could not keep from wondering how many other helpless men he'd missed. Or crushed to death beneath his keel.

When a floating sailor was found unconscious, or proved too weak to grab a lifeline and haul himself in, the strongest swimmers in the *Tabby*'s deck crew did the unthinkable and tied their life preservers onto thread lines and plunged in to haul the floaters back in life rings. More than once, rescue swimmers were lost under the eave of the rolling vessel's deck. On one occasion the *Tabby*'s gunnery officer, reservist Lt. (j.g.) Howard Korth—a burly, blond, former Notre Dame football player from Bay City, Michigan—was on duty at the cargo net and dived beneath the ship to pull in both a survivor and his floundering rescuer.

During another attempted rescue, Bosun's Mate 1st Class Louis "Skip" Purvis, a rugged and fearless twenty-four-year-old from

Chatham, New Jersey—who had once survived being washed overboard into the icy waters off Casco, Maine—reached a man who he thought was unconscious, but turned out to be dead. Purvis yanked the floater's dog tags from around his neck, and as he swam back to the ship, the slack in his lifeline fouled on the bulbous sonar dome welded to the bottom of the DE.

Twice the rolling *Tabby*'s suction pulled him beneath her keel; twice he broke the surface for an instant and managed to gulp a lungful of air before being dragged back under. On his third descent, unable to disentangle his line from the keel, he barely managed to wriggle out of his life jacket altogether and breach the surface on the other side of the vessel. He hollered for help, and surprised lookouts hoisted him aboard.

"Dammit," the lantern-jawed Purvis said after being hauled in. "I bet I'm the first sailor to be keelhauled in two hundred years." He was back in the water within an hour.

Not long after his brief encounter with Captain Marks, Archie DeRyckere literally bumped into two *Hull* crewmates, Seaman 1st Class Tom Spohn and Seaman 2nd Class George Guy. They were both wearing kapoks and asked the chief if they could tie in with him. DeRyckere laced the life preservers' lines together, and the three formed a tight circle in the somewhat becalmed ocean. Rain spouts still drenched them, the wind still howled, and the swells remained huge. But the whitewater at their crests had abated, and there was no longer any need to bodysurf.

At one point they saw a ship's running lights on the horizon, and DeRyckere unhooked the tiny flashlight from his kapok. Using Morse code, he began blinking repeated SOSs. When the vessel did not respond, he flashed another message.

"S-E-N-D H-E-L-P."

Now the ship seemed to return their entreaty. It was disheartening.

"W-E A-R-E L-E-A-V-I-N-G T-H-E A-R-E-A."

DeRyckere thought, "Those bastards are gonna abandon us." Then the vessel's lights disappeared.

As they drifted, DeRyckere, Spohn, and Guy kept up a running conversation. The chief thought it would improve everyone's emotional state. They did not speak about whether they were going to drown, but, rather, what they could do to stay alive. DeRyckere recounted his bodysurfing experience, and the two seamen, obviously disoriented, and perhaps succumbing to hypothermia, promised DeRyckere they would hang on until another rescue ship arrived.

DeRyckere saw a Bermuda onion floating by. He scooped it up and offered it to his floatmates. Both declined, and he stuffed it into the front pocket of his dungarees. The two enlisted men were by now on the verge of delirium, and the discovery of the onion apparently steered the conversation to food, specifically the next morning's breakfast.

"I'm going to have hot dogs and french fries," Spohn said.

"Naw, I'm gonna have pancakes, man, with sausage, and eggs, and ham," Guy said.

And though DeRyckere did not answer them, he was struck by a "crazy idea," and thought with a breezy quarterdeck laugh, *"Well, Arch, you're not in such bad shape. These two guys are gonna have breakfast, and you're tied into them. What the hell are you worried about?"*

Not long past midnight, as the *Tabberer* made slow search headway through the gales and high seas, she again made visual contact with Capt. Raymond Calhoun's now-stackless *Dewey*. The vessel was but a shadow in the distant mist, but recognizable from the *Tabby*'s wheelhouse, even without her funnel, as an American destroyer.

Ralph Tucker had managed to repair the communications gear to the point where it could receive fleet communiqués, although it could transmit only a short range. Doubting he could reach the destroyer with Tucker's makeshift antenna, Plage ordered his young signalman John Cross to flash the identity of the *Tabberer* via Morse code blinker, and inform the ship's skipper that his deck crew was pulling *Hull* survivors from the water. The possibility of a Japanese submarine intercepting his message crossed Plage's mind. But since no enemy had yet to see his searchlights, and with the possibility of more Americans still in the water, it was a chance he had to take. Moreover, he asked himself, what Japanese commander would be foolish enough to surface a sub in these seas?

He was perplexed when the American destroyer flashed back the message, "WE ARE LEAVING THE AREA." And she did, her running lights disappearing in the troughs of the roiling Pacific.

Captain Calhoun had, in fact, spotted the white shafts of the *Tabberer*'s searchlights far off his port beam and assumed that some vessel was conducting rescue maneuvers. But such was his ship's perilous condition that when he tried to turn to investigate, the pounding and slamming sea nearly scuttled his shambling vessel. Water poured into the hole in her deck left by the stack's disintegration, and across her foredeck ropes and lines were snarled and iron posts and ammunition lockers had been twisted into "queer shapes." The tip of the mainmast was bent at a 90-degree angle, and the galley was out of commission. The *Dewey*'s crew was subsisting on plates of cold beans and stale, soggy bread.

By then Halsey had ordered all ships to rendezvous at an assembly point well south of their position, but the admiral had exempted the *Dewey* upon learning of her wreckage. Calhoun was directed to shape course directly for Ulithi.

Hours later, as they neared the atoll's anchorage, Calhoun and his staff began rummaging through the pile of decoded dispatches received over the past twelve hours. They came across the *Tabberer*'s flashed message.

"*Hull* capsized with little warning," it read in part. "Only two life rafts launched and neither yet sighted by us. Have ten enlisted survivors and will remain in area searching."

Calhoun thought of his Academy classmate Jim Marks. His heart sank.

* * *

After drifting alone for what he guessed was a good twelve hours, treading water, occasionally trying to conserve energy by paddling in an awkward, modified backstroke, Bob Ayers came across a floater net carrying a large cluster of *Spence* crewmates. He was too weary and spent to determine their exact number.

Floater nets are huge circular affairs, their "decks" meshed with two-and-a-half-inch open weave lines and equipped with enough rubber disks, or blocks, secured at intervals around their perimeters, to support kegs of water, medicine, rations . . . and, optimally, twenty-five men. As opposed to rigid balsa life rafts, floater nets are flexible to the motions of the seas, and survivors thrust their feet through the weave and ride atop the swells without risking being overturned. At least, theoretically, such is the case. But at this point on the evening of December 18, conditions were still so atrocious, with breakers rolling in constant sets, that Ayers had no more than grasped a rubber block with his fingertips than a wave hit and tossed him, the net, and everyone riding it high into the air.

Heads knocked and bodies tangled, and when Ayers splashed down he found himself trapped beneath the meshed lines. *"I can just see myself tied up in a knot in this thing with my head facing down,"* he thought. Better to drown on his own terms. He broke free and, with neither a life jacket nor his long-gone potato crate to buoy him, began stroking away. Ayers would never again see the sailors he left on that float ring. Yet soon enough he had recovered several life jackets from the detritus about him. He spent the remainder of December 18 on a lonely vigil, battling the confused seas.

He guessed it was sometime around midnight when he spotted another floater net and swam for it. This one's mesh bottom had torn away, and sailors were clinging to the lines and the buoys forming the outer ring. Those with life jackets paired up with those without, and someone took a head count. There were tweny-seven frightened men clutching for life. One of them would not stop talking. It was the *Spence*'s chief watertender, George Johnson.

* * *

Shortly after the *Tabberer*'s fleeting encounter with the *Dewey*, Captain Plage, via his jury-rigged receiver, confirmed Halsey's fleetwide order directing all stray ships to rendezvous at sunrise, about ninety miles south of his current position. From this site all surviving ships were to finally refuel, and convoy together either back to station off Luzon or on to Ulithi.

But as soon as Plage pointed his vessel south, another drifting sailor was spotted. He was rescued, as was another survivor fifteen minutes later. Again the *Tabberer* set her course for the rendezvous with Halsey. To Plage, "Everyone aboard the *Tabby* wore a hang-dog look, not because they were exhausted, but because they hated to give up the hunt."

The hunt, however, was far from over. At 1:10 A.M. another floater was spotted and retrieved, and another at 2:50 A.M. Twenty minutes earlier the *Tabby* had managed to get off a brief radio message to the passing destroyer USS *Benham*, giving her location and status. Before the *Benham* sailed out of radio range, Plage also informed her skipper that he was plucking from the sea sailors from the capsized destroyer *Hull*.

Pat Douhan could make out the search beacons just over the horizon. They resembled long, sweeping ovals of frozen moonlight reflecting off the gray cloud cover. But the water current was too strong, carrying him in the opposite direction, and the lights soon vanished behind the gray veil of rain. He recalled his experiences mistakenly "pinging" whales for submarines as the *Hull*'s rookie sonar operator. He banished the hope. No sonarman would ever pick up a lone man drifting across the Pacific.

Just then something "whomped" Douhan in the back of his neck. He froze. Shark? Barracuda? In 1944 there were dozens, hundreds, of contradictory "shark antidote" theories circulating through the ranks of the U.S. Navy (as there are today). Punch them in the nose; poke at their eyes; roll up in a ball, become horizontal, and remain perfectly still; thrash as hard as you can to scare them away; get hold of their fins and ride them. Then (again, as today), no one could say for certain what worked. The navy found it prudent not to dwell on the subject in boot camp, bad as it was for morale, and most Third Fleet sailors had given as much thought to shark attacks as they had to capturing Tojo. *Sure, it might happen, but not likely to me.*

In a near panic, Douhan turned and threw a punch. His fist grazed the bristles of a floating push broom. It had "USS *Hull*" stamped into its handle. He clutched at it "like a long-lost friend," and after a time he began to experiment. He realized that if he turned on his back and positioned the long handle just so along his spine, he could prop his legs on the shoulders of the broom. He floated this way for some hours.

Douhan guessed it was around midnight when he saw the next light. It wasn't a ship's searchlight, too small for that, but it wasn't an optical illusion either. His throat was raw and his voice was hoarse, but he yelled for all he was worth.

"Who is it?" came the reply.

"It's Pat! Pat Douhan! Off the *Hull!*"

The light moved closer, and Douhan recognized sixteen shipmates crowded onto a donut-shaped raft. Its balsa latticework deck had collapsed from the weight of so many men, but it remained suspended by ropes, perhaps three feet below the surface. His fellow survivors were standing chest-deep in water inside the ring, their arms draped over the side. They pulled him aboard. They told him they had no food, and no fresh water.

He recognized Lt. (j.g.) E. B. Brooks, one of Captain Marks's few friends on the *Hull*. Brooks was the ship's assistant communications officer, and when he'd come aboard he was anxious to learn as much as he could about the sound gear apparatus. Douhan had spent hours teaching the man the intricacies of the machine. It wasn't but a week later that the know-it-all Brooks had returned and berated Douhan for not operating it properly. *Typical officer bullshit.* It didn't matter now.

Pat Douhan again had something solid, albeit submerged, beneath his feet. He was relatively safe. He was no longer alone.

At 2:30 A.M. on December 19, Halsey's flag plot sprang to life with the news that the *Tabberer* was still afloat. The message was relayed via TBS from Capt. William Rogers's limping *Aylwin*, which reported that she had in turn received word from the *Hickox*, which had steamed past the little DE with the *Benham* and intercepted the message Plage had sent out. Rogers gave the approximate coordinates of the sighting—latitude 14° 52' north, longitude 127° 28' east—just under one hundred miles from the rendezvous site. The jubilant reaction on the *New Jersey*'s bridge was tempered when Rogers added that the *Tabberer* reported that she was recovering survivors from the capsized destroyer *Hull*.

"Mick" Carney added the *Tabberer*'s name to the roster of surviving vessels and crossed the *Hull* off the list. One witness in Halsey's wardroom noticed "the lifting of eyebrows as soon as word about the *Tabberer*'s rescue effort got around. Wasn't a destroyer escort just a little out of its element on an operation of this sort in the wake of a typhoon?"

By this time, Third Fleet vessels that had been scattered over three thousand square miles of ocean were now coalescing around Halsey's flagship. With Typhoon Cobra swirling away to the northwest, it was finally possible to recommence fueling and servicing. The seas, however, remained highly confused and continued to hinder the effort. The admiral resigned himself to the fact that the operation would most likely take all day. Now, he realized, he was even shaving close on his promise to MacArthur to steam Task Force 38 back to its station off Luzon by December 21. This time, chastened, he did not wait to inform the general. That morning, at 9:22 A.M., he also sent a coded communiqué to CINCPAC Nimitz at Pearl:

"Typhoon center passed thirty miles north of fleet guide midday 18th. Tracked by surface radar. Gusts to 93 knots. Fleet took beating. *Tabberer* (DE418) reports *Hull* (DD350) capsized with little warning at 10:30. Only ten enlisted survivors at time of report. Several other stragglers still unreported."

Halsey further informed Nimitz that he had already ordered several ships, including the *Tabberer*, back to Ulithi and would "strike intentions and movements of cripples in separate dispatches." In other words, as soon as he knew where these cripples were. Or, in the cases of the *Monaghan* and *Spence*, if they were.

Then, draping sea charts over any available space, Halsey's staff began planning the rescue mission. His navigators studied equatorial currents and trade winds, making allowances for the longest possible distance in every direction a single floating man or raft could drift. Aerologists factored in a natural phenomenon called the Leeway Effect, that is, the correlation among a floater's exposed body surface, the local ocean currents, and the typhoon's gales. In essence, this meant that men drifting alone in sodden kapoks, or in low-to-the-waterline groups aboard floater nets, would be more apt to be carried southwest toward central Luzon by the current. Conversely, survivors aboard rafts would be pushed northwest by Cobra's winds.

As soon as his larger ships were refueled, Halsey would direct them to cover every square inch of ocean into which a drifting sailor might have carried. Hundreds of airmen prepared to take to the sky. Thousands of lookouts were designated. It was all well and good that the *Tabberer* had stumbled upon a few floaters. But one really couldn't expect a little destroyer escort to bear the brunt of a rescue so enormous in scope.

CHAPTER 22

"Them sharks, they don't like onions for breakfast."

—Ship's Cook 1st Class Paul "Cookie" Phillips,
USS Tabberer

Sometime past midnight, one of Pat Douhan's raftmates pointed and said, "Hey, there's something out there on the horizon."

Another sailor said, "Yeah, looks like an island."

There was indeed some sort of dark hulk lurking in the distance. It had no running lights; in fact, it was shining no lights at all. It was too big to be a raft. Why couldn't it be land? The twenty-five or so men began yelling, screaming, waving, until one voice cut through the celebration.

"Shut up!" he hollered. "You smell that?"

The men quieted, and Douhan recalled sailing near several Japanese-held islands the *Hull* had skirted in previous campaigns. They all had a distinctive odor from the enemy's cook pots; a little fishy, but much more pungent, like a strong incense. It was, however, an odor combat veterans never forgot, and now each man on the raft smelled it, too. But there was something else, another scent, and it seemed to dawn on the Americans all at once. *Diesel oil.*

"It's a Jap sub," someone whispered. "Surfaced. Recharging its batteries. Keep quiet. Douse those flashlights."

A blanket of silence descended upon the raft.

* * *

Beloved by his crew for his amiable disposition, in an emergency Henry Plage proved cool and hard. If he were weather, he'd be sleet. The *Tabberer*'s all-night boxed searches had carried her over twenty-five square miles of liquid cordilleras, and despite the fact that nearly 90 percent of her officers and crew were untested reservists, not one of them had been lost or injured. The *Tabby* had cut through the tossing seas like a clarinet glissando, and as December 19 dawned steel gray, the ship carried thirteen *Hull* survivors in her sick bay. Sharks had bitten several of the rescued sailors, and one had had his foot slashed deep by a scavenging barracuda.

Numerous species of shark—makos, white tips, blues, and the rapacious tigers, which have been eviscerated with objects ranging from reindeers to monkeys to barrels of nails in their gullets—have coursed through what is now known as the Philippine Sea for millions of years. Though marine biologists and shark experts maintain that the carnivores have never acquired a taste for stringy, sinewy human beings, they are, in the end, scavengers. The scent of blood from wounded survivors was a strong attraction, and seamen recovering aboard the *Tabby* told gruesome tales of watching fellow shipmates being torn apart by the "hyenas of the sea" before slipping forever into the depths. Hearing these, Plage ordered a squad of riflemen ready on deck each time they spotted a drifting sailor.

Some floaters, like Louis Purvis's poor seaman, were found dead. The little *Tabby* had no spare room to store bodies, so the corpses had their dog tags removed and were cut loose from their life jackets to sink to the bottom, accompanied by a crewman on deck reading a prayer aloud. Empty kapoks were gaffed and taken aboard to avoid redundant searches. With each dead sailor, or even an empty life preserver, the thoughts of the *Tabby*'s young crew turned to the telegrams parents and wives and sweethearts back home in the States would soon receive. *We regret to inform you . . .*

Though the seas still ran choppy, with daylight came more moderate winds, and for the first time in three days the *Tabberer*'s fatigued crew felt that they were through the worst of the weather.

All night, as Plage conducted his boxed search, his destroyer escort had climbed and descended endless ranges of white-lathered combers. Lookouts, deck gangs, and rescue swimmers had been beaten black-and-blue, and the crew manning the cargo nets had, at times, been completely submerged as the ship rolled and heeled.

Belowdecks, the ship's black gang had squeezed enough power out of the *Tabby*'s engines to escape capture in the still-cavernous troughs. Now, although she continued to pitch down waves like a toboggan on a volcano, at least her constant rolls had decreased to "only" 30 degrees.

The *Tabberer* missed her sunrise rendezvous with the rest of the fleet, yet not one crewman gave it a second thought. There was no time. Shortly after 6:00 A.M., two more survivors were spotted and hauled in, one more thirty minutes later, and another thirty minutes after that. Among them was twenty-two-year-old Ship's Cook 1st Class Milburn "Spiz" Hoffman, who had never been outside of landlocked Oklahoma before enlisting and being billeted on the *Hull*.

Hoffman had virtually "floated up" from the *Hull*'s forward galley when the destroyer capsized, and upon clearing the sinking vessel through an air vent, he had snagged a drifting life preserver and tied in with an injured *Hull* shipmate. During the night the two sailors had spotted the *Tabberer* and recognized that she was conducting boxed searches, but Hoffman's partner said he was too weak to swim for it. Hoffman removed his trousers, draped them around the man's shoulders, and began towing him like a lifeguard toward the searchlights in anticipation of her next turn. But the ship remained too distant to flag down.

Hoffman then passed out, and when he came to the next morning his floatmate was dead. He untied their connecting lifelines, removed the sailor's kapok, and watched him sink from view, swirling down through the clear blue water until he was no bigger than a toy soldier. His crewmate's death sent Hoffman into a kind of despair, and he slipped out of his own kapok and tossed it away. "I gave up," he said.

Then Hoffman began thinking about his mother. He hadn't thought of her lately. He was an only child, and his father had passed away ten months earlier. He decided he could not die this way; he could not leave his mother alone. He swam after his kapok and re- covered it floating beside a waterlogged horsehair mattress. Fasten- ing the life jacket to the mattress, he fashioned a makeshift raft and climbed aboard.

He'd lost his pants during his tow-rope duty, and while float- ing on the mattress he used all his remaining clothes, including his skivvies, to try to shield his eyes from the unrelenting morn- ing sun that beat down on him between rainsqualls. Eventually the wind whipped every stitch away, and that is how the *Tabberer's* deck gang found him: splayed across his mattress, naked, sun- burned, half dead.

Plage immediately dubbed him "Lord Godiva"—as if the skip- per was one to talk, Hoffman thought later. For the *Tabby's* skip- per was by now himself half naked, stripped to only a borrowed pair of ill-fitting trousers and his officer's peaked cap. He had not slept in close to sixty hours, most of it spent pacing the open bridge during the height of the storm, when his uniform had been shred- ded to tattered rags. He was no longer "Cary Grant," unless, that is, Grant was starring as Robinson Crusoe, and his XO Surdam even noted that the skipper's bruised, swollen eyes were in worse con- dition than most of the survivors' they were pulling from the ocean.

This, naturally, only endeared Plage further to the *Tabberer's* in- dustrious young crew, which seemed to gather strength from their skipper's unfaltering energy and good cheer. By 10:00 A.M., Decem- ber 19, the *Tabby's* rescue total had reached twenty-seven *Hull* sail- ors and, in fact, the reason Plage had had to borrow a pair of trousers was because he had loaned his backup uniform to the nineteenth man plucked from the sea—the *Hull's* Lt. Comdr. James A. Marks.

A delirious Marks was hauled in clutching a hatchet, which the *Tabby's* crew assumed he was carrying to ward off sharks. Soon enough, however, word spread across the ship from other *Hull* sur- vivors in sick bay. As one crewmate told the *Tabby's* shipfitter

Leonard Glaser, "He had that hatchet to make sure nobody from his own crew would try to get rid of him."

Recovering in officers' country, Marks told Plage that while bouncing over the whitecaps he'd become so sick from inadvertently swallowing saltwater that his body's involuntary reflex to retch had probably saved his life by keeping his head and face above the surface. There was little food in his stomach to throw up, he added, since he had not eaten a thing since December 17, the day before Cobra struck. But after puking for hours, he'd inexplicably become so ravenous that he'd started chewing, first on his kapok's whistle, and then on a strip of leather torn from his shoe. When he failed to visit his crew in sick bay for the entire journey back to Ulithi, several *Hull* seamen had other suggestions as to what Lieutenant Commander Marks could chew on.

Although the rain had tapered to soft showers, at a few moments past sunrise on December 19 it was still bleak, overcast, and depressing in the quadrant through which Chief Quartermaster Archie DeRyckere was drifting. Suddenly he caught sight of a column of gray smoke rising, as if from a chimney, on the western horizon. He nudged Tom Spohn and George Guy awake.

All three watched as a ship, no one was sure what class, steamed back and forth—right to left, left to right—inching a bit closer with each vector. DeRyckere recognized the movements as a "traffic square," or boxed search, and he told Spohn and Guy to unhitch the kapok tag lines that had lashed them together throughout the night. His plan was to spread out in a triangle pattern, to put perhaps a quarter of a mile of sea between them.

"They'll have a better chance of spotting us this way," he said. "Splash a lot, splash all you can. And don't forget, if one of us gets picked up, there's still two more of us out here."

For emphasis, he repeated, "There's still two more of us out here!"

The sailors wished each other luck, and separated.

By this time DeRyckere's eyes were nearly completely swollen shut and so scabbed over from saltwater sores that he considered it a small miracle that he'd even spotted the smoke from the ship. He had stroked only a few dozen yards when something knocked, hard, against his back. A frisson of electricity ran up his spine as he wheeled. Through blurred vision he barely made out the outline of a large dorsal fin. The shark had to be six feet. *"A big bastard,"* he thought, and said aloud, "You know, God, first you take my ship. Then you have me swim around in this ocean all night. And now you're gonna feed me to the sharks? That ain't right."

The chief was unaware that the navy had only a year earlier experimented with a shark deterrent called the Life Jacket Shark Repellent Compound Packet, a noxious mixture of ammonium acetate, black dye, and decaying shark flesh. The plan had been to equip navy-issue life preservers with this witches' brew should it prove effective in driving away sharks. It had not, and the navy had dropped the project. Even had DeRyckere known of the tests, however, they would have offered no solace. As the monster circled him, he felt in the pocket of his dungarees for the Bermuda onion. He wondered if sharks ate onions.

The big fish continued to stalk him as he squinted to watch the *Tabberer* trawl up, first George Guy, and minutes later Tom Spohn. The way the DE maneuvered herself upwind and then tumbled sideways, DeRyckere thought at first that her captain was crazy, and that his shipmates would be crushed. But once he saw Spohn and Guy plucked from the sea, he realized that this was the only feasible manner with which to approach a drifter, given the gale and the enormous swells. His admiration for this skipper's seamanship ticked up several notches. *"Must be a real shellback,"* he thought.

Within twenty minutes the *Tabberer* was closing on DeRyckere, and .30-caliber Springfield rifles and Thompson submachine guns erupted from her foredeck. The sea around him pocked with bullets. A rescue swimmer was swiftly beside him, tying him into a looped line, and he was being hauled up the cargo net slung over the side of the ship's port beam. Two sailors, one under each arm, supported him, and one asked if he could stand.

"Hell, yeah, I'm fine," he said. They let him go, and Archie DeRyckere fell flat on his face.

He was helped down to the crowded sick bay, where a corpsman examined him for broken bones, and poured eyedrops over his crusted-closed eyelids. Then Cookie Phillips handed Archie DeRyckere a pear. DeRyckere hated pears. But he ate that pear down to the stem, seeds and all. As he swallowed the last of it, he told Phillips the story of the shark, and pulled the sodden Bermuda onion from his dungaree pocket.

"Well, then, that's what saved you," Cookie Phillips said. "Them sharks, they don't like onions for breakfast."

At 9:00 A.M. on December 19, the Third Fleet's chief aerologist, Comdr. George F. Kosco, strode into Admiral Halsey's flag plot in search of the latest weather reports. He was intercepted by Capt. Leonard Dow, the fleet's communications officer, who handed him a decoded report just delivered by chute from the intelligence shack belowdecks.

Kosco stared at the message tape. He was, he said, "literally stunned by surprise." The communiqué had been filed from the seaplane tender *Chandeleur* early on the morning of December 17. It detailed how, at 5:00 A.M. on that date, a reconnaissance pilot flying out of Palau in the Western Carolines had come upon, and marked on his charts, the coordinates of a nascent typhoon developing just southeast of the fleet. For some reason, when the report had been dispatched to the *New Jersey*, a copy had not been sent to Fleet Weather Central at Pearl. Kosco reeled at the what-ifs.

When he regained his composure, the aerologist marched down to the code room. Why had it taken nearly forty-eight hours for this message to be delivered? No one had a satisfactory answer. The best Kosco could determine was that it had merely been buried under a stack of reports while higher-priority communications from

MacArthur, CINCPAC, and Washington, D.C., had been decoded. It was, someone said, just the navy way.

Moments past 10:00 A.M. on December 19, the *Tabberer*'s crew picked up the distant drone of aircraft. Soon two Helldiver SB2C ("Son of a Bitch, Second Class") dive bombers were circling the destroyer escort, close enough for Plage to get off a message via his jury-rigged antenna. He requested their assistance in his search. An airman replied that they were en route to their own search grid coordinates. In minutes the two planes were specks in the sky.

Three hours later, Plage received a radio message from Halsey, giving the coordinates of a second rendezvous site, this one scheduled for sunset, again some ninety miles due south of the *Tabby*'s current position. The admiral ordered Plage to break off his search-and-rescue and rejoin the remainder of the fleet. But as soon as Plage abandoned his boxed search and shaped a southerly course, another floater was spotted. By the time the survivor was picked up and the *Tabberer* had again turned back south, Plage realized he would not meet the sunset deadline.

This was confirmed when, at 3:15 P.M., one of the *Tabby*'s lookouts saw a group of men floating some two miles distant. This was the farthest away they'd yet spotted any floaters. The survivors turned out to be seven *Hull* seamen, led by Lt. (j.g.) George Sharp, the destroyer's chief engineer and son of the rear admiral commanding the Pacific Fleet's minesweepers. At Sharp's insistence, the group had abandoned a capsizing raft and lashed themselves together with belts, kerchiefs, and lengths of rope the night before, "tied up like a bunch of asparagus." Sharp had convinced them that they'd be easier to spot floating in a large cluster.

One seventeen-year-old seaman, quite smaller than the rest, had joined the group only that morning when the mattress upon which he had been floating for almost twenty-four hours finally fell to pieces. The boy had no life jacket, and the rest had taken turns boosting him on their backs to keep his head above water. He weighed only 120 pounds, but this was nonetheless an incredible act of strength for fatigued and frightened men treading water, trying to keep their own noses and mouths above the surface.

This knot of survivors had watched through most of the day as the *Tabberer* conducted her expanding squared search, and several sailors had wanted to swim for the ship when it first hove into view. But Sharp, realizing she was too far away, and recognizing the systematic hunt, persuaded them to stay together until she eventually came to them. The men had just been carried aboard—only one sailor, the bantamweight, could walk under his own steam—when another *Hull* officer, Lt. (j.g.) Cyrus Watkins, was spotted several hundred yards off.

The *Tabby* closed on Watkins, and the deck crew recognized that he was barely conscious and being circled by an eight-foot shark. Again rifles and tommy guns crackled, and the shark was momentarily driven away. But Watkins was still a good thirty yards from the *Tabby* when XO Bob Surdam saw the fin heading back toward the struggling floater.

Surdam stripped off his uniform blouse and, without a life jacket, dived from the signal bridge. He reached Watkins and began towing him by his life preserver collar toward the ship. He was still fifty feet away when Torpedoman 1st Class Robert Cotton, manning the cargo nets, saw that Surdam was flagging. He, too, dived in. With the shark coiling about them, the two lifted Watkins aboard.

Four more rescues followed within the next hour, interrupted by frequent wild goose chases after empty life jackets. By 4:30 P.M. the *Tabby* had forty survivors in sick bay. The sensate men all kissed the deck.

Here the twenty-nine-year-old Henry Lee Plage made a calculated decision to countermand Admiral Halsey's orders. He assumed he was sailing the same ocean currents that were carrying *Hull* survivors toward his ship, and decided to remain on this grid throughout the night and early morning of December 20. At least until daybreak, he told his officers; if he saved just one more man, the insubordination would be worth it. Privately, he thought he'd get either a medal or a court-martial.

The *Tabberer*'s crew, whose zeal was contagious, let up a great cheer when word circulated about the skipper's "rebellion." The rescues had become, one *Tabby* sailor put it, "a proud and wonderful chore." Plage, however, would later admit to feeling "a little shaky inside because of the high-handed disregard for orders I had shown." Yet, as he told Surdam, "In [our] battered condition, this ship is no good to the fleet. But it can still save lives."

The captain's hazard paid off almost immediately, as the *Tabberer* pulled in her forty-first survivor a little after sunset. Moreover, through radioman Ralph Tucker's yeoman efforts, Plage was able to pick up a message from Halsey's flagship changing the DE's orders. The admiral now instructed the *Tabby* to continue its searches until relieved by an escort carrier the following day.

CHAPTER 23

"Well, if He wants to test me, I guess I'll show Him what I'm made of."

—Lt. (J.G.) Lloyd Rust, CIC Officer, USS Hull

Communications officer Lt. (j.g.) Lloyd Rust was at his station in the *Hull*'s combat information center, just back of and below the bridge, when the destroyer capsized. The shack filled with seawater almost instantaneously. He was forced to swim underwater to escape but, as fate would have it, such was his lack of confidence in Captain Marks's seamanship that he'd strapped on his kapok long before the ship went over. Before Rust freed himself completely, he'd become tangled up in the shack's electric lines, which had cut his hands badly. Then a renegade life raft carrying several shipmates had dropped from the sky directly on top of him and nearly drowned him. Those crewmates were the last men he had seen for twenty-four hours.

After bouncing from wave to wave throughout the night, sometime after daybreak on the morning of December 19, Rust spotted a floatplane skimming the waves. It was obviously searching for survivors. Earlier, he had kicked off his shoes and doffed his pants, as he felt they were dragging him below the ocean surface. Now, with nothing to wave at the floatplane, he took off his white boxer shorts and brandished them as high as he could reach. The aircraft's crew did not see him.

Sometime that afternoon Rust saw a destroyer bearing down on him. She was so close that he could make out the actions of her deck crew. But when she came within several hundred yards, she took an abrupt turn to starboard and steamed back over the horizon.

That was the final straw for Lloyd Rust. He was ready to give up hope. He was ready to die. Only his anger saved him. He decided that he was "mad at the Good Lord"—angry with Him for sinking his ship, and even angrier with Him that two rescue searches had failed to spot him. But then he turned some kind of spiritual corner.

"He's just testing me," Rust decided. "He just wants to see if I really want to stay alive. Why else would He have my rescue ship make a hard right turn out in the middle of nowhere on the ocean? Well, if He wants to test me, I guess I'll show Him what I'm made of."

Rust began stroking west, and vowed to swim all the way to the Philippines if necessary. He swam under the searing sun. He swam under the glittering stars. He swam until the eastern horizon bloomed with the faint glow of sunrise on December 20, when he could swim no more. It never occurred to Lloyd Rust that the ship he had seen the previous day was conducting a boxed search, and he'd undoubtedly carried himself away from its vector.

He rolled over on his back and lapsed into unconsciousness.

Ralph Tucker was proud of himself. He felt like a modern Edison, coaxing crackling life from an inert mare's nest of wires and cable snaking about a backup steel antenna atop the *Tabby*. Granted, his makeshift TBS could not transmit very far, but it could pick up coded American communiqués beamed across the entire Western Pacific. Now, his skipper, Captain Plage, could overhear Third Fleet radio transmissions, although he was still unable to send messages more than a short distance.

Thus it occurred that sometime before midnight on December 19, Plage intercepted an ominous directive from Halsey's flag plot. Two destroyers were ordered to peel off from their screening task group to investigate "a suspicious radar contact" not far from what Plage guessed were the *Tabby*'s coordinates.

Plage's first thought was, "It could be us."

Without his radar, Plage had no idea in what direction the fleet was, nor from which bearing the two destroyers would approach. He was well aware, however, that with her mast and radar rigging carried away, from even a short distance the *Tabby* could easily be mistaken for a Japanese man o' war, or even a surfaced sub. It had already happened with more than a few survivors. But survivors didn't carry cannons.

Over the TBS, Plage could hear the two Tin Can skippers speaking to each other about "the enemy target" as they steamed closer. The pilothouse was fraught as the *Tabby* cut her lights. Her bridge crew expected shells to start raining down upon them at any moment, and Plage himself had visions of being run down in the darkness. He found it "maddening" being able to listen to his own fellow captains, probably men he had met at some point, discuss zeroing in on his ship while not being able to call them off.

But the same confused seas that had so battered the *Tabberer* now saved her. Because of the giant swells, neither destroyer commander could get a fixed radar bead on the little DE. They were forced to move closer than normal firing range, and after several heart-pounding moments, the two ships sailed to within hailing distance of the *Tabby*'s short-range transmission power.

Plage frantically identified his vessel just as, he was to later learn, not only the destroyers, but the big guns of the Third Fleet's heavies were preparing to open fire. As he put it, "All the guns of the *New Jersey* and other fire-support ships were aimed at us, ready for business."

After nearly being blasted from the sea by her own task force, the *Tabberer* searched in vain for survivors throughout the evening of December 19 and into the morning of December 20. The seas were calmer now, placid enough, Plage knew, for a Japanese sub to surface to periscope depth. He ordered his searchlights turned off. Yet without the lights, it was entirely too dark to spot any drifting men in the rolling, and still dangerous, swells. Not one did the *Tabby*'s crew sight.

Nonetheless, it was to the great good fortune of men floating about the Philippine Sea that Lt. Frank Cleary, medical officer of the DEs in Task Group 30.7, had chosen the *Tabberer* for his maiden sea voyage. Cleary was a greenhorn, a California kid but six months in the service, though he had a natural physician's touch. Assisted by the *Tabby*'s two pharmacist's mates, his sick bay as well as an adjacent cabin were soon overwhelmed. He knew what he was dealing with.

When the recovered drifters were strong enough, Cleary directed that they be helped out of their clothes and immediately given hot showers, wrapped in blankets, and administered spoonfuls of fruit juice and hot soup. Immobile men were carried by stretcher to tables in the wardroom next to sick bay, stripped, and inspected for injuries. All had their blood pressure and heart rates monitored.

Since so many had been only half clad, if that, when they went into the water, dungarees and T-shirts were dug out of the *Tabby*'s meager stores, and precious cigarettes were scrounged from across the ship. Most of the survivors had not eaten since the day before Typhoon Cobra struck hardest, December 18, and Cookie Phillips and his galley mates prepared mountains of sandwiches and brewed gallons of coffee. "Spiz" Hoffman, the *Hull* cook, had even recovered enough to volunteer to help out.

Sailors pulled from the sea were suffering from a host of maladies, including exposure, saline poisoning from drinking saltwater, saltwater lesions, and shark and barracuda bites. Nearly all had swollen, red-and-purple-tinged eyes and faces from battling the huge surf. Cleary knew that a boy or young man robust enough to serve in the United States Navy carried, on average, about 20 percent body fat and could live under ordinary circumstances for perhaps three weeks without food, and a week without potable water. But for most of the survivors, these were no ordinary circumstances.

Aside from large predators such as sharks and giant barracuda, the Western Pacific teemed with bacteria and other tiny organisms and smaller fish that feasted on open flesh wounds, of which few Typhoon Cobra survivors were free. Navy scientists had determined that men could live, theoretically, for many days drifting about the warm, 80-degree surface waters of a body such as the Philippine Sea (unlike, say, in the frigid waters off the Aleutians, where washing overboard ensured nearly instant death). But navy doctors also knew that over the same period of time the stripping of a human's epidermal layer of naturally protective oils through saltwater immersion would turn sailors' skin either as fragile as papier-mâché or as coarsened as beef jerky.

Even immersion up to twenty-four hours would result in painful, acidic ulcers similar to bedsores that could eat through exposed flesh down to muscle and bone. And pulmonary edema, brought on by the ingestion of saltwater—whether inadvertently while being tumbled by combers or out of delusional thirst—would lead to breathing problems and, if left untreated, quickening, irregular heartbeats and pneumonia. Swallowing seawater, with its high sodium chloride content and trace elements of potassium, boric acid, magnesium, and sulphate, was like drinking a toxic cocktail. Those chemicals would seep from a man's lungs into his bloodstream and begin breaking down red blood cells. This would hasten anemia, and weakened men become delusional and subject to visions. The *Tabby*'s crew listened in disbelief to stories of hallucinating survivors swearing they heard mermaids' voices.

The one factor Cleary counted in the survivors' favor was that the capsized destroyers had been so low on fuel, and sunk so rapidly, that little or no oil had coated the sea's surface, as was common in most shipwrecks. The roiling waves that had so quickly scattered the drifting sailors had actually helped in this regard, as men swallowing toxic fuel oil not only become violently ill, but the acidic, viscous liquid ate into the seams of life preservers. Eventually, it would rot their kapoks from the inside out.

But, Cleary also knew, this small run of luck did not amount to much. A single overnight of drifting about the ocean, even at these equatorial latitudes, would most likely trigger hypothermia. The heart rates, respiratory rates, and blood pressures of desperate men would all plummet until the hapless sailors, passing from stupor to unconsciousness, died. He informed Plage that rescue had best arrive sooner than later for drifting seamen battered and beaten to pulp by Cobra's waves and winds.

From the movement of the sun, Ray Schultz guessed it was close to noon on December 19 when he caught sight of another floater, the first human being he had seen in close to twenty-four hours. Striking out, Schultz soon recognized the sailor as the teenage storekeeper Ken Drummond. How he knew this boy, he did not remember.

The young sailor appeared near death and wore a blank look on his face, a sphinx without a riddle. Schultz attempted to buck him up by convincing him the storm was finally ebbing. It was true. The sky was loosening, and though the swells were still huge, the wind had softened and the rainspouts had become less violent and less frequent.

"I'm sure you'll get picked up really soon," Schultz yelled to Drummond. He added that he was certain he'd spotted search-lights on several occasions during the night. He had, he said, even tried to swim toward them. "Somebody knows we're out here," he said.

Drummond did not reply. In fact, he did not say a word as he drifted away. The boy was in shock, and Schultz was too weak to help him.

The chief floated alone for several more hours before, sometime late in the afternoon, he drifted into a cluster of five *Hull* shipmates who were trying to keep one of their crewmates alive. It was another boy, and though Schultz did not know his name, he almost wept. The kid had been pounded so viciously by waves that at least one rib had snapped and punctured his lung. He was in excruciating pain, barely able to swim, and with every breath he coughed up mouth-fuls of blood.

Not long after Schultz joined the group, the boy died, and the other survivors looked to the ranking chief bosun's mate for guidance. Schultz saw no option other than to relieve him of his dog tags, life jacket, and white undershirt, and allow the corpse to sink.

Schultz was still herding these sailors when, just before sunset, the *Tabberer* steamed over the horizon. The chief eyed this demasted vessel with its superstructure so torn up and, like so many others, was convinced she was a surfaced Japanese submarine. They would all spend the rest of the war in a prisoner-of-war camp. At this point, however, no one seemed to care. Selecting the smallest and lightest seaman in the group, they lifted him as high in the air as they could. He waved the white T-shirt from the boy dead with the punctured lung.

When the DE neared, Schultz and his drifting crewmates recognized the sailors on her foredeck as Americans. But the *Tabby*'s deck gang seemed agitated, pointing, waving, and before long muted yells could be heard, but not made out, above the wind. The floating survivors had no idea what to make of this pantomime until, soon enough, the familiar ring of automatic rifle fire split the air, and the circling sharks were dispersed.

Ray Schultz was finally lifted on deck after floating for thirty-three hours across the Philippine Sea. Like his friend and fellow chief Archie DeRyckere, he assured the *Tabby* sailors that he could walk on his own. By now this reaction had become predictable, and when Schultz tried to take a step, he fell face-first. *Tabby* sailors caught him before he hit the deck.

"I guess I'm closer to dead than I think I am," he said as they guided him down to sick bay. Schultz was led to a bunk adjacent to that of DeRyckere, whose eyes had gotten so bad he was temporarily blinded. Their exchange could have been lifted from an Abbott and Costello routine.

"Hey there, Archie, how ya doing?"

"I'm doing good, great, glad to be here. Who are you?"

"I'm Schultz."

"No, I haven't seen Schultz. But who are you?"

"It's me, Arch, Ray Schultz."

"No, I told ya, I haven't seen Schultz."

"Fer cripesakes, Arch, what the hell's the matter with you, anyway? It's me, Ray Schultz."

"Ray! God, Ray! You're alive! Oh, Jesus, am I glad to hear your voice. I can't see nothing. They say I'm blind, but just for a little while, from all the salt coating my eyes."

Minutes before 5:00 A.M. on December 20, flag plot received a report from the jeep carrier USS *Rudyerd Bay*. Four hours earlier, one of the DEs in her rescue group had picked up five survivors from the destroyer *Spence*.

"Statements indicate," the message continued, "*Spence* capsized suddenly and believe few personnel survived."

Halsey's shoulders slumped. He stood, crestfallen, as "Mick" Carney removed the *Spence* from his fleet roster. The admiral prepared to compose another depressing communiqué for Nimitz.

Since the evening of December 18, all Third Fleet vessels had been conducting ad hoc searches for survivors despite the unlikelihood of spotting an individual floater, or even a small raft, from a heavy's towering deck. Lookouts tied into gun sponsons, some hastily equipped with "shepherd's crooks" lashed to long poles, on the carriers USS *Cabot* and USS *Hancock*, as well as the battleship USS *Iowa*, and the carrier USS *San Juan* reported seeing flashing kapok lights and hearing whistles (later determined as most likely being from *Hull* survivors). But they could not reach the men, and when destroyers arrived thirty-nine hours later to search each area, they discovered no one.

Similarly, specific DD searches for *Hull* survivors launched toward the coordinates at which she was believed to have capsized proved futile. The only object recovered was a small, empty whaleboat washed off the cruiser USS *Pittsburgh*. ("Have sighted a suburb of *Pittsburgh* and have taken it in tow," radioed the recovering ship's commander.)

The day after the storm, Halsey had designated the jeep carriers *Rudyerd Bay* and *Anzio* to accompany three destroyers and two destroyer escorts—including Lt. Comdr. Raymond Toner's *Robert F. Keller*—in the van of what he was to label "the most exhaustive and extensive sea search ever organized in maritime history." As a wide arc of reconnaissance planes and vessels fanned out to the west-northwest, on December 20 the *Robert F. Keller* picked up not only four teenage *Hull* sailors who were certain they had been abandoned, but a seaman from the *Anzio* who had been washed over the side when the carrier took green water over her bow. One oddity, noted by the *Keller's* Captain Toner, was that as he sighted the *Hull* survivors through his binoculars, they all appeared to be wearing white gloves. Later, after they were brought aboard, the *Keller's* medic informed him that their white skin was a medical condition known as "immersion hands," caused by exposure to the sun and saltwater. Toner personally broke out a bottle of brandy and gave each lad a dram.

Meanwhile, at 8:25 A.M. on December 20, the destroyer USS *Cogswell* nearly ran down the *Hull's* Tom Stealey, the fireman who, moments before she'd capsized, had volunteered against his better judgment to crawl into the aft boiler room to try and stoke her doused fires. Stealey had seen two of his crewmates eaten by sharks before his glazed eyes, and when the *Cogswell's* deck crew hauled him in, he was semiconscious and near out of his head. Following a hot shower, he told a harrowing story through the swollen and bloody saltwater sores that lacerated his mouth.

He had begun his ordeal in the water with fourteen to fifteen shipmates, he said, each gripping a single, floating ship's line perhaps fifty feet long. Some men wore life jackets; others did not. But, one by one, every one had been either picked off by sharks or given up and slipped, exhausted and traumatized, below the surface, as if off on some far greater mission. Stealey had awakened that morning drifting beside the last, dead body, floating facedown in its kapok. The *Cogswell* sailors listened rapt until one thought to offer him a meal.

"Anything," Stealey muttered.

"How about a nice steak, and some potatoes?"

"Oh, man, that'd be great."

A few minutes later, when Stealey cut his steak and tried to bite down, he howled in pain. His mouth and tongue were too swollen and sore. His lips began to bleed again. He placed his silverware aside and began to weep.

CHAPTER 24

"Take care of the others first. Take care of the others first."

—LT. (J.G.) ALPHONSO KRAUCHUNAS, USS SPENCE

On the afternoon of December 20, the destroyer USS *Knapp* sent a message to flag plot that it had recovered three more *Hull* sailors. One was Seaman 1st Class Al Taylor, Archie DeRyckere's body-surfing buddy, whose face was so battered by the wind, rain, and sun that one *Knapp* seaman thought it had been seared by a blowtorch. The sea was still too volatile for the *Knapp* to lower its high-sided, flat-bottomed Higgins boats, and Taylor had been recovered by the ship's rescue swimmer, Owen "Red" Atkinson. Atkinson, a twenty-year-old seaman from Georgia, subsequently brought aboard an unidentified dead man whose dog tags were missing.

The sailor's body had been fairly mutilated by sharks, his thighs bloody stumps nearly to the hem of his kapok, and the *Knapp*'s skipper ordered that his fingerprints be taken before preparing a burial at sea. A burial detail sewed the corpse into a canvas shroud and weighted it with 40mm shells, and sailors lined each side of the destroyer's fantail as selections from the "Service for the Dead" and *The Book of Common Prayer* were read aloud. *"We therefore, Oh Lord, commit the body of our shipmate unto Thy hands and into the depths."*

Not long after the ceremony was completed with a heartrending splash, Atkinson was back in the water, this time swimming toward a man floating faceup in his kapok. When Atkinson reached him, he slid a bight under his arms and, remembering his last "save," gingerly slapped the seaman's cheeks to see if he was still alive.

At that the floater's eyes blinked open and his arm shot up from beneath the surface. In his hand he held a death grip on a pair of white boxer shorts.

"Lieutenant Lloyd Rust, CIC, USS *Hull*," the officer said to a befuddled Red Atkinson. "The Good Lord has tested me, and it appears that I have passed His test."

As the deck crew from the *Knapp* "reeled" Atkinson and Rust back toward the ship, their herky-jerky movements replicated those of a large wounded fish and acted as a lure for sharks, which began to shadow them. Moreover, because the destroyer had shut off her engines during the rescue, huge swells began to crash over her fantail deck, the lowest point of the vessel above the sea surface, where a swimmer would normally be hoisted aboard. Atkinson and Rust had to be towed nearly completely around the *Knapp*, and guns blazed as the two were lifted atop the cargo head.

Around the same time, the *Keller*'s sister DE, the USS *Swearer*, rescued nine *Spence* crewmen, including six clinging to a float ring. Among them was Lt. (j.g.) Alphonso Krauchunas.

Krauchunas's floater net had escaped the sinking *Spence* with twelve desperate sailors clutching its mesh lines and rubber blocks. Six traumatized souls were lost as the days passed. The float ring had originally contained sufficient stores—two 5-gallon kegs of water and, cached in an empty shell casing, two K-ration food kits, a medical kit, flares, a signal mirror, two cans of dye marker, a hatchet, and two small medicinal bottles of whiskey. But as the night of December 18 wore on and waves pounded the craft, first the medical kit, then the food kits, and finally the flares were wrenched loose and swept away.

When the seas calmed somewhat, Krauchunas assigned each sailor a specific compass point around the net to prevent any one side from overloading and rolling over. The men were all weak, soaking, and freezing, barely holding their heads above water. At some point that first night, one of them snagged a large canvas bag washing by. It contained an uninflated, twenty-man yellow rubber raft, which a seaman managed to inflate by yanking on the toggle that sparked a CO_2 cylinder. Krauchunas and three other sailors climbed aboard, but Krauchunas decided he did not trust the craft's stability and swam back to the float ring. The wind and currents soon tore the raft away. Its three occupants were never again seen.

On the morning of December 19, Krauchunas and his party sighted two search planes far off on the horizon. He broke one of the die marker cans into the sea as his crewmates hollered, waved, and flashed the signal mirror. But the rough swells dissipated the dye and the aircraft did not see them. Like the *Monaghan*'s McCrane, as the ranking officer, Krauchunas had taken charge of doling out one swallow of fresh water to each man every three hours. The water kegs were actually sagging with the meshed net under the ocean's surface, and since they were too heavy to lift, in order to drink men would have to submerge themselves and place their mouths over the spigot, as if siphoning a gas tank, while Krauchunas opened and closed the valve.

For some it was not enough, and they resorted to drinking salt-water. One was Ens. George W. Poer, who sometime after noon on that second day floated away from the raft while the others slept. When Krauchunas awoke, he saw Poer's body, buoyed by its kapok and drifting facedown, perhaps fifty yards from the net. He felt obliged to retrieve the ensign's dog tags, and swam out. When he lifted the sailor's head out of the water to grab the silver chain around his neck, Poer opened his eyes and sputtered, "Why did you wake me? I want to sleep! Let me alone!"

Krauchunas was astonished. When he regained his composure, he convinced Poer to return to the net. Sometime later that day, again as his dog-tired raftmates napped, Poer drifted away a second time, never to be seen again. Soon thereafter two other sailors, Lt. (j.g.) John Whalen and Seaman 1st Class James Heater, also went out of their minds from drinking seawater. For eight or nine hours stronger shipmates held their heads above water, but by nightfall both had slipped beneath the surface for good.

When another seaman suddenly bolted from the float ring and stroked a short distance before returning, Krauchunas asked him what he was doing. The man answered that he'd seen a Coca-Cola sign lit up by a grocery store, and he'd swam out for a drink. But instead of Coca-Cola, he continued, he'd brought back an apple. He brandished a fist-sized chunk of rubber that had broken off from a buoy block, and bit down on it. Krauchunas's cracked and swollen lips hurt just watching.

The group drifted aimlessly throughout the afternoon, their corneas painfully inflamed by the shattered-glass glare of the intense, lemon-colored sun. It hurt just to blink, and men buried their faces in the crooks of their arms in order to avoid even a glimpse of the reflective sea.

Sometime before dusk, small fortune smiled. Seaman Charlie Wohlebb, the first man Krauchunas had encountered in the water after the *Spence* went down, lifted his head and noticed the metallic flash of something bobbing on the surface perhaps a hundred yards away. He dived in, and returned pushing before him an industrial-strength can of vegetable shortening.

Krauchunas hacked it open with the hatchet and passed it around as sunblock. Krauchunas then peeled off his woolen socks and slathered his feet, which had swollen to twice their size. Some on the floater net were buoyed by the rumor that vegetable shortening acted as a shark repellent, although no one could say where it started.

That night, as the men shivered and moaned, Krauchunas led them, alternately, in prayers and songs in an attempt to revive their spirits. But by the early morning of December 20, Krauchunas realized their situation was bleak. He was dreading the dawn, and another day of blistering sun. By 3:00 A.M. he barely had the energy to raise his head when someone shouted, "A ship! It's a ship!"

It was, in fact, a jeep carrier steaming into view, its running lights visible for miles. It had developed a leak in its fuel lines and been ordered to return to Ulithi for servicing. Krauchunas and his shipmates had thought their throats too parched and swollen to scream, but now they shouted hoarsely and waved their shirts. The flattop passed them by in the darkness, no more than one hundred yards away, and vanished over the horizon. Despair prevailed.

Unknown to the survivors, however, a lookout had heard their cries, and the escort carrier had dropped rafts and flares, invisible to the drifting men because of the large swells. Her skipper had also broken radio silence and informed the destroyer escort *Swearer* of the sighting. Presently Krauchunas saw the DE's lighted mast steam into view. As the vessel closed on their port side, again the men screamed with all that was left in their hoarse throats. This time a returning voice blared over a loudspeaker system.

"Survivors in the water, we hear you but cannot see you. Yell once if you want us to turn to starboard, or yell twice if we are to remain on course."

A single yelp, loud and clear, pierced the night. The *Swearer* swerved to starboard, and when it came to within fifty yards of the net, the men all began hollering, "Stop! Stop! You're running us down!"

The DE slowed, turned broadside, and a searchlight swept the sea. The first several times the beam was aimed at their net, swells rose between the floaters and the ship and they were not sighted. Finally the light shone on nine upturned faces, as pale as cadavers, followed by another blaring announcement. "We have spotted you. Remain where you are."

Next a rescue swimmer appeared from nowhere. Someone said, "What took you so long?" and the swimmer smiled. He tied a line to the floater net and signaled the ship. The net was pulled broadside to the destroyer escort, rolling deep in the swells. Timing the rolls as the net rose on the crests, deckhands clasped hands and linked arms with the *Spence* survivors and, one at a time, hoisted them aboard. Krauchunas was the last. He was caught by two husky officers before he collapsed to the steel deck.

He was out of his head, and suddenly the most drained he'd ever felt in his life. It was as if, after nearly three days of keeping his wits sharp to shepherd his floating flock, his life force was slowly leaking out of him. For some reason he demanded that an accounting of his possessions be officially taken—eighteen dollars was found in his saturated wallet—and he repeatedly mumbled, "Take care of the others first. Take care of the others first." Someone assured him that everyone was being seen to.

By the fifth or sixth cup of strong, black coffee, Krauchunas began to come back around, as well as regain the feeling in his legs. This was not delightful. He sat wrapped in blankets, drinking the hot joe, while a pharmacist's mate cut away his woolen socks, revealing two grotesquely swollen feet streaked with bright orange and inky black stripes. The pharmacist's mate told him his socks had shrunk in the water and cut off the circulation to his lower limbs. The last thing he recalled of the night was thanking the mate treating his "immersion feet" for a second shot of morphine.

Twenty-one hours later, as the *Swearer* steamed toward Ulithi, Krauchunas awoke in a sweat-soaked panic. "The ship is rolling over!" he screamed. "The ship is rolling over!"

He bolted from his bunk, pushed past a young seaman assigned to watch over him, and sprinted on throbbing feet for the deck. Along the companionway he burst into the ship's dimly lit wardroom. There his minder caught up to him and found him staring at a pitcher of water and several glasses. They were not moving, much less crashing to the floor.

The young seaman placed a reassuring hand on his shoulder, and Alphonso Krauchunas again regained his wits. The sailor led him back to his bunk.

The sharks had begun to circle Pat Douhan's raft sometime after daybreak on December 19. Huge dorsal fins atop ghostly gray shadows, one after another, sometimes a dozen at a time, like Indians making a war dance. First Charybdis, now Scylla. Every so often one of the predators would make a close pass at the floating balsa craft, turn on its side, bare its teeth, and roll its huge saucer eyes far back in its head. There was an open gap of two to three feet between the sides of the raft and the sunken deck, and though no snout had yet probed it, all hands stood ready to beat and kick any that tried.

Douhan was vaguely aware that sharks had been known to trail deepwater ships, feeding on the scraps of garbage disposed in their wake. Their "sonar" sensors were also attracted to the low-grade electrical currents emitted by modern motorized vessels. And though it is logical to assume that the riverine-like underwater currents churned by Typhoon Cobra may have thrown them off the scent of the *Hull*, chances were good that the subsonic vibrations from the sinking ship's detonating boilers and depth charges, filled with the explosive Torpex, had refocused their attention.

Moreover, though sharks are notorious for their poor eyesight, they are not blind, and the contrasting colors of, say, a pale white naked arm, leg, or torso against the aquamarine hue of the deep South Pacific made for an attractive lure. In all likelihood, up to this point they had scavenged as many dead sailors as possible, and per their opportunistic eating habits, were now seeking a meal from the fresh meat still floating about them.

It was during one of these "shark runs" that a *Hull* sailor reached out over the side with his knife and sliced a big fish, opening a foot-long gash in its back. The cheers at this moral victory died instantly when the school went into a feeding frenzy at the smell of the blood in the water. The sea boiled and gushed, and Douhan wondered if one of the writhing sharks would wing into the raft.

Several of Douhan's raftmates were near death from shock, dehydration, diarrhea, or a combination thereof. And despite the tropical latitude, hypothermia had also begun to set in among some floaters. As night had fallen the previous evening, the air temperature had dropped nearly 20 degrees, down to the low 80s. The human body can function only over a very narrow range of internal core temperature, normally between 97 and 100 degrees Fahrenheit, and survivors drifting in even the warm waters of the Philippine Sea lost anywhere from six to eight degrees of body temperature after the sun set.

As this drop in the body's heat-balancing mechanisms occurred, cellular chemical changes began to induce intense shivering, blurred vision, and a lack of coordination. The survivors' skin turned pale, cold, and rubbery, speech became slurred, and muscles stiffened to the point of rigidity. But mostly, Douhan noticed, his raftmates' mental acuity had become impaired and disoriented.

At first the heartier and more lucid sailors had tried to prevent the delirious from drinking seawater, making them spit it out whenever they caught them. But it proved impossible to police every man. Geysers of water broke over the raft, and the thirstiest would simply open their mouths and swallow. As the hours passed, this ingested saltwater overwhelmed their kidneys and circulatory systems and, in the most simple medical explanation, shorted out the neurons in their brains. Some slipped over the side and died in quiet agony, their blood-red pupils unclouded by consciousness. Others foamed at the mouth in violent fits, their tongues curled and their swollen blue lips inverted, before closing their eyes and taking a final breath.

Several of the surviving seamen had gone into the water nearly naked, and others had had their clothes torn off by the bashing waves. Thus, before the dead were lowered into the sea with a prayer, their garments were removed and distributed among the neediest. By the morning of December 20, Pat Douhan's raft was down to a dozen men.

As the day wore on and the relentless sun beat down, even those men not suffering from delirium were too spent to stand vigil over weaker shipmates. Finally, the anguished sailors could only watch as a surreal drama began to play out. First, one man leapt into the sea, swam a little distance among the sharks, and returned with a tale of visiting his uncle's farmhouse. He said he had even tried to drive back his uncle's old Model A Ford to pick up his crewmates, but the car would not start.

Now two more men jumped the raft, disappeared beneath the surface, and popped back up saying they had just been to the *Hull*'s galley, where they'd feasted on bologna sandwiches. A crewmate, angry that they hadn't brought sandwiches back with them, dived in, saying he was going to retrieve a case of 7-Up for everyone to share.

When he failed to reappear, Fireman 1st Class Nick Nagurney dived in after him. Nagurney was no more than five feet from the raft when the shark struck. It was a classic "bump and bite" attack. The fish shot like a guided missile from deep beneath the fireman and knocked him almost completely out of the water. Its jaws, capable of applying over ten tons of pressure per square inch, locked on the meaty, upper portion of his arm and began sawing, tearing away hunks of flesh. Nagurney screamed, the shark loosened its grip, and Douhan and several others reached out and hauled him back aboard.

Nagurney was bleeding badly from his shoulder to his elbow, and sailors began desultorily stripping off their shirts to make bandages. There was nothing they could do for their pitiful shipmate who had gone over the side to salvage the case of 7-Up. Everyone noticed that the sharks now seemed to be coiling about the raft in an ever-tightening ring.

Two planes passed high overhead, too high to spot a speck on the sea. Douhan guessed they were not search planes at all, but aircraft busy with the business of war. Still, the men about him waved T-shirts and hollered. The aircraft were soon gone. The day wore on, the silence broken only by the swish of the dorsal fins and the occasional soft keens of injured and defeated men.

Douhan could not stop thinking about his pregnant wife. Who would help her raise the baby? His unborn child had become his only lifeline. That child he would live for. The moment you give up hope, he told himself, is the moment you are lost. He played name games, both girls and boys, and wondered what he'd say if his wife gave birth to a son who would one day ask his permission to join the navy. Would he tell him about shipwrecks and drowning sailors and man-eating sharks? He thought less, dreamed more.

By December 21, after drifting for seventy-two hours, Douhan and his raftmates faced the sunrise feeling like a collection of passages from the Book of Job. Most were sleeping when a young lieutenant surreptitiously began scooping seawater into his mouth. The fireman Nagurney, recuperating from his shark wounds, was the only one to see him. He yelled for the officer to stop.

"Drop dead," came the reply. The fireman pounced like an angry badger and pinned the lieutenant's arms and legs. He jammed a finger down his throat.

"Puke that stuff up before it kills you," he hollered.

The officer obliged, but not before clamping his teeth down so hard on Nagurney's finger he nearly bit it clean through.

Conflating the time in his near delirium, the confused fireman said, "Jesus, I gotta be the only guy who ever got bit by a shark and a lieutenant on the same day."

Like the unhinged lieutenant, Douhan was near out of his head, and thus certain the man lolling next to him was hallucinating when he unexpectedly croaked, "Hey, look, over there. On the horizon. It's the task force."

Douhan could barely rouse himself. *They're no more still searching for us than they're searching for the man in the moon.* Yet others stirred. It was their weak shouts that finally prompted Douhan to turn and gaze. He rubbed the salt from his eyes to make sure he was not seeing things. There were indeed many ships on the horizon. American ships, Halsey's ships—carriers and cruisers and battlewagons. They looked like floating blocks of apartment buildings. They had drifted into the goddamned task force.

Within minutes every Tin Can sailor on the raft recognized the thick puff of black smoke emanating from the stack of one destroyer in particular. Black smoke meant that the vessel was "lighting off" all boilers and answering all bells to steam at full speed. Someone had spotted them. Now two fighter planes circled the raft, banked, and waggled their wings. *I see you!*

For Pat Douhan the next moments were a blur, literally and metaphorically. The sharks went into a frenzy, poking their snouts into the gap beneath the waterline, as if realizing their floating feast was on the verge of vanishing. A ship, the destroyer, closed on them and tossed a line. Small-arms fire echoed above him, and tiny splashes erupted from the ocean about the raft. A shark's nose butted Douhan's ankle. He jumped and kicked. Now he was being lifted by the shoulders, his feet guided into the footholds of a cargo net draped over the side of the vessel.

"No, I can walk," he heard himself say. The words were slurred, and distant, as if echoing from a place far away.

Between small sips of water, someone poured a shot of whiskey down his throat, and it blazed all the way to the soles of his feet. Now a steaming mug of soup was placed in his cupped hands, and he burned his crusted lips and tongue inhaling it. He was addled, more confused than he ever remembered being, and asked one of his rescuers why in the world he was speaking English.

"This is a Russian submarine, isn't it?" he said.

The sailor smiled and gently draped a blanket over Douhan's shoulders. The rescuers were aghast at the survivors' appearances. Here were boys their own age, some not yet out of their teens, yet they resembled wizened old men. Sunburned, their features raw and flaking, swollen tongues protruding, it was as if their faces had been subtly adjusted by a funhouse mirror.

"No, sir," the sailor said. "You're on the USS *Brown*." The same man led Pat Douhan down to a bunk in sick bay.

When he awoke the next day, he was told that his raft had drifted sixty-six miles from the coordinates where the *Hull* had capsized.

CHAPTER 25

"That one reunion was worth the entire effort."

—LT. COMDR. HENRY LEE PLAGE, CAPTAIN,
USS TABBERER

Within forty-eight hours of the height of Typhoon Cobra's deadly lashing, delirium and exposure had taken a toll on survivors across the Philippine Sea. On the same morning, December 20, that Pat Douhan and his *Hull* crewmates had begun to count the number of sharks ringing their raft, a few miles over the horizon the roster of *Monaghan* survivors under "oil king" Joe McCrane's command had shrunk from twelve to nine.

The previous night the ship's cook, Ben Holland, had succumbed from his head wounds, and two other seamen had gone "berserk" from drinking saltwater and swam off to their deaths. Not long afterward, nine became eight when another man who had swallowed too much seawater bit a shipmate on the shoulder, leapt over the side, and drowned.

Just past sunrise on December 20, a sailor jumped up and yelled that he could see land and houses. He dived off the raft with several men in his wake. They hadn't made it far before McCrane and the fireman Evan Fenn somehow persuaded them they were hallucinating. Fenn was particularly convincing, hollering to his crewmates that he possessed a special sixth sense, and he was sure they were about to be rescued. The men stopped stroking, turned around, and made it back safely.

At one point during the ordeal, one of McCrane's shipmates broke out a short rope and decided to "fish" for shark, using a chunk of salty Spam as bait. Many sailors knew that all fish eyes contain fresh water, and in their delirious state it sounded quite reasonable that a buffet of sharks' eyes would slake their incessant thirst. The fellow sunk his line about ten feet below the surface and, sure enough, his shipmates watched in fascination as a five-foot shark nosed forward to investigate.

As the shark came closer, the man pulled in the line bit by bit, until it was clear out of the water. The shark followed, as if hypnotized, to the point where its head was resting on the side of the raft. Then another sailor plunged his small penknife into its scaly snout, directly between the large, dark nasal passages. This only seemed to rile the animal, which rolled and thrashed, its leathery tail fanning gallons of water over their heads. The *Monaghan* seamen decided that perhaps their quest for shark eyes was not such a good idea after all.

Not long after McCrane and the rest spotted an unoccupied raft skimming across the surface, perhaps a quarter of a mile away. Thinking it might carry additional stores, two sailors decided to brave the sharks and dived in after it. They boarded it just as it disappeared behind a huge swell. McCrane, Fenn, and a third weary seaman tried to paddle after them, using their hands and the one remaining oar.

It was impossible. They never saw the men again. They were now six.

As the day wore on, Fenn was the first to notice that one of the freshwater kegs was missing. He guessed that one of the parched and crazed sailors had tried to sneak an extra ration sometime during the night and failed to resecure the canister. Fenn's legs were raw and bleeding, the lacerations racked by saltwater ulcers, but he kept his theory to himself. He saw no purpose in speaking ill of the dead.

Scattered showers throughout the second afternoon brought some relief from the incessant thirst, but by dusk the sky turned pink, russet, and purple, depending upon the vagaries of the light streaking through the loosening cloud cover. That night the sky was a sparkling dome of constellations and shooting stars. They were a mere 15 degrees north of the equator, and each man knew the morning would bring a merciless South Pacific sun.

The survivors slept fitfully, and as dawn broke on December 20, rose-tinged and unwelcome, McCrane began applying sulfa powder, ointment, and salt-crusted bandages to the wounds of his injured shipmates. Abruptly two American fighter planes appeared overhead. The six seamen realized they were close to land, or at least to an American carrier. Their spirits soared as the aircraft banked and dropped dye-bomb water markers. Twenty minutes later the black smoke of the destroyer *Brown*, nearly bursting her boilers racing toward the coordinates, appeared on the horizon.

For their part, seamen aboard the *Brown* were relieved to have again struck paydirt. After rescuing the *Hull* survivors from Douhan's raft earlier that morning, her lookouts had spotted but three empty life rafts and a solitary floater net. The net had a single, scourged body, its limbs devoured by sharks, entangled in it.

When the *Brown* sailors tossed the *Monaghan* men a rope ladder, Evan Fenn, despite his ravaged legs, scurried up the lifeline like a squirrel. The rest had to be carried. McCrane was the last up, and as he reached the deck a *Brown* sailor told him that his raft had been shadowed during the entire rescue by a huge shark, the largest he'd ever seen.

The Oil King was nonplussed. "Well," he said, "he's welcome to the rest of the Spam, anyway."

Thus, three days after she had capsized, did Admiral Halsey discover the fate of the USS *Monaghan*. Navy chief of staff Adm. Ernest King had been monitoring the rescue operations from Washington, D.C. He was aware of the sinking of the *Hull* and *Spence*, and pressed CINCPAC Nimitz at Pearl for updates on the

Monaghan. On the morning of December 23, Nimitz wired King, "Monaghan believed lost." Hours later, after hearing from Halsey that "Mick" Carney had crossed the legendary destroyer from his list, Nimitz amended his "belief."

"Six survivors recovered from *Monaghan,*" he radioed King. "State she capsized and remained afloat about one half hour thereafter."

To this day, United States Naval Bureau records count the six sailors rescued by the *Brown* as the only survivors from the capsized destroyer *Monaghan.* They neglect the "ghost sailor," Keith Abbott.

Periodically—to keep himself awake to spot rescue ships, to stay alert, "to keep from going crazy"—Keith Abbott would slip over the side of his lonely raft and tread water beside it. This also helped minimize his exposure to the burning sun, which had risen like a red dahlia with blossoms ablaze on the morning of December 20. Although he was still wearing his standard-issue navy dungarees, T-shirt, and canvas shoes, the rays seemed to burn right through his clothes.

To avoid becoming waterlogged, not to mention shark bait—he had seen several dorsal fins—he tried to time his "dips" by the movement of the sun across the periwinkle sky: one hour in, one hour out. Nonetheless, as the temperature edged past 100 degrees, blotchy red blisters began to appear on his arms and face.

The blue of the ocean and sky seemed fused, and Abbott felt as if he were floating in the interior of a sapphire. He thought constantly of his wife, and of the baby daughter he had never seen, waiting for him back in Utah. At his lowest points, he told himself, over and over, that he had too many reasons to hang on.

The seas had reduced from mountainous to hilly to choppy by the time Abbott spotted the smoke from the *Brown*'s stack. It seemed like an eternity before the destroyer steamed alongside him and the rescue gang threw him a line. He was too weak to grab it, so the destroyer sent in a swimmer to pull his little raft athwart her starboard beam and lowered a rope ladder. He tried to climb it; it was no use. Members of the *Brown*'s deck gang scrambled down to assist him.

As he lay in the *Brown*'s sick bay, one thought seared Keith Abbott's mind. What if he had died? As a "ghost sailor," no one would ever have known how, or when, or where, or why.

Not long after daybreak on December 20, two destroyers hove out of the waves on either beam of the *Tabberer* and, at 8:40 A.M., after fifty straight hours of search-and-rescue operations, she was relieved of her duties by the jeep carrier *Rudyerd Bay*. Instructed to steam for Ulithi, Captain Plage was also notified by the *Rudyerd Bay*'s skipper to be on the lookout en route to the atoll for survivors of the *Spence*, who appeared to be drifting in that general direction.

Two hours later, as the *Tabby* steamed southeast, her lookouts spotted a floater net.

Bob Ayers and his *Spence* crewmates had been drifting for close to forty-eight hours. By the night before, December 19, every man on Ayers's floater net was battered black and blue, and all had bruised eyes from being beaten by waves. As their kapoks became more and more waterlogged, Chief Watertender George Johnson had decided that sleepy men were sure to drown, and he talked himself hoarse to keep his shipmates awake.

Johnson had spoken about anything that came to his mind—the grub in the chow hall, the best bars on Pearl, the worst officers he'd ever served under, movie stars his crewmates most wanted to date. He chattered on about his family, particularly his wife, and the baby daughter he hadn't yet seen back home in Fresno, California. By now nobody was listening, not even grunting in response to the conjured images of Hollywood starlets. Johnson's voice, rasping, so gravelly it could scour a stove, was no more than white noise in the background. The chief watertender did not care. Even if he was losing his mind, he was determined to keep a sunny side up.

There had been one keg of water on the float ring, but a delirious sailor had tried to swim off with it in the night, a scuffle ensued, and its contents had become fouled with saltwater. As the hours passed with no sustenance, Ayers began to lose his floatmates.

One young crewman passed away from head wounds he had received just before the *Spence* sank. In the throes of the typhoon, he had climbed into the housing holding one of the gun mounts. But when the ship overturned, a 5-inch shell had rolled off its shelf and slammed into his forehead. His head was stove in and now, his skull most likely fractured, Ayers watched helplessly as the boy removed his ring from his finger, asked a shipmate to see that his mother got it, and quietly died.

Others just drifted away out of sheer exhaustion and hallucinations. One seaman announced, "I'm going to swim over that wave and catch a plane home." A fellow sailor said, "I'll go with you." The two left the floater net and were never seen again.

By the morning of December 20, there were ten miserable souls remaining on Bob Ayers's float ring. Like his lieutenant, Alphonso Krauchunas, two days earlier, Ayers began to wonder how he would die. Though some of his floatmates assumed they were sure to be picked up—to the point where George Johnson led a sort of giddy roundtable discussion asking each how and where he planned to spend his survivor's leave—Ayers realized there was a distinct possibility that by this time all rescue searches had been called off.

After fifty hours in the water, he had reached his lowest psychological ebb when, a little after 11:00 A.M., he glimpsed the outline of a ship on the horizon. From that distance the superstructure looked stripped bare—no mast, no radar gear, a giant tear in the roof of its pilothouse—and Ayers took it for a Japanese submarine. He laughed out loud. He was aware of the horrors of Japanese prison camps, that is, if they didn't just machine-gun him and his crewmates and be done with it right here. He also realized he was not supposed to feel such joy over the prospect of being captured by the enemy. He did not care.

But as the vessel closed on his bedraggled float ring, it slowly dawned on Ayers that he was watching a much-battered American destroyer escort. Finally he was able to make out her lettering. USS *Tabberer*. Jubilation. But there was still one more adventure left for Bob Ayers.

When the *Tabby* approached Ayers's floater net, a deckhand tossed a heave line to the drifting sailors. At the end of the rope was a monkey fist, a lead weight encircled with twine. It landed short of the ring. Mustering the last vapors of adrenaline remaining in his system, Ayers decided to swim for it. He took no more than a half dozen strokes before the *Tabby*'s deck crew opened fire. Bullets whizzed into the water about him. Ayers knew damn well what they we aiming at. Later, witnesses told him he took "ten strokes out after that line, but only two strokes back."

The sharks dispersed, and Ayers and his crewmates were hauled in by the *Tabberer*, which began to circle the area. Ostensibly relieved of rescue duties, Henry Plage refused to give up, and the *Tabby* subsequently picked up four more disparate floaters from the *Spence*.

One of them was a chief petty officer whose best friend, also a chief petty officer, had been stationed on the *Hull* and been rescued by the *Tabby* on the night of December 18. The *Hull* chief had recovered enough to spend the past twenty-four hours pulling in survivors alongside the *Tabby*'s crew, and as the *Spence* sailors were taken aboard, he approached each one separately, asking after his buddy. When they finally came face-to-face, both men cried.

To an exhausted and emotional Plage, "that one reunion was worth the entire effort."

But theirs was not the only reunion to take place on the *Tabberer*'s deck that morning. A rescued *Spence* survivor, Chief Machinist's Mate Henry Deeters, happened to be a neighbor of the *Tabby*'s radioman Ralph Tucker back in Somerville, Massachusetts. And, finally, one of the last sailors the *Tabby* hauled aboard was Bob Ayers's newfound friend Floyd Balliett.

Upon their return to dry ground, both vowed to avoid bacon sandwiches for the rest of their lives.

Admiral Halsey called off the search for survivors at sundown on December 22. The final sailor to be recovered was Seaman 2nd Class William Keith of the *Spence*, who by a stroke of great good fortune had been swept by the currents into a shipping channel and was spotted on the afternoon of December 21 by a lookout from the destroyer USS *Gatling*. Keith was floating alone, his waterlogged kapok punctured in several places and losing buoyancy.

Upon being hoisted to the deck, the dazed and hollow-eyed sailor was in such a deranged state he fought his rescuers, broke free, and tried to leap back into the sea. As they tackled him, Keith ranted that he had been riding a torpedo, which he intended to convey all the way to Japan to blow up the city of Tokyo.

Of the roughly 900 men who had seen their ships go into the Philippine Sea four days earlier, only 93 officers and enlisted men were recovered. The *Tabberer* rescued 55 of them—5 officers and 36 seamen from the *Hull*, and 14 seamen from the *Spence*. The destroyer *Brown* had taken aboard 13 *Hull* survivors as well as the only 7 seamen to make it off the *Monaghan*. The destroyer escort *Swearer* had picked up 9 *Spence* floaters, and her sister DE *Robert F. Keller* 4 more from the *Hull*. The destroyer *Knapp* accounted for 3 more men from the *Hull*, including the officer Lloyd Rust. And the destroyers *Cogswell* and *Gatling* had found one man apiece, from the *Hull* and the *Spence*, respectively.

By this time Typhoon Cobra had turned sharply and begun curving northwest, and Halsey, gathering what was left of his armada, hoped to employ the same "Dirty Trick" he had used over two months earlier, when his task force had sneaked in behind the screen of "Good Guy" Typhoon Zero-Zero to shell Okinawa.

This time luck eluded him. Despite cobalt skies and a burning white sun off the east coast of Luzon, the residue of the typhoon had left the Philippine Sea too turbulent and the winds far too gusty for Halsey to launch aircraft from the bobbing flattops of Task Force 38. Continuation of the Big Blue Blanket would have to wait. The admiral radioed MacArthur, "Regret unable to strike on 21st due to impossible sea conditions. Am retiring eastward."

He seethed at having to give the general "an excuse instead of an attack." Unlike the proverbial British field marshal, "who talked of action tomorrow when he should have talked of action today," Halsey preferred his action yesterday. But his hand was stayed by the weather. He set a return date for early January 1945, to coincide with MacArthur's long-anticipated invasion of Luzon, and shaped course for Ulithi to service his ships and personally assess the damage to his fleet.

Meanwhile, far to the northwest, Typhoon Cobra was done in by the same cold front through whose peripheral edge she had churned on the night of December 17. By 9:00 P.M. on December 19, Cobra had penetrated the bulk of this blanketing front's frigid air mass, about one hundred miles off the northeastern tip of Luzon. Deserted by the warm water and languid air that stoked her engine, she was encompassed by the enormous accumulation of cold air and "literally chilled into disintegration."

During her death throes, according to navy weather scientists, "gargantuan chunks of charged atmosphere flew in all directions as the air masses and typhoon clawed and chewed at each other high over the ocean surface; torrents of rain slammed into clouds as if forced from gigantic pressure hoses; mighty winds struck with diabolical force. This great eruption of violence spread in all directions over hundreds of oceanic square miles in every direction of the compass and caused severe weather conditions along the coast of Luzon, over which the Third Fleet planned to stage those launching operations, which had to be canceled."

The crippled *Tabberer* was one of the last of Third Fleet's vessels to steam through the Mugai Pass and into Ulithi's vast harbor on December 22. Plage had gone belowdecks to check on the survivors several times over the preceding three days, and many, including Archie DeRyckere, had ventured up to the bridge, wishing to shake his hand.

Now, as he neared the atoll, Henry Lee Plage lined up the *Tabby*'s crew on her foredeck and invited the rescued seamen who could walk to personally thank their saviors. Battle-hardened sailors hugged, and wept.

The death toll of U.S. Navy officers and seamen lost in the wake of Typhoon Cobra was enormous, more than twice the number of sailors and airmen killed in action at the Battle of Midway, and nearly as many as at Midway and the Battle of Coral Sea combined. As one eyewitness was to write in the wake of the killer storm, "Compared to the staggering total of some 790 men who were lost or killed during Cobra's attack, the rescue ratio . . . seems pitifully small. But when the circumstances that governed the majority of these rescues are brought into consideration, they become a monumental tribute to the skills and courage of our sailors and the binding bonds of the Brotherhood of the Sea."

When the *Tabby* limped into Ulithi's anchorage, most of Halsey's ships, in various states of disrepair, were already in dry dock or having their battered keels and hulls attended to by divers wielding underwater welds. Before reaching the atoll, Plage had received a "Well done for a sturdy performance" communiqué from the admiral for his ship's epic heroism and selfless service. But as she entered the harbor, no one seemed to take particular notice of the scalped and battered little destroyer escort.

When she shaped toward her mooring across from the *New Jersey*, however, she received a blinker message from the behemoth battleship.

"What type of ship are you?" it asked.

Plage was tired, and irritated, and in no mood to be condescended to. He felt it was about time a destroyer navy man, even a reservist, set the smug BB boys straight, insubordination be damned. With no hesitation he ordered his signalman to blink back the following response:

"Destroyer escort. What type are you?"

EPILOGUE

The last thing Archie DeRyckere remembered seeing was the huge dorsal fin, gray with dark blotches, circling him like a hangman's noose. Now he bolted awake and gaped at the wooden slats of the bottom of the bunk a few feet before his face. He rubbed his tender eyes—they were wet and gooey from the drops administered by Doc Cleary—and reached up to touch the latticework to make sure he was not dreaming. He turned to the bed beside him in the *Tabberer*'s sick bay and recognized Ray Schultz, whose own eyes had also crusted over.

"Man, oh man, oh man, this is living, huh, Ray," he said. Schultz grunted.

Simultaneously, similar scenes were being played out belowdecks aboard the small flotilla of rescue ships steaming toward Ulithi.

DeRyckere's shipmate Pat Douhan, on the destroyer *Brown*, could never recall so many officers being so friendly to him. The entire ship's complement visited the sick bay, on each occasion laden with fruit juice, soup, coffee, and ice cream. When the *Brown*'s regular galley ran short of supplies, the officers' galley was thrown open. Between these goodwill visits and much-needed sleep, Douhan and his *Hull* crewmates spent most of the time comparing the experience of having a ship sink out from under them with the survivors off the *Monaghan*. Only a few men recounted stories from the water. Shark attacks were an especially taboo topic of conversation.

Aboard the destroyer escort *Swearer*, the *Spence*'s Lt. Alphonso Krauchunas felt healthy enough to venture topside to air out his sore feet. They were still swollen and slightly streaked but didn't hurt nearly as much, and the fresh breezes and sunlight instilled in him a new vigor. On the destroyer *Cogswell*, the *Spence* seaman William Keith had recovered enough to feel sheepish about brawling with his rescuers when they plucked him from the sea.

When the *Tabby* arrived at Ulithi on December 22—the first vessel to return with Typhoon Cobra survivors—most of the injured men were transferred to the hospital ship USS *Solace* berthed in the lagoon. Over the next several days, as more sailors from the doomed *Hull*, *Spence*, and *Monaghan* joined them, emotional reunions and surreal events took place. Evan Fenn, the *Monaghan* fireman, his legs still raw and scarred, was carried aboard the *Solace* on Christmas Eve and, aided by the morphine, thought the nurses singing Christmas carols were the voices of angels. On Christmas morning the *Swearer*'s nine *Spence* survivors came aboard, the last to arrive. To Krauchunas, the turkey-and-trimmings dinner he and his crewmates were treated to was the most memorable they'd ever eaten.

Although sailors like Douhan were initially astonished to discover so many fellow crewmates crowding the *Solace*—the sonarman fell into the arms of Chiefs DeRyckere and Schultz upon his arrival—after the *Swearer* contingent came on board, it gradually dawned on everyone that no more were coming. Elation turned to anguish, the living mourning the dead.

Among those killed by Typhoon Cobra were Lt. Comdr. Bruce Garrett of the *Monaghan* and the *Spence*'s Lt. Comdr. James Andrea. The *Hull*'s Lt. Comdr. James Alexander Marks was thus the only captain of a lost ship to survive the storm. On December 26, 1944, four days after he'd walked under his own strength down the *Tabby*'s gangway, he was designated a "defendant" by the three-admiral court of inquiry investigating what was even now being commonly referred to as "Halsey's Typhoon." Marks was the only man so named.

The court, executed swiftly and well out of public view, assigned Marks a defense attorney, and in the most dramatic flourish of the entire proceedings convened in the pilothouse of the destroyer tender USS *Cascade* to hear his testimony. This was done, Judge Advocate Capt. Herbert Gates said, "in order to best approximate the conditions on the *Hull*'s bridge during the storm."

Marks's face was a rash of saltwater sores and, like all the other survivors, his eyes remained bruised and blackened as he paced the *Cascade*'s wheelhouse. He told the court that had the *Hull* been released from her screening station early on December 18, she just might have been able to outrun the typhoon south. The point was moot; she had not been released. He was, he said, merely following orders.

In earlier testimony, Capt. Preston Mercer, commander of the destroyer squadron of which the *Hull* was a member, had diplomatically sidestepped questions concerning Marks's command capabilities. Mercer's several brushes with death sailing through Cobra aboard Capt. William Rogers's battered destroyer *Aylwin*, tempered by an innate service loyalty, left him unprepared to cast stones. "The commanding officer of the *Hull* had served in the North Atlantic and experienced very heavy weather," Mercer told the court, "and perhaps did not appreciate that the *Hull* was not as stable as previous destroyers in which he was embarked."

In a tortuous evasion of the judge advocate's follow-up question regarding his view of Marks's overall leadership, Mercer added that it had to be taken into consideration that all his squadron commanders, Marks included, "are the most junior in destroyers." No telling endorsement, that.

Now Marks's narrative of the final, tragic hours of the *Hull* was read aloud in the makeshift floating courtroom. It contained no hint of the panic and tension permeating her bridge at the time. Judge Advocate Gates asked Marks if he had an official complaint to register against any surviving officers or crew. Archie DeRyckere, seated in the gallery, leaned forward in his chair and peered expectantly through eye sockets swollen to the size and color of small plums. He was still weak, and the skin on his ears and nose had been sloughed off by wind and waves, leaving ugly red scabs.

DeRyckere exhaled deeply when Marks said he had no accusations to make. When the court addressed the same question to the *Hull*'s survivors, eyes shifted downward and feet shuffled. Each man's face resembled a hard winter breaking up, but not a single sailor said a word. DeRyckere stole a glance at sullen Chief Bosun's Mate Ray Schultz, and thought of the XO Griel Gherstly. No man is an island. Gherstly was dead.

DeRyckere was heartsick. But, like his shipmates, he felt he had no other option but to remain silent. Who was he, a twenty-five-year-old enlisted man, to vouchsafe an officer's testimony under oath? He planned to make a career of the navy. It wouldn't do to call out one's superior in public. "What did they expect us to say in there?" he asked the coxswain transporting him and his crewmates across Ulithi lagoon back to the white hospital ship. "What with everywhere you look, all you see are them braided admirals boring holes through you with their eyes."

The court of inquiry would eventually reach the conclusion that the commanding officers of the *Hull, Monaghan,* and *Spence* "maneuvered too long in an endeavor to keep station, which prevented them from concentrating early enough on saving their ships." But after poring over the minutiae of the case and paying special attention to the engineering faults and failures of the top-heavy destroyers, to Judge Advocate Gates the pelts of three young junior officers, two of them deceased, were but stray doggies compared to the snorting "Bull."

When Halsey took the stand, on the day after Christmas, Gates bored in on the admiral's contradictory testimony. Nearly all of Third Fleet's officers, he noted, saw the storm coming. He read back testimony definitively illustrating that each of Halsey's three task group commanders, as well as several subordinate ship captains, had already surmised that they were steaming into a typhoon as early as the afternoon and the gloaming evening of December 17. In fact, Gates suggested, it was the admiral who seemed to be the last to realize that the storm posed a danger to his ships.

It was not until 4:00 A.M. on December 18 that the weather—"for the first time," in Halsey's words—suggested "that the Fleet was confronted with serious storm conditions." Further, it took an additional eight hours before Halsey thought "to issue orders to the

Fleet as a whole to disregard formation keeping and take best courses and speeds for security."

"Why?" Gates demanded.

Storm warnings, Halsey replied, "were nonexistent until the horse was out of the stable." Hewing close to his warrior script, he added, "The thought of striking Luzon was uppermost in our heads right up to the last minute."

Virtually ignoring these inconsistencies and contradictions, on January 3, 1945, the naval court of inquiry returned a single-spaced, typewritten, two-hundred-page document that delineated 84 separate "Findings" regarding the facts surrounding Third Fleet's encounter with Typhoon Cobra, 63 separate "Opinions," and 10 "Recommendations."

In brief, the court found that the losses of the *Hull* and *Monaghan* were due primarily to the inherent instability of the top-heavy *Farragut*-class destroyers, and further suggested that Bruce Garrett of the *Monaghan* and James Marks of the *Hull* had not been experienced enough commanders to realize they should have broken station and tended to the safety of their ships. Capt. James Andrea of the *Spence*, unable to defend himself, was faulted posthumously for "probably" failing to ballast his ship's bunkers and remove extraneous topside weight from her decks.

The court attached no blame nor reprimand for damage to or the loss of aircraft to any of the jeep carrier commanders or officers whom, it found, had reacted as best they could given the dreadful circumstances. Similarly exonerated were the commanders of the wrecked, if still floating, destroyers *Dewey*, *Aylwin*, and *Hickox*.

The fleet aerologist, Comdr. George F. Kosco, was mildly admonished for relying too greatly on far-off weather reports and analysis from Pearl and other outlying stations, and task force commander Vice Adm. John Sidney "Slew" McCain was held responsible for briefly turning the fleet into the heart of the storm on the morning of December 18. Oddly, they never questioned McCain about this decision.

Finally, the court made clear, the liability to Third Fleet for damages during Typhoon Cobra, and specifically for failing to issue a fleetwide typhoon warning on that same morning, accrued to Admiral Halsey.

After a meticulous listing of the damage and losses to the fleet, the court's final statement read, in part, "The preponderance of responsibility for the above falls on Commander Third Fleet, Admiral William F. Halsey, U.S. Navy. In analyzing the mistakes, errors, and faults included therein, the court classifies them as errors in judgment under stress of war operations, and not as offenses."

The judgment went on to compare the catastrophe to an act of God, and concluded, "The extent of blame, as it applies to Commander Third Fleet or others, is impractical to assess."

And there it was. Some, not least those seamen who had drifted across the Philippine Sea for days and witnessed their shipmates die under the most horrific circumstances, saw the ruling as a whitewash. When, nine days later, CINCPAC Nimitz's office issued its own meager, three-page summary of the court's findings, there were murmurs that the entire inquiry had become, in a distinctive swabbie acronym, FUBAR—"Fucked Up Beyond All Recognition."

Nearly 800 men had died and over 80 were injured; 3 destroyers had capsized and another dozen ships had been rendered inoperable; 146 aircraft were lost or damaged beyond repair; and America's Big Blue Fleet was literally decimated. It seemed no wonder that some naval observers viewed the court's conclusions as distinctly lenient.

Following the court's "Recommendations," it was up to Nimitz to decide whether disciplinary action should be taken. During the proceedings, CINCPAC and his staff had lived up to their reputation for thoroughness by spending much of their Ulithi stopover informally interviewing those survivors who were strong enough to speak. In addition to Nimitz's personal conversations with Halsey, his staff had visited the hospital ship *Solace* and invited seamen aboard the *New Jersey*, where Nimitz was billeted. One of the first of these was the "ghost sailor" Keith Abbott. His story was of particular interest to the investigators, as he was the only man who had made it off the *Monaghan*'s bridge alive.

The room was crowded for Abbott's appearance—everyone was curious—and CINCPAC's staff officers listened rapt as the radar technician related the story of Captain Garrett's heroic efforts to save the ship, of watching the inclinometer's needle surge past its stop, of the titanic waves that preceded the destroyer's final, terrifying moments.

On the basis of these interviews and the court's findings, CINCPAC composed a "classified" overview of the catastrophe as well as a new set of future fleetwide weather guidelines. These included more reconnaissance aircraft and weather ships stationed across the Western Pacific, a new "weather central" station established on Leyte, and an expansion of the existing station on Guam. He also instructed the Bureau of Ships to initiate a design study of destroyer stability. In Nimitz's "confidential" letter dated January 1945—which was not released from "classified" status until ten years later, in 1955—an angry CINCPAC called the disaster "the greatest loss that we have taken in the Pacific without compensatory return since the First Battle of Savo."

His official memorandum of January 22, 1945, however, was somewhat more modulated. In it Nimitz officially approved the Proceedings, Findings, Opinions, and Recommendations of the court of inquiry. In the terse Recommendation Number 8, he wrote, "No further proceedings recommended in case of Lt. Comdr. James A. Marks, U.S.N., CO Hull."

Regarding Halsey, Nimitz was "of the firm opinion that no question of negligence is involved." Mitigating the court's findings somewhat, he softened its language toward the admiral by removing the word "faults" and wrote that Halsey's mistakes "were errors of judgment committed under stress of war operations and stemming from a commendable desire to meet military requirements."

In conclusion, he said, "No further action is contemplated or recommended."

The Navy Department concurred. In fact, such was Halsey's fame and reputation that Adm. Ernest J. King, commander in chief of the U.S. Navy, further moderated the judgment by substituting the words "firm determination" for Nimitz's phrase, "commendable desire," in the final official report.

All in all, it appeared that most navy brass were more than anxious to put this typhoon unpleasantness behind them and move forward with the business of warfighting. MacArthur's Luzon invasion was slated for January 1945, with Task Force 38 again scheduled to provide "Big Blue Blanket" air cover.

Survivors of the capsized *Hull*, *Monaghan*, and *Spence* were transported in stages to hospitals at Pearl Harbor. Upon sufficient recovery from their wounds, they were given back pay and granted four weeks of Stateside shore leave. Their lives, and stories, scattered to the four winds.

On January 2, Lt. (j.g.) Alphonso Krauchunas, along with the other 23 *Spence* survivors, was transferred from the *Solace* to the receiving ship USS *Sturgis*. Every man was asked to write down the names of any shipmates they had seen in the water following the *Spence*'s capsize. They reported spotting an additional 23 shipmates in the high seas. These names were incorporated into the roster of 294 officers and men presumed to have gone down with the ship. This was about 45 more men than the *Monaghan* and *Hull* had each lost.

Not long afterward, the *Hull*'s chief bosun's mate, Ray Schultz, was being conveyed to Pearl on an ancient minesweeper when, fifteen days out of Ulithi, the vessel broke down. Fearful that her skipper would issue the order to abandon ship, he nearly collapsed in relief when she was instead attached to a freighter's towline and lugged into port. Similarly, during Pat Douhan's Stateside journey from Pearl aboard an old four-stack destroyer, a fire broke out in her engine room and her skipper was contemplating abandoning ship. When Douhan and several other typhoon survivors heard this, they raced belowdecks to assist the firefighting gang in dousing the flames. There was no way they were going back into the water.

Monaghan fireman Evan Fenn remained on the *Solace* for a month while being treated for the saltwater ulcers on his legs. Arriving finally at Pearl, he hitched a ride on a destroyer to the naval base at California's San Pedro Island. He slept on the cold steel deck and developed a hacking cough. From San Pedro he was transferred to a naval station in Utah, where the freezing weather exacerbated his condition, and he was diagnosed with tuberculosis. He was shipped back to a California naval hospital, where his diagnosis was downgraded to pneumonia. He spent the next eight months in sick bay before being transferred to a naval hospital in New Mexico, where he recovered fully.

Tragicomic indignities continued to shadow the *Monaghan's* "ghost sailor" Keith Abbott. As he had never officially been stricken from the roster of the destroyer escort *Emery*, he was immediately transferred back to her without any shore leave other than the few days he spent recovering on Ulithi. From Ulithi, Abbott was unable to contact either his wife or his parents, and worried that his brother, a naval intelligence officer based in Florida, had surely heard of the *Monaghan's* sinking and delivered to his folks the bad news. He hadn't, as Abbott learned when he finally exchanged telegrams with his brother. So Abbott evasively wrote his wife and parents that he "had gotten off the Monaghan," deliberately trying to give the impression that he had already transferred back to the *Emery* before she went down. He knew he was to remain in the Pacific Theater for the remainder of the war and didn't want his loved ones to worry needlessly.

On December 29, 1944, Halsey was piped aboard the *Tabberer* to personally award Lt. Comdr. Henry Lee Plage the navy's Legion of Merit. A day earlier, when inquiring about Plage's experience, Halsey had been flabbergasted to find that the skipper was not only just twenty-nine years old, but a reservist to boot. "I expected to learn that he had cut his teeth on a marlinspike," he wrote. "How can any enemy ever defeat a country that can pull boys like that out of its hat?"

After pinning the medal on Plage's tunic, the admiral turned to address the *Tabby*'s crew.

"Captain Plage, officers and men of the *Tabberer*," he began. "I am greatly honored, privileged, and it is with great pleasure that I come over here this morning to tell you what I think of you as the commander of Third Fleet. Your seamanship, endurance, and courage, and the plain guts that you exhibited during the typhoon that we went through, is an epic of naval history and will be long remembered by your children and their children's children.

"It is this plain guts displayed throughout the world by the American forces of all branches that is winning the war for us. How those yellow bastards ever thought they could lick American men is beyond my comprehension. Keep going until the final thing, and the final thing should be the complete destruction of the Japanese empire. If I had my way there would not be a Jap yellow bastard alive, but I guess I won't have it my way."

Despite wartime protocols, by mid-January 1945 military censors realized it was no longer possible to keep the story of Typhoon Cobra under wraps. The Navy's Public Affairs Department reminded reporters of the need to hold back detailed information regarding specific Third Fleet losses and damages—which could render aid and comfort to the enemy—and released the account with an emphasis on the rescue operation. Lt. Comdr. Henry Lee Plage and members of his crew were made available to the press. Their first-person accounts made front-page headlines across the United States—a deft counteraction to the bad news emanating from the disturbing Nazi advances at the Battle of the Bulge.

"Courage and Plain Guts," the *Atlanta Constitution* called it. "Destroyer Crewmen Risk Lives to Save 55 During Typhoon," bannered the *Honolulu Advertiser*. The narratives of individual *Tabby* sailors whose hometowns were nearby were provided to the *Boston Globe*, *Kansas City Star*, and *San Francisco Examiner*, among other newspapers. The front-page, January 20, 1945, account in the *New York*

Times began, "One of the most dramatic play-by-play accounts of rescue at sea to come out of the war in the Pacific was told here today by the commanding officer of the USS *Tabberer*." Two days later correspondent Webley Edwards in Pearl Harbor filed an audio report for CBS *World News Today*, which included a live interview with Plage.

This initial burst of publicity obscured the fact that the transcript from the official court of inquiry was classified "Top Secret," and so buried for decades to come.

The *Tabby* spent several weeks in January reservicing at Pearl. As she was being fitted with a new mast and had her superstructure repaired, her crew was housed in the swank Royal Hawaiian Hotel and feted with free beer and ice cream. Rumor had it that Adm. Alexander Sharp, father of rescued *Hull* lieutenant George Sharp, had personally arranged for the accommodations. No one complained. Nor was there any objection when the entire crew was awarded, en masse, the first-ever Navy Unit Commendation Ribbon from Secretary of the Navy James Forrestal.

Meanwhile, on Capt. Henry Plage's recommendation, Lieutenants Robert M. Surdam and Howard J. Korth, Torpedoman's Mate 1st Class Robert Lee Cotton, and Bosun's Mate 1st Class Louis Anthony Purvis were each awarded the Navy and Marine Corps Medal for heroism. For Purvis the honor was particularly freighted with irony. After completing basic training in 1941, Purvis had been assigned to the light cruiser USS *Juneau*, but a case of the mumps had kept him from reporting to the ship and it sailed without him. He was thus billeted on a destroyer escort on Friday, November 13, 1942, when the *Juneau* went down off Guadalcanal with all hands, including the five Sullivan brothers memorialized by Hollywood in the 1944 film *The Fighting Sullivans*.

Within a month of her completed repairs, the *Tabberer* returned to bombardment and submarine screening duties during the landings on Iwo Jima. One day, when Plage was summoned ashore, he anchored the *Tabby* close enough for the crew to watch the American flag being raised on Mount Suribachi. From Iwo Jima she subsequently saw action during the invasion of Okinawa, bombarding the island and fending off kamikazes as her crew watched in horror from the aft fantail as Japanese women and children, so petrified at the arrival of the "barbarian" Americans, jumped to their deaths from the seaside cliffs.

On April 24, 1946, less than a year after Henry Plage had been transferred to the Naval War College at Annapolis, Maryland, and two years and a day after she had been commissioned at the Brown Shipbuilding Yard in Houston, Texas, the USS *Tabberer* was decommissioned. She had steamed over 110,000 miles, none so important as the few hundred of her boxed search on December 18, 19, and 20, 1944.

In the name of the President of the United States, the Commander, Third Fleet, United States Pacific Fleet, takes pleasure in awarding the Legion of Merit to

LIEUTENANT COMMANDER HENRY L. PLAGE
UNITED STATES NAVAL RESERVE

for service as set forth in the following

CITATION

For exceptionally meritorious conduct in the performance of outstanding service to the Government as Commanding Officer of the U.S.S. Tabberer operating in the Western Pacific war area from December 18, 1944 to December 20, 1944. During this period, while his ship was combating a storm of hurricane intensity and mountainous seas causing severe damage, Lieutenant Commander PLAGE directed the rescue of fifty-five survivors from two destroyers which foundered as a result of the same storm. In spite of seemingly insurmountable hardships and adverse conditions, he persisted in the search for survivors for fifty-one hours. Lieutenant Commander PLAGE's courageous leadership and excellent seamanship through treacherous and storm-swept seas and his timely reports aided materially in the rescue of additional survivors by other ships which later arrived at the scene. His outstanding conduct was in keeping with the highest tradition of the United States Naval Service.

W. F. Halsey
Admiral, U.S. Navy

THE SECRETARY OF THE NAVY
WASHINGTON
The Secretary of the Navy takes pleasure in commending the

UNITED STATES SHIP TABBERER

For service as follows:

For extremely meritorious service in the rescue of survivors following the foundering of two [sic] United States Destroyers in the Western Pacific Typhoon of December 18, 1944. Unmaneuverable in the wind-lashed seas, fighting to maintain her course while repeatedly falling back into the trough, with her mast lost and all communications gone, the U.S.S. TABBERER rode out the tropical typhoon and, with no opportunity to repair the damage, gallantly started her search for survivors, steaming at ten knots, she stopped at short intervals and darkened her decks where the entire crew topside, without sleep or rest for 36 hours, stood watch to listen for the whistles and shouts of survivors and to scan the turbulent waters for small lights attached to kapok jackets which appeared and then became obscured in troughs blocked off by heavy seas.

Locating one survivor or a group, the TABBERER stoutly maneuvered to windward, drifting down to her objective and effecting rescues in safety despite the terrific rolling which plunged her main deck under water. Again and again she conducted an expanding box search, persevering in her hazardous mission for another day and night until she had rescued fifty-five storm tossed and exhausted survivors and had brought them aboard to be examined, treated and clothed.

Brave and seaworthy in her ready service, the TABBERER, in this heroic achievement, has implemented the daring seamanship and courage of her officers and men.

All personnel attached to and serving on board the TABBERER, during the above mentioned operation, are hereby authorized to wear the NAVY UNIT COMMENDATION RIBBON.

James Forrestal
Secretary of the Navy

AFTERWORD 2006

History would be kind to Adm. William Frederick Halsey Jr., for he intended to write it. And though he did devote four pages to the Third Fleet's encounter with Typhoon Cobra in his 1947 autobiography *Admiral Halsey's Story* (written with Joseph Bryan III), true to his word, he never spoke nor wrote about the ensuing court of inquiry for the rest of his life.

That task was left to naval historians, the most penetrating of whom, the Harvard professor Samuel Eliot Morison, defended Halsey vociferously in volume 13 of his fifteen-volume masterpiece *History of the United States Naval Operations in Wold War II*. Wrote Morison, "In my opinion—after rereading the testimony fourteen years later, and examining the meteorological data then available to Admiral Halsey—the court was not fair to Commander Third Fleet. It assumed that the typhoon sent out warnings long before there were signs of anything more than a normal tropical disturbance."

From the perspective of sixty-odd years of hindsight, this sounds about right. Shining what the American revolutionary Patrick Henry called the "lamp of experience" on the typhoon incident, Morison spotlighted the primitive meteorological facilities available to Halsey at the time and contrasted this to the admiral's inherently bold leadership, and strategic and tactical attack instincts. These same instincts again came to the fore during the final operations against Japan in the summer of 1945.

Halsey's brilliant use of air strikes and "Slew" McCain's "Big Blue Blanket" in the war's closing hours further pulverized what was left of the enemy's meager naval and air forces, and decimated the Japanese mainland's industrial base and war industries. After the atomic bombs detonated over Hiroshima and Nagasaki, Halsey would maintain that his life reached its climax at 9:25 A.M., September 2, 1945—when he joined MacArthur in formally accepting Japan's unconditional surrender from Emperor Hirohito's envoys aboard his flagship battleship USS *Missouri* in Tokyo Bay.

Four months later Halsey was awarded his fifth star and promoted to fleet admiral, a position the U.S. Congress amended to "for life" in April 1946. "My only fear," he wrote to a friend, "is that the extra stripe is going to interfere with my drinking arm."

That same year Halsey embarked on a tour of Latin America at the request of President Harry Truman, and upon his return eschewed several lucrative private-sector job offers to accept the chairmanship of the development fund drive at the University of Virginia, the school he attended for a year before enrolling at Annapolis.

Now sixty-five, he and his wife settled briefly in Charlottesville, but the old seaman's character remained his fate, and the "sheer boredom" of moving from command of the world's greatest fleet to pleading with alumni for donations left him unfulfilled and discontented. When the offer came to join the board of directors of the International Telephone & Telegraph Company, he jumped at the chance to move to New York City.

As IT&T's—and America's—goodwill ambassador, Halsey circled the globe collecting shelfloads of foreign awards, national orders, and Grand Crosses from grateful allies. Through these years the admiral occasionally battled with historians and journalists who questioned his decisions during the Battle for Leyte Gulf (as Morison did) and Typhoon Cobra. His fiery defenses can be fairly well encapsulated by the ancient Greek proverb, "It is the sins we don't commit we regret."

In 1957, while raising money in a failed effort to turn his old flagship, the carrier USS *Enterprise*, into a naval museum, he suffered a mild stroke. He recovered enough to travel to California to visit his son, now married to Admiral Nimitz's daughter. While there, he also took a trip to the production set of *The Gallant Hours*, the movie based on his book, starring James Cagney. But, now walking with a cane, afflicted by cataracts, on August 15, 1959, the admiral was vacationing on Fishers Island in Long Island Sound—not far from the Halsey family's ancestral home in Sag Harbor, New York—when he took his usual wade through the beach surf, retired, and failed to appear for breakfast the next morning. He was discovered in his bed, dead from a heart attack at the age of seventy-six. He was given a state funeral in Washington's National Cathedral and buried in Arlington Cemetery.

As Petrarch observed, a good death does honor to a whole life, and Admiral Halsey departed this vale within hailing distance of his beloved sea. He ranks among Jones, Perry, Dewey, and Farragut in the pantheon of American sailors. Like them, he kowtowed to no man, and his naval status and repute remain as fierce and honored as those of his legendary predecessors.

Adm. Chester Nimitz, who represented President Dwight Eisenhower at Halsey's funeral, furled his CINCPAC flag at Pearl Harbor on November 26, 1945, in order to succeed Fleet Admiral Ernest J. King as Chief of United States Naval Operations. After two years in this post, he was appointed in 1949 by the United Nations as a roving goodwill ambassador, and two years after that moved home to San Francisco for good. Like Halsey, Nimitz was named five-star admiral "for life," and also became an honorary president of the Naval Historical Foundation. He served for eight years as a regent of the University of California.

Ironically, Nimitz did much to foster postwar amity between the United States and Japan by raising funds to restore the battleship *Mikasa*, Adm. Heihachiro Togo's flagship at the victorious Battle of Tsushima in 1905, during the Russo-Japanese War. Nimitz died on February 20, 1966.

The navy was not as kind to Vice Adm. John Sidney McCain. Having been awarded his second Distinguished Service Medal for actions off Iwo Jima, McCain was again at Halsey's side, in command of Task Force 38, in June 1945 as it bombarded Okinawa and took heavy losses from kamikazes. Warned that a typhoon was approaching the American task groups from the south-southwest, Halsey ordered McCain to steam his ships due east. Once again the vessels sailed directly into the curving storm's path. Though this time only 6 sailors were killed by what the navy dubbed Typhoon Viper, 36 ships were damaged and 76 aircraft destroyed. McCain became the scapegoat.

Following the court of inquiry investigating Typhoon Viper, a livid Navy Secretary James Forrestal was prepared to relieve both Halsey and McCain of their commands, but again Halsey's reputation saved him. Admiral King convinced Forrestal that the demotion would be too great a blow to morale. This didn't stop the Navy Department, however, from disciplining McCain. Halsey, ever loyal, rode for the brand and insisted McCain be present for the Japanese capitulation aboard the *Missouri*. But "Slew" left for the States as soon as the surrender papers were signed. He arrived home in California four days later. In the middle of a "Welcome home" party the following evening, he told his wife he felt ill, and fell dead from a heart attack. He was sixty-one.

McCain's son, John Sidney "Jack" McCain Jr., a submarine commander during World War II, rose to the rank of four-star admiral as commander of all United States forces in the Pacific during the Vietnam War. It was during this conflict, in 1967, that his son, John Sidney McCain III, a naval aviator, was shot down over Hanoi, captured, tortured, and held in a North Vietnamese prison camp for five and a half years.

Fourteen years earlier, in 1953, the seventeen-year-old John S. McCain III had traveled to Bath, Maine, with his mother to witness Halsey deliver the dedication speech at the commissioning of the navy's newest destroyer, the USS *John S. McCain*, named for his grandfather. Although "Slew" had been dead for eight years, Halsey began his speech haltingly, and midway through began to sob before announcing he was too overcome to speak any longer.

Later that evening, after the ceremony, the young McCain met Halsey at the reception. "Do you drink, boy?" the admiral asked.

The future United States senator eyed his mother warily and answered, "Well, no, I don't."

Halsey looked from the young McCain to his mother, and then back again. "Well, your grandfather drank bourbon and water." He flagged a passing waiter. "Bring the boy a bourbon and water," he said.

The two clinked glasses, and silently toasted the crusty and gnarled "Slew."

Following Typhoon Cobra, Comdr. George F. Kosco remained the Third Fleet's chief aerologist, serving on Halsey's flagships *New Jersey* and, later, *Missouri*, for the duration of the war. He would later explore, by air and sea, the meteorology of both poles, and there is a glacier named after him in Antarctica. Like Kosco, Charles Calhoun, commander of the demasted *Dewey*, continued his career in the navy and retired at the rank of captain. In retirement he devoted time to researching and writing the book *Typhoon: The Other Enemy*, a detailed, first-person chronicle of the plight of his destroyer. It was published by the Naval Institute Press in 1981. When last contacted, in 2006, Calhoun was a hale and hearty ninety-three.

A decade after the deactivation of Destroyer Squadron 23's "Little Beavers" so saddened its commander, Capt. Arleigh "31-Knot" Burke, DS23 was reactivated by then Adm. Arleigh Burke, Chief of United States Naval Operations, and has operated continuously since within the U.S. Navy's Pacific Fleet. And after making way for Nimitz as Chief of Naval Operations, Adm. Ernest J. King served in an advisory capacity in the office of the secretary of the navy, and as president of the Naval Historical Foundation. He died at the Naval Hospital, Portsmouth, New Hampshire, on June 25, 1956.

Excepting Halsey, by far the most prominent name to escape the gales and giant combers of Typhoon Cobra was the *Monterey*'s Lt. (j.g.) Gerald Rudolph Ford. Ravaged by wave, wind, and fire, the *Monterey* was declared unfit for service and dispatched Stateside for repairs. Ford, meanwhile, was transferred to the Navy Preflight School in California, and from there to the Naval Reserve

Training Command Air Station in Illinois. Promoted to lieutenant commander, he received his honorable discharge in 1946 and won his first U.S. congressional seat in his home state of Michigan in 1948.

Known as a reliable and loyal Republican, he served on the Warren Commission investigating the assassination of President John F. Kennedy and, in 1973, was appointed to the vice presidency under Richard Nixon after the resignation of Spiro Agnew. In 1974, after Nixon resigned, Ford took office. As president, Ford pardoned Nixon of any crimes ("Our long national nightmare is over"), and was the target of two assassination attempts. He ran for reelection in 1976, but lost to the Democrat Jimmy Carter.

Ironically, for all the glory and praise heaped upon the *Tabberer* and her crew, by far the most famous ship to survive Typhoon Cobra never existed. Following World War II, former Pacific Theater naval officer Herman Wouk immortalized the destroyer-minesweeper USS *Caine* in his 1952 Pulitzer Prize–winning novel *The Caine Mutiny*. It was subsequently made into an award-winning Broadway play, and a movie starring Humphrey Bogart.

Although Wouk had not been present for the typhoon, the setting for his fictional mutiny against the overmatched Captain Queeg is believed, especially among old tars, to be based on the actions in the pilothouse of the USS *Hull* on the fateful morning of December 18, 1944.

Following the war, the less-heralded actors in the drama that was Typhoon Cobra returned home, relocated, married, raised families, divorced, found God, took solace in the bottle, ran companies, worked in factories and farms, doted on grandchildren and great-grandchildren, lived productive or desperate lives, and—in many cases—never spoke about the events of December 1944 for years, if at all.

Some, such as the *Hull*'s Archie DeRyckere and the *Spence*'s loquacious Chief Watertender George Johnson, made a career of the navy. DeRyckere spent twenty-eight years in the service; Johnson, "from a navy family," served for twenty-one.

Others, like *Hull* communications officer Lt. (j.g.) Lloyd Rust—who drifted for forty-four hours across the Philippine Sea—followed Ford into public service. Rust returned to Texas, earned his law degree, and raised four daughters as a widower while serving as a district attorney, a county judge, a district judge, and a twice-elected representative to the Texas state legislature. And at least one, *Cape Esperance* seaman Paul Schlener, fulfilled a promise he had made to his Lord for saving him that frightening night. Paul and his brother and their wives spent over forty years as missionaries in the Amazon section of Brazil.

Spence "deck apes" Floyd Balliett and Bob Ayers lost touch with each other. After Balliett's discharge, he remained in Long Beach, California, and spent a career working for the Ford Motor Company. Ayers, meanwhile, was stationed in Utah for the remainder of the war, where he met and married a local girl, and when his enlistment expired he took her back to Chicago. Ayers's bride did not care for the big city, and the two moved on to Iowa, where Ayers became a traffic manager for a trucking firm before starting his own small freight-hauling business. The old Great Lakes schooner sailor admitted in 2004 that he never lost his love of the sea.

After being hospitalized for pneumonia in New Mexico, *Monaghan* fireman Evan Fenn was discharged and remained in the Southwest, becoming an Arizona rancher. "I finally lost that fluid in my lungs and got well," he said in 2005. "And I haven't been sick since."

Fenn's "ghost sailor" crewmate, Radar Maintenance Technician Keith Abbott, rode out the end of World War II aboard the destroyer escort *Emery*, taking part in the landings on Iwo Jima. From there the *Emery* sailed to San Francisco for reservicing in preparation of the invasion of mainland Japan. Abbott was in San Francisco when the atomic bomb was dropped on Hiroshima. He never went back to sea. Plagued by nightmares for six months following the typhoon—"survivor's guilt dreams," he called them—Abbott said in 2005, "I was glad to get them out of my system before I brought them home to my family." Honorably discharged in November 1945, the navy gave Abbott $32.30 in mileage allowance to make his way home to St. George, Utah. From there he moved his family to California, where he became a successful businessman.

Like many survivors, for fifty-eight years Abbott never told a soul, not even his spouse, about his experience in and after Typhoon Cobra. In 2004, at the urging of his wife, the couple booked a cruise through the South Pacific tailored specifically for World War II veterans. His cruise ship skirted the waters of seven of the *Monaghan*'s campaigns as well as sailed to within a few hundred miles of where the destroyer now lies on the ocean floor. This inspired Abbott to begin, first, a journal, and finally a brief record of his adventures for his family.

Many of the men who endured the typhoon kept in touch, and ships' reunions that lasted through the 1980s and 1990s were common. The *Hull*'s were usually organized by the sonarman Pat Douhan who, following the typhoon, returned to the States on survivor leave in time to be present for the birth of his son (who grew up to become a Seabee and serve two tours of duty in Vietnam). Of the thirteen *Hull* sailors who had left pregnant wives behind on the vessel's last voyage, Douhan was one of three to make it home alive.

Afterward, Douhan was assigned to duty in the Fleet Post Office in San Francisco, and was responsible for forwarding mail to the remaining *Hull* survivors or—"the saddest part"—stamping "Return to Sender" on letters and packages addressed to dead crewmates. He had been a trumpet player before enlisting, and he soon found himself playing with the Fleet Post Office's dance band in small San Francisco nightclubs and halls. He enjoyed it so much that when his hitch was up, he enlisted for six more years. Upon his discharge, he and his family moved back to his hometown of Madera, California, just north of Fresno. As a member of his local VFW Honor Guard, Douhan still plays taps at funeral services for local veterans and remains an avowed "water bug," swimming laps every morning.

Hull chiefs Ray Schultz and Archie DeRyckere became regular attendees at the reunions Douhan organized, which were, needless to say, often bittersweet. Schultz married a Seattle girl, moved to the Pacific Northwest, and became a Seattle firefighter. He arrived at one reunion with cartons of ball caps to hand out to his former shipmates. Above the brim they read "Halsey's Swimming Team." To this day, he said in 2005, "I don't go near the water."

Not to be outdone, DeRyckere showed up at the next reunion with ball caps that read "USS Hull Bodysurfing Team." Unlike Schultz, his experience of capsizing and drifting across the waves did nothing to dim DeRyckere's enthusiasm for the sea. He went on to command a U.S. Navy fleet tug in Alaska, run the Navy Hydrographic Office in Honolulu, and rise through the ranks to become an operations officer and amphibious training officer aboard various vessels. He retired in 1968 as a lieutenant commander, still studying his Bowditch, still loving the *Hull*.

"You say, 'How can you love a ship, it's just a piece of steel,'" he replied in response to a reporter's question in 2005. "But it's not just a piece of steel. It's an accumulation of personalities and people. The captain, the exec, all of your shipmates, they all become brothers to you. The admiration is just there. And when you see a ship like that in danger, when you lose it, you lose a part of yourself."

As the years passed and the ranks at the reunions thinned, Douhan began inviting former seamen from the rescuing ships to the affairs, and among the *Hull* crewmen were always sprinkled men from the *Knapp*, the *Brown*, the *Swearer*, and most especially the *Tabberer*.

"We didn't feel like heroes at the time, it was just our job," *Tabby* shipfitter Leonard Glaser said in 2005. Nonetheless, the captain of that little destroyer escort holds a special place in the hearts not only of the fifty-five men she plucked from the sea, but of the men who served under him. Through campaigns that encompassed the Mindoro landings, Typhoon Cobra, the invasions of Iwo Jima and Okinawa, and the bombardment of the Japanese mainland in the final days of World War II, the *Tabberer* never sustained a single casualty. She was a lucky ship . . . for her crew and for others.

"I just thank the good Lord for Henry Plage," said the *Hull*'s Ray Schultz. "I have more respect for him than anyone in the world." Added the *Spence*'s Bob Ayers, "If he hadn't disobeyed orders and kept looking, they wouldn't have found us. Thank God for Henry Plage."

For the remainder of his life Henry Plage corresponded with the sailors who served under him not only aboard the *Tabberer*, but also from the *Donaldson* and the *LeHardy*. In 1997 he addressed a letter to the entire surviving crew of the *Tabby* via the ship's newsletter. "This I do know," he wrote. "We will never give up our ties with each other and our mutual love. We came together during perilous times and survived by working together and looking out for each other, and by the Grace of God, Marge and I will look forward to future contact with each of you. Marge joins me in sending our everlasting love."

In 2005 the former enlisted man Lawrence Howard, who sailed with Plage aboard the *LeHardy*, summed up his former commander thusly: "You'd have to know the man to understand exactly the way he was, so gentle, so concerned, but a man's man through and through."

On the occasion of the fortieth anniversary of "Halsey's Typhoon," in 1984, Marjorie Plage penned the "Ode to the Men of the 418." It reads, in part:

> But, soon, you formed firm bonds
> Of friends that were tried and true
> Together you brought the Tabberer
> Through Hell—safe—what a crew
>
> The caps with Tabberer 418
> Made each especially glad

For it showed that they were one
Of the best ships the Navy ever had

So again we salute you
Always hold your head high
For the record of your "Tabby"
Will never, never die.

Ten years later, on May 23, 1994, the exact date of the fiftieth anniversary of the USS *Tabberer*'s commissioning, survivors and shipmates of the *Hull* and *Tabberer* gathered on the grounds of the Admiral Nimitz Museum in Fredericksburg, Texas—since renamed the National Museum of the Pacific War—to dedicate a plaque to Plage and the crew of the *Tabby*.

When Henry Plage appeared before the court of inquiry in late 1944, his testimony was limited to any suggestions he might have as to how to technically improve the stability of ships caught in a typhoon. He was not asked his opinion regarding Admiral Halsey's complicity in the disaster, and for years never offered one. Later in life, however, he did volunteer to a reporter that he felt Halsey "was working blind," and that the court of inquiry had been too harsh on the "old man."

"I felt that was a bad decision because your hands are tied without the information," Plage said in his Florida home. "You can't predict a storm's path. Or, you couldn't back then, anyway."

There was one more plaque to be dedicated. That was at the church of Henry and Marguerite Plage in Ocala, Florida, in December 2003. Services for "Mrs. Tabby" had been held there several years earlier, and more recently for her husband. The beloved captain had died on September 24, 2003, almost sixty years after he, his crew, and his little ship stayed in a typhoon to rescue men from the sea. The plaque, paid for by survivors' donations, reads:

IN MEMORY OF
HENRY L. PLAGE
CAPTAIN USS TABBERER DE418
WITH GRATITUDE FOR THE 55 LIVES
HE SAVED
12-18-1944
FROM THE SURVIVORS AND CREW OF
THE USS HULL DD350

Recently, those survivors—led by Archie DeRyckere and supported emphatically by former President Gerald Ford—have mounted a letter-writing campaign and public relations drive to have Comdr. (Ret.) Henry Lee Plage awarded a posthumous Medal of Honor, the United States' highest military award (www.typhooncobra1944 .net).

In DeRyckere's petition to the secretary of the navy, he cites Plage's distinguished and conspicuous gallantry and, "intrepidity at the risk of his life above and beyond the call of duty." And Ford, in a 2005 letter to the Department of the Navy's Board of Decorations and Medals, offers "my strong support for a favorable decision on behalf of LCDR Henry L. Plage for the award of the Medal of Honor."

The navy, as of this writing, has yet to render a decision.

ACKNOWLEDGMENTS

Without the recollections, documents, memorabilia, and support of the brave men who sailed through Typhoon Cobra in December 1944—including those who survived the sinking of their ships—we would not have been able to write this book. Our debt to them, and to their families, is beyond reckoning.

For taking the time to recount their experiences, we wish to offer our sincere thanks to: Keith Abbott, Owen Atkinson, Harley "Bob" Ayers, Michael Bak, Floyd Balliett, Alvin Barras, John Bedrosian, Tom Bellino, Herbert Brooks, Charles C. Calhoun, William Christensen, J. Frank Cross, Les Denton, Archie DeRyckere, Pat Douhan, John Dowd, James Elder, Richard Fanning, James Felty, Evan Fenn, President Gerald Ford, Earl Frosch, Leo Gauthier, Ronald Gift, Phil Gingerich, Leonard Glaser, James Grimes, James Haveman, Linus Hawkins, Marion Hicks, J. W. "Bill" Hillis, John Hoagland, Lawrence Howard, George Johnson, O. J. King, David Loomis, Donald McCarthy, William McClain, John Mehill, Edward Miller, William Ogden, Gene Perry, Paul Phillips, William Pihl, O. K. Poulson, Paul "Ray" Ramirez, Walter Roberge, John Rosas, Lloyd Rust, Paul Schlener, Herman Schnipper, Ray Schultz, Lloyd Speulda, Tom Stealey, Robert Traver, Leon Vanderschaaf, John Walker, Elijah Watlington, Leonard Watson, Bob Winn, John Wisse, and Ray Zasadill.

We also received encouragement and invaluable assistance from relatives of sailors and airmen who served aboard Admiral Halsey's Third Fleet during World War II and survived, or perished, in the great storm. We are particularly beholden to Tom DeFranco, Dorothy Glaser, Guy Lester, and Richard Strand. Arthur "Russ" Plage's generosity—both in spirit as well as in providing us with his father Henry's personal papers—enriched our work.

We were also blessed to find research sources that were over-seen by courteous and exceptionally competent people. The Web sites and newsletters maintained by Ray Booher, Leon Krog, John McKechnie, Pete Smith, and Donald Steffins fall into this category. We thank them. We would also like to acknowledge the invalu-able contributions of Pamela Browne and Martin Hinton of the Fox Network, Jennifer Scott of Towers Productions, Inc., Jim Ryan, Lisa O'Neil, Anne S. Atkinson and Carrie Trimmer of the A&E Television Networks, Ruri Kawashima of the Japan Society, and Jann Wenner, Corey Seymour, and Nina Pearlman at Wenner Media.

A book, even one with two authors, cannot be written in a vacuum, and at important junctures the insights and suggestions of Bill Boyle, Arthur French, David Hughes, Capt. (USN) Michael Jacobsen, Bob Kelly, and Tom Kelly were instrumental in steering us down the correct path. Further, special thanks must be extended to the staff researchers, librarians, and directors of the Library of Congress, the National Archives and Records Administration, and the Naval Historical Center. Finally, Archie DeRyckere's persistent effort to secure a posthumous Medal of Honor for Lt. Comdr. Henry Lee Plage must be recognized.

The wisdom of family and friends was put to great use in both practical and emotional ways during the process of writing *Halsey's Typhoon*. Our heartfelt thanks to Nancy Bartolotta, John Bonfiglio, Heather Buchanan, Kathryn and Brendan Clavin, Gertrude Clavin, James Clavin, Liam-Antoine De Busschere-Drury, Joe Flood, Michael and Shelly Gambino, Michael Griffith, Harry Kohlmeyer, Kate Lawton, Denise McDonald, Kitty Merrill, Kelly Olsen, Amy Patton and David Winter, Danny Peary and Suzanne Rafer, Bill Phillips, Valerie Pillsworth, Allen Richardson and Karen Curry, Tony and Patty Sales, Bob Schaeffer, Simon Smith and Janet Palmer, and David Zinczenko.

This book originally took form as a story in *Men's Journal*, and without the foresight and demanding editing of Bob Wallace, Michael Caruso, and Larry Smith it would not be complete.

We are also grateful to our editor, Morgan Entrekin, for his enthusiasm, editor's touch, and omniscient range of knowledge. Jamison Stoltz's, Brando Skyhorse's, and Jofie Ferrari-Adler's insights, unfailing courtesy, and professionalism throughout the production of this work will not be forgotten.

Thank you to Jennifer Unter of RLR Associates for her consistent support. Finally, this project would not have been possible without the insight, unrelenting encouragement, and acute eye of Nat Sobel, whose strong shepherding brought this book to life. He is more than a literary agent and adviser. He is a great and good friend.

APPENDIX

U.S. Navy Personnel Killed in Typhoon Cobra

The demands of war at the time and the suppression of information about the Typhoon Cobra tragedy resulted in lists of the deceased that are not completely reliable. The authors relied on lists created by the Navy's Bureau of Personnel immediately after the event and then classified for over half a century. We apologize for any errors. As readers will note in the case of the *Hull* victims, first names were not supplied. Also, men swept overboard and men who died of injuries on other ships can account for the discrepancy between the number of men listed and the total of 793 who died in the typhoon.

We urge readers to visit the Web site www.typhooncobra1944.net, which has been created by Archie DeRyckere and the USS Hull Survivors Association. The site is dedicated to "those true heroes who made the supreme sacrifice," as DeRyckere puts it. Donations made via the Web site go to a plaque honoring the victims of the typhoon at the National Museum of the Pacific War in Fredericksburg, Texas.

USS Hull

1. Gherstly, G.I.	Lt.	8. Anido, Alfred	Ensign
2. Baker, H.C.	Lt.	9. Korinko, D.L.	Ensign
3. Smart, Jr., F.G.	Lt. (jg)	10. Johnson, W.G.	Ensign
4. Snodgrass, F.L.	Lt. (jg)	11. Schuerman, O.E.	Ensign
5. Kappus, K.H.	Lt. (jg)	12. Abreu, M., Jr.	
6. Bryant, H.H.	Lt. (jg)	13. Ackerman, J.F.	
7. Nelson, G.C.	Lt. (jg)	14. Adams, M.	

15. Albrecht, H.G.
16. Alexander, S.C.
17. Anderson, H.E.
18. Anderson, J.W.
19. Ashley, F.
20. Banes, D.R.
21. Banfill, D.P.
22. Belden, J.I.
23. Born, P.
24. Burleson, E.G.
25. Carlstrom, R.D.
26. Cobb, I.
27. Connor, J.T.
28. Cook, J.
29. Cooke, R.E.
30. Cosgrove, G.J.
31. Cothran, C.R.
32. Cotten, J.O.
33. Dean, B.B.
34. Deck, A.L.
35. De Vaney, W.F.
36. Eichen, D.J.
37. Eisenbach, A.E.
38. Eiskle, E.F.
39. Ellis, R.H.
40. Farrell, E.V.
41. Fenderson, R.N.
42. Fernandez, A.
43. Fisnefska, G.L.
44. Foster, H. L.
45. Fowler, R.B.
46. Gabler, D.M.
47. Gaulke, D.J.
48. Geddert, G.F.
49. Gilberg, J.A.
50. Gillette, W.F.
51. Gipson, R.B.
52. Gower, W.H.
53. Granby, H.
54. Green, O.L.

55. Gruner, H.
56. Gundel, H.E.
57. Guthrie, R.M.
58. Hahn, L.A.
59. Haislip, C.J., Jr.
60. Halladay, J.R.
61. Hart, W.F.
62. Haydon, M.R.
63. Henkel, E.
64. Henry, G.W.
65. Hicks, L.F.
66. Hicks, R.H.
67. Hill, L.G.
68. Hixson, M.B.
69. Homaug, G.
70. Horton, J.T.
71. Houghton, D.C., Jr.
72. Howland, W.K.
73. Hoy, M.L.
74. Hughes, S.N.
75. Ingraham, T.M.
76. Jambor, J.J.
77. Juson, R.D.
78. Karnopp, W.E.
79. Kelley, K.W.
80. Kelly, W.L.
81. Kendrovios, A.
82. Kennedy, W.H., Jr.
83. King, J.P.
84. Knadler, G.F.
85. Korponai, Z.A.
86. Kraus, G.W.
87. Kreidler, J.E.
88. Kunz, E.W.
89. Lagow, L.S.
90. Lane, A.B.
91. Leabo, D.C.
92. Leombrone, J.
93. Lewis, G.J.
94. Loney, D.W.

95. Mabius, J., Jr.
96. Macchio, J.
97. Martin, D.R.
98. Martin, P.A.
99. McDonough, W.T.
100. McGee, T.M.
101. McGill, C.J.
102. McGlauchn, W.M.
103. McIntyre, J.F.
104. McInvale, R.R.
105. McKeehan, L.
106. Melancon, C.F.
107. Miller, C.P.
108. Miller, E.H.
109. Millsaps, S.
110. Mink, M.S.
111. Mohr, O.E., Jr.
112. Moldenhauer, A.E.
113. Moon, R.R.
114. Moreno, J.
115. Mullins, L.C.
116. Mullins, L.W.
117. Murie, J.H.
118. Newsom, E.T.
119. Niss, A.W.
120. Northey, G.W.
121. Oakley, R.D.
122. Ostlee, M.L.
123. Papcke, F.A.
124. Parker, R.E.
125. Parrott, R.T.
126. Peek, J.T.
127. Peterson, J.M.
128. Pfander, S.E.
129. Pfeiffer, J.W.
130. Phillippi, E.A.
131. Phillips, F.B.
132. Phillips, L.O.
133. Piccin, E.R.
134. Pickett, F.M., Jr.

135. Pierce, C.W.
136. Pippins, W.E.
137. Poe, C.L.
138. Pratt, G.L.
139. Preisser, T.E.
140. Preston, A.R.
141. Price, C.E.
142. Pruitt, P.Q.
143. Rattaro, J.J.
144. Rotter, I.F.
145. Ruby, G.E., Jr.
146. Runyan, J.K.
147. Ryals, S.V.
148. Sackmaster, H.E.
149. Scarletta, J.A., Jr.
150. Scherer, K.R.
151. Scherzinger, R.J.
152. Schmiderer, J.A.
153. Schrader, H.D.
154. Sego, J.F.
155. Simons, M.E.
156. Skapsik, J.J.
157. Sloane, F.C.
158. Smith, J.H.
159. Smith, P.A., Jr.
160. Smith, W.W., Jr.
161. Snow, H.M.
162. Solano, H.J.
163. Spencer, C.C.
164. Stacy, A.J.
165. Stennett, J.
166. Stephens, J.H.
167. Stercula, W.V.
168. Stevens, P.Q.
169. Stipetich, G.L.
170. Stoddard, K.C.
171. Szente, G.A.
172. Tabor, H.G.
173. Teiffel, W.S.
174. Tenholder, A.J.

175. Terrio, L.L.
176. Thomas, K.
177. Thornton, K.G.
178. Torkildson, K.B.
179. Trapp, B.G.
180. Travis, A.H.
181. Updegraff, G.J.
182. Vaughan, A.L.
183. Vernon, W.H.
184. Vulcano, S.J.
185. Wall, C.J.
186. Ward, E.M.
187. Webb, W.
188. Weibel, A.J.

189. Weimers, G.L.
190. Weiss, V.J.
191. Whitehair, W.W.
192. Whitney, R.A.
193. Williams, C.E.
194. Wilson, R.
195. Wolfe, G.J.
196. Wolff, T.A.
197. Wolkins, M.W.
198. Wright, J.E.
199. Yarbrough, H.G.
200. Yonts, C.W.
201. Zawne, R. O.
202. Zielinski, L.A.

USS Monaghan

1. Garrett, F.B., Jr.   Lt. Comdr.
2. Elliott, F. J., Jr.   Lt.
3. Van Iderstine, D. H. Lt.
4. Mills, R. C.   Lt.
5. Siegesmund, E.W.   Lt.
6. Stark, S.F.   Lt.
7. Gavin, R.C.   Lt. (jg)
8. Hargrave, R.K.   Lt. (jg)
9. Prather, J.W.   Lt. (jg)
10. Burden, R.C.   Lt. (jg)
11. Pedersen, R.F.   Lt. (jg)
12. Blittersdorf, C. H.   Lt. (jg)
13. Carlson, L.A.   Lt. (jg)
14. Nolop, R.E.   Lt. (jg)
15. Davidson, H.E.   Ens.
16. Dubpernell, J.   Ens.
17. Cochran, E.M.   Ens.
18. Weber, H.H.   Ens.
19. Adler, Victor L.
20. Alessi, Joseph R.
21. Allen, Fred A.
22. Amis, Hugh B.
23. Anspach, Roy R.
24. Anthony, James C.

25. Attaway, James R.
26. Aubrey, John T.
27. Austin, William J.
28. Bailey, Clarence A.
29. Baker, Willard R.
30. Barber, Horace L.
31. Bard, Richard F.
32. Barszczewski, Edward J.
33. Bassett, William M.
34. Beach, Gurney A. Sr.
35. Benfatti, John J.
36. Berger, George W.
37. Bingham, Eugene D.
38. Binner, Clyde R.
39. Borouff, Jerome J.
40. Britton, Thomas L.
41. Brunkow, Ferdinand
42. Bryant, Leonard R.
43. Burgess, Fred J.
44. Burnett, Raymond O.
45. Burtch, Charles D.
46. Busch, Martin L.
47. Butler, Ralph J.
48. Cain, Frank A.

49. Camunez, James C.
50. Carbone, Richard E.
51. Carriker, Robert R.
52. Casson, Orval K.
53. Caswell, Floyd A., Jr.
54. Chapin, Gail W.
55. Cieszynski, Stanley J.
56. Cimino, Ceasar D.
57. Clark, George M.
58. Cochran, James H.
59. Coleman, William D.
60. Conrad, Carl E.
61. Cooper, Carl L.
62. Corley, Howard W.
63. Cote, Leonard G.
64. Cotton, Almer A.
65. Cradduck, Raymond A.
66. Crater, Ray E.
67. Croft, Edward J.
68. Culp, Donald A.
69. Debord, John G.
70. Dedmore, Gale A.
71. Delis, John S.
72. Devault, Francois L.J.
73. Doyle, George W.
74. Driscoll, Charles J.
75. Dumas, Frank S.
76. Eggen, Wendell J.
77. Ellis, John H., Jr.
78. Entrican, Carroll V.
79. Etheridge, Lindsey E.
80. Evans, Paul R.
81. Fantozzi, Frederick C.
82. Faught, Laurence M.
83. Felton, Russel B.
84. Ferrero, Robert E.
85. Ferrier, James J.
86. Finch, Lester J.
87. Fisher, Roland D.
88. Foster, Victor W.

89. Fox, Loyd S.
90. Gastmann, Harm
91. Geier, Donald C.
92. Givens, Robert P.
93. Godfrey, Harvey H.
94. Goetz, Otto J.
95. Gostyla, Bruno
96. Green, James B.
97. Grubham, Fred William
98. Haight, Benjamin E.
99. Hally, William
100. Hankins, Marvin R.
101. Harris, Harry L.
102. Heitner, Henry
103. Heflin, Dewey L., Jr.
104. Higginbotham, Sherman
105. Hill, Horace C.
106. Hirsch, Leonard H.
107. Holt, Jack L.
108. Hommel, John W.
109. Hudgins, Wendell R.
110. Iler, George Jr.
111. Ingoe, James E.
112. Jeffery, Charles W.
113. Johnson, William E.
114. Johnson, William L.
115. Jones, Alfred H.
116. Jones, Forest E.
117. Jordan, Harold L.
118. Karns, Forest E.
119. Karpinski, Milford J.
120. Kell, Ralph O.
121. Kimmel, Donald
122. Kowalk, Bernard A.
123. Kurikjan, Edward A.
124. Lamb, Arthur G.
125. Larson, Joseph J.
126. Larson, Simon P.
127. Lee, James S.
128. Lenig, Walter L., Jr.

129. Lewellen, Roy L.
130. Litton, John A.
131. Lindsey, Ben H., Jr.
132. Lindsey, David F.
133. Lomax, Clenn C.
134. Lopez, Jose E.
135. Lowe, Jefferson T.
136. Lyste, Chester M.
137. Maldonado, Alex J.
138. Malveau, Chester
139. Mann, Boyd
140. Manochi, William M.
141. Martin, Hubert M.
142. Mattern, Robert Allen
143. Matzener, John F.
144. Maxwell, Earl T.
145. Mayer, Kenneth G.
146. McConnell, Harley M.
147. McCormack, William
148. McFalls, Charles J.
149. McGough, Joseph N.
150. McIntosh, R. C. P.
151. McNally, Joseph L.
152. Meisen, Francis P.
153. Messa, Louis
154. Mickelson, Max L.
155. Mills, Houston E.
156. Moore, Carlus B.
157. Moore, John C., Jr.
158. Moran, Voy G.
159. Morrison, Melroy E.
160. Nichols, Robert J.
161. Nutting, Roland B.
162. Ogborn, John "J"
163. Osterby, Albin E.
164. Panas, Peter
165. Peerenboom, Donald G.
166. Perry, Joe E.
167. Peterson, Wayne L.
168. Phister, Harold C.

169. Platt, Bryce L.
170. Ragland, Ralph K.
171. Ravnell, Stacks
172. Richmond, Ganis J.
173. Ricker, Doyle L.
174. River, Francis N.
175. Rogers, Harry A.
176. Ross, Charles L.
177. Sables, John A., Jr.
178. Sanford, Clyde H.
179. Sanford, James L., Jr.
180. Schubert, Elmer H.
181. Schuler, Carl F., Jr.
182. Shalkowski, Louis P.
183. Shaner, Leonard P.
184. Sherrill, Harvey "J"
185. Shoemate, Roy C.
186. Sigafoos, Jack R.
187. Simmons, William W.
188. Smith, Dewey L.
189. Smrkolj, Harry
190. Spence, Louis L.
191. Stapleton, James "N"
192. Stark, Robert M.
193. Stevenson, James H.
194. Stewart, Harold B.
195. Stewart, Robert F.
196. Stewart, Robert L.
197. Still, Frederic P.
198. Stimolo, Sam, Jr.
199. Stone, Edward
200. Stoner, Howard A.
201. Stopher, Robert H.
202. Storz, Andrew "J"
203. Stowe, Marvin E.
204. Strahan, Everett N.
205. Stravinski, John J.
206. Strength, Luther N.
207. Strickland, Henry P., Jr.
208. Strickland, "J" "M"

209. Stricklin, Arthur G., Jr.
210. Stutes, Lee R. J.
211. Sullivan, Earl P.
212. Sutherin, Donald G.
213. Swartwood, James N.
214. Thomas, Cyril J.E.
215. Tondreau, Joseph A.
216. Tripp, Alonzo W.
217. Trostel, William J.
218. Tschimperle, Matthew J.
219. Tyler, Fred D.
220. Tyler, George "L"
221. Varazo, Siver C.
222. Varvil, Kenneth E.
223. Villanueva, Gustavo B.
224. Wallace, Ronald J.

225. Walters, William, Jr.
226. Warren, Coleman Y.
227. Warren, Robert F.
228. Weaver, William D.
229. Werbelow, Louis C.
230. White, Clifton J.
231. Willenborg, Ervin E.
232. Willhite, Lawrence W.
233. Willis, Edward
234. Wilson, Willie
235. Witcher, Leroy
236. Working, James W.
237. Wright, Evert
238. Wright, Paul
239. Wright, Ralph J.

USS Spence

1. Andrea, James P.   Lt. Comdr.
2. Andrews, Frank V.   Lt.
3. Sundin, Lawrence D.   Lt. (jg)
4. Collins, David H.   Lt. (jg)
5. Harnish, Paul R.   Lt. (jg)
6. Isham, George P.   Lt. (jg)
7. McClelland, Vincent   Lt. (jg)
8. Robinson, Lester V.   Lt. (jg)
9. Bellion, John J.   Lt. (jg)
10. Whalen, John   Lt. (jg)
11. Gaffney, John C.   Lt. (jg)
12. Smith, Donald H.   Ensign
13. Bickel, Charles P.   Ensign
14. Poer, George W.   Ensign
15. Ligon, William R.   Ensign
16. Kissinger, Rexal H.   Ensign
17. Brightman, Robert W. Ensign
18. Sellers, William I. F. Ensign
19. Luebbe, Herbert   Ensign
20. Adams, Vern Oliver
21. Adams, William Jerome
22. Akers, James Robert

23. Alarie, Karl Joseph
24. Aldrich, Raymond Earnest
25. Alexander, George James
26. Alexander, Thornton Ross
27. Allen, Edgar Arthur
28. Alley, George William
29. Anastoff, Carl (n)
30. Anderson, James (n)
31. Armbrust, Almon Lee
32. Arvold, Arthur Allen
33. Ashcraft, William Davis
34. Ashworth, Jr., Ernest (n)
35. Asmus, Charles Benjamin
36. Aube, Harold Nicholas
37. Aulenbach, Edward Joseph
38. Baeder, Francis Elmer
39. Bailey, Jr., Walter Richard
40. Bair, Allen George
41. Bair, Lewis John
42. Baren, Lionel
43. Barr, Robert Neil
44. Barras, Sidney Theo

45. Beachy, Jonas Elijah
46. Bean, Charles Reed
47. Bearrows, Charles Gordon
48. Beaty, Douglas Clinton
49. Beaumont, Cletus Edward
50. Billengsley, Jr., Ernest Edmond
51. Blackburn, Oliver
52. Blanton, Sr., Warren Thomas
53. Bloom, Jr., Axel Warner
54. Bloomquist, Harold Edward
55. Bodag, Michael
56. Boone, Joseph Patrick
57. Bowman, Richard Glenn
58. Bradshaw, Jr., Raymond
59. Brandl, Harry George
60. Britzman, Glen Gerald
61. Broch, Peter
62. Bronchu, Edward Albert
63. Bronis, Henry
64. Brown, Paul Thomas
65. Browning, Alva Leon
66. Bruchert, Jr., Albert John
67. Bryant, Harold Lester
68. Buck, Walton Grayson
69. Buckley, William Joseph
70. Buczek, Edward Clarence
71. Busby, Wallace Hugh
72. Butts, Harry Lee
73. Byrd, Joseph Elmer
74. Cahill, Christopher Daniel
75. Campton, Gilbert George
76. Carls, Jack William
77. Carrigan, Harlan Kenneth
78. Cayer, Albert Fredrick
79. Chalfant, George Raymond
80. Champagne, William Anthony
81. Chastain, James Wilson
82. Christiansen, George Lewis
83. Christiansen, Wesley John
84. Clark, Donald Cleon
85. Clark, Stillman
86. Cloutier, Marcel Gregorie
87. Cobb, Robert Marcus
88. Coleman, Manuel William
89. Connolly, John Emmett
90. Cook, Jr., William Wickliff
91. Cooper, Frederick
92. Cope, Robert Earl
93. Copeland, Roosevelt
94. Coppens, William Arthur
95. Corder, Frank Bill
96. Craver, Charles Robert
97. Crawford, Newton Craig
98. Criteser, Gordon Lee
99. Crooks, Fred Thomas
100. Crump, Walter Ray
101. Culler, Alvin Jay
102. Dalrymple, Jr., Arthur Garfield
103. David, Calvin Martial
104. David, Jerome Anthony
105. Davis, Edward Nelson
106. De Vaughan, James Frank
107. Dewan, Jr., Benjamin Thomas
108. Di Stanislao, Frank "S"
109. Dommeleers, Daniel Victor
110. Duda, Alfred Francis
111. Edwards, Simpson
112. Elburn, Charles Franklin
113. Ellison, Lowell Eugene
114. Ellwanger, Fred Otto
115. Elwell, Jr., Roland Douglas
116. Esler, Gilbert John
117. Faust, Kyle Howard
118. Ferguson, George Joseph
119. Filannino, Frank Carl
120. Finch, David Lawrence
121. Finch, Hugh Alvin
122. Finn, Martin Francis
123. Ford, Joel LeRoy
124. Forry, Dudley Clair

125. Frost, Frank Bert
126. Frost, Myron Delbert
127. Gary, Leroy Joseph
128. Gehle, Willard Fred
129. Gehr, John Thomas
130. Gibbons, William Henry
131. Giffin, Freeman Franklin
132. Gill, Francis Joseph
133. Goodwin, Edward Walde
134. Gordon, Jack
135. Governile, Frank Paul
136. Grabowski, Joseph Charles
137. Graddy, George Washington
138. Gray, John Merrill
139. Gray, William Howard
140. Greenwald, Jr., Henry William
141. Grillo, Roy Robert
142. Haak, Menno Martin
143. Hakenson, Warren Irvin
144. Hampton, David Dillon
145. Hansen, John Howard
146. Hariskevich, Rudolph
147. Harris, Earl Robert
148. Healy, Lorin Carson
149. Heater, James Patrick
150. Heaverlo, Clarence Joseph
151. Heckart, Billy Dean
152. Heintz, Sr., Edwin Thomas
153. Hensley, George William
154. Hill, Harold Homer
155. Holland, Clarence Everette
156. Horkey, Franklin William
157. Hosford, Leonard David
158. Huffman, Walter Lewis
159. Huppert, Carlton Joseph
160. Jackson, Lawrence Nathaniel
161. Jankowski, Stanley Edward
162. Johnson, Clarence Elmer
163. Johnson, George Albert
164. Jones, Bennie Joe

165. Jorden, Jr., Harry Ellsworth
166. Karl, John William
167. Kaufman, Harold Donald
168. Kaufman, John Clarence
169. Kelin, Vernon
170. Kelley, Jr., Thomas Raymond
171. Kelly, Brady Leon
172. Kelly, Carlyle Xavier
173. Kelly, John Joseph
174. Kendall, Leonard Forest J.
175. Kestle, James Raymond
176. Kittle, James Robert
177. Kleckley, William Woodrow
178. Kosters, Henry Anthony
179. Lara, Eddie Manual
180. Lasorsa, Louis Joseph
181. Leschinski, Thaddeus John
182. Lesher, Robert Louis
183. Lewis, John Franklin
184. Lindseth, Theodore Sverre
185. Loughery, Edward Alexander
186. Lundgren, Arthur Lee
187. Lundgren, Lloyd Otto
188. Luther, Francis Eugene
189. Lybrand, Robert Lenoye
190. Mahaffee, Lawrence Morgan
191. Mahan, Henry Ford
192. Manchisi, Peter Paul
193. Marconi, Carl Carmen
194. Marget, Glenn Edwin
195. Martin, Andrew Joseph
196. Marvel, Robert Edward
197. Massa, John Duncan
198. Mathes, Frank Eugene
199. McCrary, Hubert Elliott
200. McEachren, Glen Ellis
201. McFaddin, William Cecil
202. McQuerry, George Pershing
203. Mergenthaler, Elmer John
204. Merrritt, Roy Lobis

205. Miley, Frank Buren
206. Miller, Cecil Louis
207. Monnig, Harold Anthony
208. Moore, John "H"
209. Murphy, Hugh
210. Myers, Frederick Paul
211. Naquin, Roy Joseph
212. Neal, Ralph Douglas
213. Neely, Clifford "E"
214. Netolicky, George Stanley
215. Nevins, William Bryan
216. Nose, Allen Jacob
217. Oesau, Andrew John
218. Orasi, Harold William
219. Owens, Muriel Grant
220. Para, Aldo
221. Pauer, Joseph Anthony
222. Payton, Russell
223. Penpraese, George Howard
224. Polhemus, John Donald
225. Powell, Curtis Thomas
226. Powell, Luther Keneth
227. Powers, Dorman Muskedward
228. Purvis, Joe Earl
229. Reams, Charles Howard
230. Redmond, James
231. Richards, Donald Garth
232. Ridge, Edwin Gerard
233. Ringuiso, Francesco Carmen
234. Roberts, Harvey David
235. Rosen, Samuel
236. Rossi, Sr., Joseph Anthony
237. Rutter, James Vernon
238. Ryan, Harry John
239. Sarli, Michael
240. Saxon, John Joseph
241. Schmidt, Frank Arthur
242. Schneider, Benjamin Monroe
243. Schnell, George Frederick
244. Schoen, Andrew Steve

245. Schult, Howard Alfred
246. Schwartz, David Ernest
247. Schwarz, Paul Frederick
248. Selders, Everett Ernest
249. Sepanski, Alexander Leon
250. Shepherd, Marion "L"
251. Sherer, Edward Gilman
252. Shropshier, Louis Howard
253. Shupek, John
254. Slagle, Benjamin Earl
255. Slaughter, Layton William
256. Small, Norman Eugene
257. Smith, Jr., Carl Glee
258. Smith, Charles Albert
259. Smith, Donald LeRoy
260. Smith, Jerome Herbert
261. Smith, Robert Eugene
262. Snyder, Karl Homer
263. Spotts, Virgil Dean
264. Spradling, Frenchy
265. Springbett, William George
266. Staffen, Howard Franklin
267. Stalder, Duane Jay
268. Stein, Warren Jacob
269. Stepp, Edgar Everett
270. Stevens, Max John
271. Stevenson, Richard Louis
272. Stewart, Jr., David Leroy
273. Stewart, Robert Wayne
274. Strand, Robert Louis
275. Straszynski, Philip John
276. Stromberg, Vernon Ardell
277. Stroup, Bernard Carlton
278. Sullivan, Francis Mathew
279. Sullivan, Robert Al
280. Sundbeck, Clarence Vincent
281. Svouros, George Anthony
282. Swerzbin, Ralph Joseph
283. Tagg, Henry Oliver
284. Tapovic, Peter

285. Tate, Ernest Jefferson
286. Taylor, Robert Jackson
287. Thompson, Frank Allison
288. Thompson, Thomas Naughton
289. Thorpe, Errol Martin
290. Tighe, Rody Joseph
291. Tryon, Perry Raymond
292. Turner, Claude
293. Vinal, Willard Henry
294. Vining, James Otto
295. Votta, Gerard Vernon
296. Wallace, John Joseph
297. Waters, Earl Joseph
298. Weaver, Carl Robert
299. Weisenborn, Wayne Wyllie
300. Weiser, Edwin Maurice

301. Whited, Cleo Parson
302. Widmeyer, Richard Clark
303. Wildenhain, Leo Joseph
304. Wilhelm, William Eugene
305. Williams, James Benjamin
306. Williams, Jr., Joel
307. Williamson, Burnis Farrior
308. Wilson, Frank Everett
309. Wilson, Murray Leroy
310. Woitkovich, John Leon
311. Wool, Jr., Frank Francis
312. Wright, Robert Arnold
313. Wright, William Philip
314. Yaksich, Jr., George Frank
315. Zinamon, Morris Louis

SELECTED BIBLIOGRAPHY

Books

Ancell, R. Manning, with Christine Miller. *The Biographical Dictionary of World War II Generals and Flag Officers.* Westport, CT: Greenwood Press, 1996.

Astor, Gerald. *Wings of Gold: The U.S. Naval Air Campaign.* New York: Random House, 2004.

Atkinson, Rick. *An Army at Dawn: The War in North Africa, 1942–1943.* New York: Henry Holt, 2002.

Bowditch, Nathaniel. *The American Practical Navigator.* Arcato, CA: Paradise Cay Publications, 2002.

Bradley, James. *Flyboys: A True Story of Courage.* New York: Back Bay Books, 2003.

———, with Ron Powers. *Flags of Our Fathers.* New York: Bantam Books, 2000.

Brinkley, Douglas, and Michael E. Haskew. *The World War II Desk Reference.* New York: HarperCollins, 2004.

Brokaw, Tom. *The Greatest Generation.* New York: Random House, 1998.

Calhoun, Capt. C. Raymond (USN Ret.). *Typhoon: The Other Enemy.* Annapolis: Naval Institute Press, 1981.

Clark, Adm. J. J. "Jocko" (USN Ret.), with Clark G. Reynolds. *Carrier Admiral.* New York: Van Rees Press, 1967.

Clavin, Tom. *Dark Noon: The Final Voyage of the Fishing Boat Pelican.* New York: McGraw-Hill, 2005.

Costello, John. *The Pacific War, 1941–1945.* New York: HarperCollins, 1981.

Donovan, Arthur J. Jr., with Bob Drury. *Fatso: Football When Men Were Really Men.* New York: William Morrow, 1987.

Drury, Bob. *The Rescue Season: The Heroic Story of Parajumpers at the Edge of the World.* New York: Simon & Schuster, 2001.

Dull, Paul S. *A Battle History of the Imperial Japanese Navy (1941–1945).* Annapolis: Naval Institute Press, 1978.

Ellis, Richard. *Encyclopedia of the Sea.* New York: Alfred A. Knopf, 2000.

Fahey, James J. *Pacific War Diary.* Seattle: University of Washington Press, 1963.

Halsey, William F., and Joseph Bryan III. *Admiral Halsey's Story.* New York: McGraw-Hill, 1947.

Hornfischer, James D. *The Last Stand of the Tin Can Sailors.* New York: Bantam Dell, 2004.

Hoyt, Edwin P. *How They Won the War in the Pacific: Nimitz and His Admirals.* Guilford, CT: Globe Pequot Press, 2002.

———. *The Typhoon That Stopped a War.* New York: David McKay Co., 1968.

Hyams, Joe. *Flight of the Avenger: George Bush at War.* Orlando: Harcourt Brace Jovanovich, 1991.

Jones, Ken. *Destroyer Squadron 23: Combat Exploits of Arleigh Burke's Gallant Force.* Annapolis: Naval Institute Press, 1997.

Junger, Sebastian. *The Perfect Storm: A True Story of Men Against the Sea.* New York: W. W. Norton, 1997.

Knight, Roger. *The Pursuit of Victory: The Life and Achievement of Horatio Nelson.* New York: Basic Books, 2005.

Kosco, Capt. George F. (USN Ret.), and Col. Hans Christian Adamson (USAF Ret.). *Halsey's Typhoons.* New York: Crown, 1967.

Leary, William M., ed. *We Shall Return!: MacArthur's Commanders and the Defeat of Japan.* Lexington: University Press of Kentucky, 1988.

Longshore, David. *Encyclopedia of Hurricanes, Typhoons, and Cyclones.* New York: Checkmark Books, 2000.

Manchester, William. *American Caesar.* New York: Little, Brown, 1978.

———. *Goodbye Darkness: A Memoir of the Pacific War.* New York: Little, Brown, 1979.

McCain, John S., and Mark Salter. *Faith of My Fathers: A Family Memoir.* New York: Random House, 1999.

Merrill, James M. *A Sailor's Admiral: A Biography of William F. Halsey.* New York: Thomas Y. Crowell, 1976.

Mooney, James, ed. *Dictionary of American Naval Fighting Ships.* Washington, D.C.: Department of the Navy, 1991.

Morison, Samuel Eliot. *History of the United States Naval Operations in World War II: Vol. 12, Leyte.* Champaign: University of Illinois Press, 1958.

———. *History of United States Naval Operations in World War II: Vol. 13, The Liberation of the Philippines.* Champaign: University of Illinois Press, 1959.

Newcomb, Richard. F. *Abandon Ship!: The Saga of the USS Indianapolis, the Navy's Greatest Sea Disaster.* New York: HarperCollins, 1958.

Nicolson, Adam. *Seize the Fire: Heroism, Duty, and the Battle of Trafalgar.* New York: HarperCollins, 2005.

Parkin, Robert Sinclair. *Blood on the Sea: American Destroyers Lost in World War II.* New York: Sarpedon, 1996.

Potter, E. B. *Bull Halsey: A Biography.* Annapolis: Naval Institute Press, 1985.

Reynolds, Clark. *The Fast Carriers: The Forging of an Air Navy.* Annapolis: Naval Institute Press, 1992.

Roberge, Walter Jr. *Dog Easy One Eight Six.* Self-published, 1995.

Schlener, Paul. *Port of Two Brothers.* Harrisburg, PA: ABWE Publishing, 2000.

Sides, Hampton. *Ghost Soldiers: The Forgotten Epic Story of World War II's Most Dramatic Mission.* New York: Doubleday, 2001.

Smith, Myron. *World War II at Sea: A Bibliography of Sources in English, 1974–1989.* Latham, MD: Scarecrow Press, 1990.

Solberg, Carl. *Decision and Dissent: With Halsey at Leyte Gulf.* Annapolis: Naval Institute Press, 1995.
Stanton, Doug. *In Harm's Way.* New York: Henry Holt, 2001.
Stewart, Adrian. *The Battle of Leyte Gulf.* New York: Scribners, 1980.
van der Vat, Dan. *The Pacific Campaign: The U.S.-Japanese Naval War, 1941–1945.* New York: Simon & Schuster, 1991.
Wooldridge, E. T. *Carrier Warfare in the Pacific: An Oral History Collection.* Washington, D.C.: Smithsonian Institution Press, 1993.

Magazine and Newspaper Articles

"Andrew Toti, 89, Dies; Savior of Many Pilots." Christopher Lehmann-Haupt, *New York Times*, March 29, 2005.
"History Is Written in Bold Sea Rescue by Gallant Sailors." Ray Coll Jr., *Honolulu Advertiser*, January 22, 1945.
"John Wayne McCain." Bill Muller, *Arizona Republic*, October 3, 1999.
"The Law of Storms." Hanson Baldwin, *Crowsnest Magazine*, October 1953.
"Revisiting Typhoon Central." Sheldon Levin, *Naval History*, December 2004.
"Ship Sunk, Two Hold Up Sailor in Sea 31 Hours." *New York Times*, February 12, 1945.
"The 'Tabby' and Typhoon Cobra." Owen Gault, *Sea Classics*, January 1989.
"3 U.S. Destroyers Lost in a Typhoon." *New York Times*, January 10, 1945.
"Trapped in a Typhoon." Erwin Jackson, *Naval History*, December 2004.
"Triumph at Trafalgar." Christopher Hitchens, *Atlantic Monthly*, October 2005.
"Typhoon!" Charles Calhoun, *Reader's Digest*, January 1951.
"A Typhoon Added to War's Horrors." Ernest McKay, *VFW*, April 1983.
"Typhoon Forecasting, 1944, or, The Making of a Cynic." Reid Bryson, *Bulletin of the American Meteorological Society*, October 2000.
"Typhoon—1944." Robert Welch, *U.S. Naval Institute Proceedings*, January 1987.
"Typhoon's Ravages Described." Keith Wheeler, *Hawaii Star-Bulletin*, January 1945.
"Typhoon Sinks Three Yankee Destroyers." *New York Times*, January 11, 1945.
"Vice President Bush Calls WW II Experience 'Sobering.'" Timothy Christmann, *Naval Aviation*, March–April 1985.
"We Got More Breaks Than Halsey." Ray Robichaud, U.S. *Naval Institute Proceedings*, October 1997.
"When the Third Fleet Met the Great Typhoon." Hanson Baldwin, *New York Times Magazine*, December 16, 1951.
"Writer Tells How Navy Lost 500 in Typhoon." Al Binder, *New York Daily News*, January 14, 1945.

Video & Electronic Sources

"Fighting Destroyer Escorts of World War II." "War Stories with Oliver North."
    Fox Network.
"Megacentric Height." Stuart Slade, www.navyweaps.com, December 19, 1998.
"Support for Mindoro Operation." Leonard Watson, www.airgroup4.com.
"Typhoon Cobra." The Weather Channel.
"Victory Is Certain." USS *San Jacinto* Web site, January 1, 2005.

Miscellaneous

Tin Can Sailor newsletter. April–May–June 2005.
The Jerseyman newsletter (online). December 2003 and January 2004.
Ernest McKay. "The Survivors: A Typhoon Added Awesome Fury to War's
    Horror," Pearl Harbor–Guam, July 1983.
World War II Histories and Historical Reports in the U.S. Naval History Divi-
    sion (partial checklist). Operational Archives, Naval History Division, May
    1973.
Court of Inquiry into the Typhoon of 18 December 1944 by Commander in
    Chief, Pacific Fleet, Microfilm NRS 1978-43.
Richard Strand, Naval History of the USS *Spence* DD-512.
E. Andrew Wilde, ed. The USS *Spence* (DD-512) in World War II: Documents,
    Recollections, and Photographs. 2001.

Library of Congress
National Archives and Records Administration
Naval Historical Center
U.S. Navy Memorial Foundation
Personal Papers of Henry Plage
www.history.navy.mil
Office of Naval Records and History

INDEX

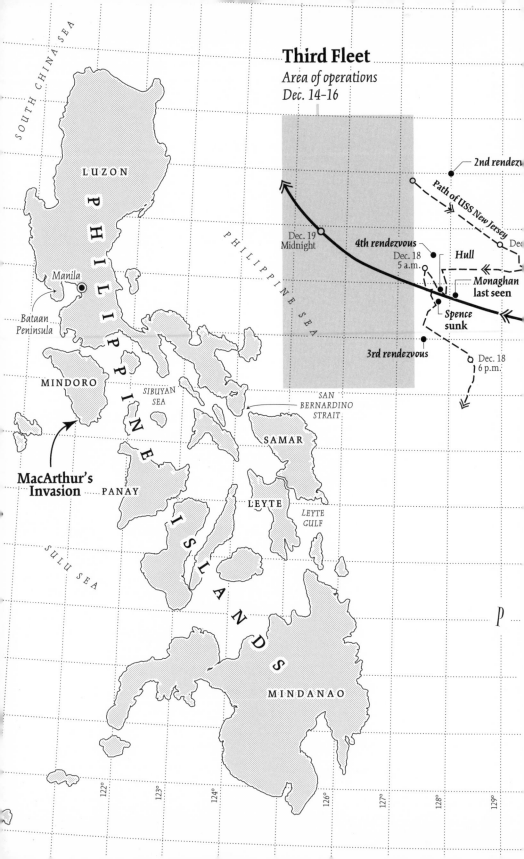

Third Fleet

Area of operations
Dec. 14-16

SOUTH CHINA SEA

LUZON

PHILIPPINE

Manila

Bataan
Peninsula

MINDORO

SIBUYAN
SEA

SAN
BERNARDINO
STRAIT

SAMAR

PANAY

LEYTE

LEYTE
GULF

**MacArthur's
Invasion**

ISLANDS

SULU
SEA

MINDANAO

PHILIPPINE SEA

2nd rendez

Path of USS New Jersey

Dec

Dec. 19
Midnight

4th rendezvous
Dec. 18
5 a.m.

Hull

Monaghan
last seen

Spence
sunk

3rd rendezvous

Dec. 18
6 p.m.

122° 123° 124° 126° 127° 128° 129°

P